David E. Malick

Narrative Art & Women in the Gospels and Acts

David E. Malick

Narrative Art & Women in the Gospels and Acts

Selected Studies in New Testament Narratives

WIPF & STOCK · Eugene, Oregon

Wipf and Stock Publishers
199 W 8th Ave, Suite 3
Eugene, OR 97401

Narrative Art & Women in the Gospels and Acts
Selected Studies in New Testament Narratives
By Malick, David
Copyright©2017 by Malick, David
ISBN 13: 978-1-5326-4509-9
Publication date 12/6/2017
Previously published by Éditions Universitaires Européennes, 2017

NARRATIVE ART & WOMEN IN THE GOSPELS AND ACTS

SELECTED STUDIES IN NEW TESTAMENT NARRATIVES

David E. Malick

χάριτι δὲ θεοῦ εἰμι ὅ εἰμι
(1 Cor. 15:10)

TABLE OF CONTENTS

CHAPTER		PAGE
I.	THE SIGNIFICANCE OF THREE NARRATIVE PARALLELS OF MEN AND WOMEN IN THE GOSPEL OF LUKE, JOHN, AND THE BOOK OF ACTS	3
II.	SIMON'S MOTHER-IN-LAW AS A MINOR CHARACTER IN THE GOSPEL OF MARK: A NARRATIVE ANALYSIS	34
III.	AN EXAMINATION OF JESUS' VIEW OF WOMEN THROUGH THREE INTERCALATIONS IN THE GOSPEL OF MARK	48
IV.	THE CONTRIBUTION OF CODEX BEZAE CANTABRIGIENSIS TO AN UNDERSTANDING OF WOMEN IN THE BOOK OF ACTS	71
V.	NARRATIVE LOGIC AND THE "SIGN-SERMON" PATTERN IN ACTS	97
VI.	THE CYCLICAL STORY AS A UNIFYING, LITERARY DEVICE IN ACTS	126

CHAPTER I

THE SIGNIFICANCE OF THREE NARRATIVE PARALLELS OF MEN AND WOMEN IN THE GOSPEL OF LUKE, JOHN, AND THE BOOK OF ACTS[1]

Introduction: A Hermeneutical Prologue

Biblical narratives are constructed word-after-word and line-after-line without the aid of tables, mechanical layouts, or images that show patterns to the reader.[2] Even though the medium is linear by necessity, the resulting narratives have contours. Even though the narratives have progression in thought,[3] their pathway is not always straight. Narrative writers provide textual, literary clues to the structure of their works through the employment of imbedded patterns like repetition, lead words, summary statements, the arrangement of units, intercalations, and the editing of known material.

One such pattern places two narratives in proximity to one another so that the reader will compare and contrast the accounts and arrive at conclusions beyond that contained in either particular narrative. The author uses duality and balance to show his theology as he invites the reader to weigh the paired stories and consider what they have to say when viewed together. Not everything is explicitly stated in the text.

By modern analogy, author Ernest Hemingway employed a theory of omission, often referred to as an "iceberg theory," where only a small portion of a story is explicitly expressed, and the reader senses the larger portion that is implied beneath the surface.[4] The pressure of implication moves the reader so that he or she probes the narrative for clues to the implied world from what is explicitly shown on the surface. Present-day novelist and short-story writer, Tobias Wolff, specifically expresses his trust in the reader to find what is not out-in-the-open but present through particular clues in the text:

---

[1] A shorter version of this article first appeared in *Priscilla Papers* 28.3 (2014): 15–25.

[2] Some may consider Hebrew poetry to be an exception to this pattern with its division of lines into cola, and its use of parallelismus memborum. A fine example of the visual structure of the Psalms may be found in J.P. Fokkelman, *The Psalms in Form: The Hebrew Psalter in its Poetic Shape* (Leiden: Deo Publishing, 2002). Nevertheless, the editorial, Masoretic marking of cola and Fokkelman's visual layout of the Psalter into individual psalms, verses, cola, and strophes are not the way in which writers originally expressed, or readers originally encountered, the biblical text.

[3] All four canonical gospels contain a plot line that includes an introduction of Jesus, a description of his ministry, his rejection, crucifixion, and resurrection. Likewise, the book of Acts unfolds the progress of the Gospel from the Jews in Jerusalem to the Apostle Paul's proclamation to Jews and Gentiles in Rome.

[4] "If a writer of prose knows enough of what he is writing about he may omit things that he knows and the reader, if the writer is writing truly enough, will have a feeling of those things as strongly as though the writer had stated them. The dignity of movement of an ice-berg is due to only one-eighth of it being above water." Ernest Hemingway, *Death in the Afternoon* (New York, NY: Schribner, 1932), 116.

I like my stories to the degree that I have felt that I have trusted my reader. That the reader is able to apprehend, perhaps even at an intuitive level, those things which I'm hoping the reader will understand without being told.[5]

Even though the canonical Gospels and the Book of Acts are not modern short stories, their writers often employ omission in their writings.[6] For instance, the logical

---

[5] The full, contextual quote is found in a discussion of Wolff's short story, *Deep Kiss*, where the interviewer, Robert Harrison, suggests that the reader is left to his own devices in determining the implied world of the protagonist, Joe Reed, whereupon Wolff explains:

> Left to your own devices only in so far as that I trust you to be able to read the story and to feel those elements of the story that might suggest a reason for his formation, for the way he sees the past -- the things that were important to him in the past, the things that led him off the conventional path when he was young. He became so obsessed with a girl that he actually had to be shipped away from his home. He was in the common parlance now stalking her in fact. And why is that? And you have to ask, and it obviously had an effect on his life, and his capacity to form emotional attachments later. And what is going on when he forms this attachment with this girl? Well, his father is dying; and they've been very close. It comes out in little ways. But he's obviously terrified and even feels in some strange way betrayed by his father's dying. And I think that the life of the senses has somehow taken over for him as a moment when he is not able to face what is actual in his life, and what is demanding things from him. And so we see that pattern somewhat played out in his life, I think, and a little below the level of his awareness. It does come to him though, in ways that are painful. I never say that in the story, but those elements are all there. And that is for me the crux of the relationship between the short story writer and the reader. I like my stories to the degree that I have felt that I have trusted my reader--that the reader is able to apprehend perhaps ever at an intuitive level those things which I'm hoping the reader will understand without being told. . . . So my relationship with the reader is one – I want to trust the reader to be as good a reader as I think I am. And I know that sometimes readers will be disappointed by a lack of what they perceive to be direction, and I'm not really helping them enough to understand. And that may be true, but I would rather err on that side than the other.

"Tobias Wolf on American Fiction," February 9, 2010, an interview on "Entitled Opinions (about Life and Literature)" with Robert Harrison. http://www.stanford.edu/dept/fren-ital/opinions/.

[6] In discussing John 2:13—3:21, Charles Talbert provides two reasons for the common feature of gaps, or lack of explicitness, in narratives: "(1) There are gaps in all artful narratives. Gaps, deliberate ambiguity, and reticence assist the narrative to avoid being boring by serving as invitations for readers or hearers to fill in the narrative according to their expectations as fostered by literary conventions or community convictions. The ancient rhetorician, DemetRuis, puts it thusly:

> Not everything should be given lengthy treatment with full details but some points should be left for our hearer to grasp and infer for himself. If he infers what you have omitted, he no longer just listens to you but acts as your witness, one too who is predisposed in your favor since he feels he has been intelligent and you are the person who has given him this opportunity to exercise his intelligence. In fact, to tell your reader everything as if he were a fool is to reveal that you think him one. (*On Style* 222)

(2) A foundation document of a group that embodies the corporate traditions and that has evolved over a lengthy period of time within the community would be telling a story that is already known to its hearers. It is not as though the readers know nothing except that has come before in the Gospel's narrative. They know the story from beginning to end and so can enjoy, as only insiders can, the stupidity of the Jews and the denseness of Nicodemus, knowing for themselves the answers to every question that arises in the story.

connection between individual units in narratives are not explicitly stated, as in Pauline epistles, with the use of conjunctions like "and," "but," "because," and "therefore." Nevertheless, the writers "trust the reader" to actively seek out the implied connections.[7] So too, when the narrative clues include stories aligned with one another, the writer intends for the active reader to compare the stories and arrive at conclusions that would not be present if the stories were read in isolation.

First Century readers may have been better at recognizing these literary expressions than the average modern reader. Today, a Westerner is more adept at *seeing* narratives than reading them.[8] However, explanations that make the implicit explicit can liberate readers to view the biblical narrative as more than a news account of what happened, but as an artful expression of narrative theology that calls the reader to fully engage.[9] These narratives are not *plain-glass windows* to be looked *through*, but *stained-glass windows* to be looked *at*.[10]

This study will examine three examples of joined stories in New Testament narratives: Gabriel's announcements to Zacharias and Mary (Lk. 1:5-38); Jesus' conversations with Nicodemus and the Woman at the Well (Jn. 3:1-12; 4:1-21); and Peter's healings of Aeneas and Tabitha (Acts 9:32-42). These three narratives each include an implied comparison between a man and a woman, and none of them are controversial in terms of biblical gender studies. Like all writers, biblical authors were selective in their

---

Charles Talbert, *Reading John: A Literary and Theological Commentary on the Fourth Gospel and Johannine Epistles* (Smyth & Helwys Publishing, 2012), 103.

[7] An example of implied narrative connections may be found in Luke 17:3-10 where Jesus instructs his disciples to forgive a brother who sins against him seven times a day and repents (Lk. 17:3-4). The apostles recognize the difficulty of what Jesus has commanded and say, "Increase our faith" (Lk. 17:5). Jesus then teaches that a little faith can do great things—"say to this mulberry tree, 'Be uprooted and be placed in the sea' and it would obey you" (Lk. 17:5). Jesus then tells a parable about a servant who works in the field, comes in and prepares a meal for his master, properly dresses and serves his master, and then later eats his own meal. The point of the story is that the master does not thank the servant for what he did, because he only did what was commanded of him. Then in verse 10 Jesus states: "So you too, when you do all the things which are commanded you, say 'We are unnecessary servants, we have done that which we ought to have done.'" The implied logical connection of the units is: (1) forgive your brother when he sins against you numerous times; (2) you do not need more faith to obey this command, since a little bit of faith can do enormous things; (3) you need to be obedient as servants.

[8] As experienced movie viewers, we intuitively grasp a flash-back without the need for text that states: "Ten Years Earlier." However, when directors, like Terrance Malick, juxtapose large sections of a movie beside one another without explanation as in *The Tree of Life* (2011), or *To the Wonder* (2012), the implied world/meaning is more difficult for the modern audience to grasp.

[9] This writer has recently experienced precisely this kind of growth as a new participant in the liturgy of the Anglican Church. For instance, at first, I only observed with the interest of a child, that the reader of the Gospels came down from the platform to read in the middle of the center isle in the midst of the congregation. Then a friend mentioned in passing that this act pictured the incarnation of Christ—who left his realm and came to dwell among us. My eyes were then opened to look at other elements in the liturgy and ask what is being impliedly communicated through these express symbols.

[10] *See* Abraham Kuruvilla, *Mark: A Theological Commentary for Preachers* (Eugene, Oregon: Cascade Books, 2012), xiv.

material (*see* Jn. 20:30-31; 21:25). Men could have been compared with men just as easily as with women. Therefore, it is significant that these writers often chose to align narratives involving men and women to show their narrative theology.[11] Each narrative discussion will be preceded by charts that attempt to *show* the narrative whole before its particulars are discussed.

---

[11] Some might protest that the narrative with Zacharias and Mary had to be told together because that is what happened—Gabriel appeared to both of them. However, the other Gospel writers did not feel a need to express this information. Mark completely omits any background information about Jesus; both John the Baptizer and Jesus first appear as adults in his Gospel (Mk. 1:1-14). John has more of a theological prelude to his Gospel than an historical account (Jn. 1:1-18), and Matthew does not identify Gabriel's appearance to Mary, but the appearance of an angel of the Lord (ἄγγελος κυρίου) to Joseph (Matt. 1:18-21). We only specifically know about Gabriel's appearances to Zacharias and Mary through Luke's pairing of the stories in his narrative setting to the Gospel. Luke not only chose *what* to include but *how* to arrange the material—by placing the stories of Zacharias and Mary next to one another.

Gabriel's Announcements to Zacharias and Mary
(Luke 1:5-38)

Luke's use of interchange, or duality and balance, in chapters 1 and 2 of his Gospel invites the reader to compare and contrast parallel narratives: [12]

	Zacharias and Elizabeth	Mary	Mary and Elizabeth	Zacharias and Elizabeth	Joseph and Mary
Historical Setting	Herod (1:5)	Nazareth (1:26)			Caesar And Quirinius (2:1-3)
Life Setting	Righteous, No children, Old (1:6-7)	A virgin, engaged (1:27)			Of the house of David, engaged (2:4-5)
Announcement	To Zacharias (1:8-20)	To Mary (1:28-37)			
Response to the Announcement	Zacharias (1:21-23) Elizabeth (1:24-25)	Mary (1:38)	Mary (1:39-40) Elizabeth (1:41-45) Mary (1:46-56)		

---

[12] This chart is adopted and adapted from David E. Malick, "A Literary Approach to the Birth Narratives in Luke 1—2" in *Integrity of Heart, Skillfulness of Hands: Biblical and Leadership Studies in Honor of Donald K. Campbell*, ed. Charles H. Dyer and Roy B. Zuck (Grand Rapids: Baker Books 1994), 94. A similar chiastic structure is set forth by François Bovon:
    a declaration of the birth of John the Baptist (1:5-25)
    a' declaration of the birth of Jesus the Messiah (1:26-38)
    b meeting between Mary and Elizabeth (1:39-56)
    c birth of John the Baptist (1:57-80)
    c' birth of Jesus the Messiah (2:1-40)
Das Evangelium Nac Lukas, Vol. 1: Lk 1,1-9,50. Evangelisch-Katholischer Kommentar Zum Neun Testament III/I. (Zurich; Benzinger/Neukirchen-Vluyn: Neukirchener Verlag, 1989), 46-47; *see also* Darrell L. Bock, *Luke: Volume 1:1:1—9:50.* (Grand Rapids, MI: Baker Books, 1994), 68, 102.; Joseph A. Fitzmyer's "The Structure Of The Lucan Infancy Narrative" *The Gospel According to Luke (I-IX): Introduction, Translation, and Notes* The Anchor Bible (Garden City, NY: Doubleday & Company, Inc., 1979), 313-14; Raymond E. Brown, *The Birth of the Messiah: A Commentary on the Infancy Narratives in Matthew and Luke* (New York, NY: Doubleday, 1977), 294-97.

	Zacharias and Elizabeth	Mary	Mary and Elizabeth	Zacharias and Elizabeth	Joseph and Mary
Birth				John (1:57)	Jesus (2:6-7)
Response to the Birth				Neighbors and Relatives (1:58)	Angles and shepherds (2:8-20)
Circumcision				Fact (59-64) People (1:65-66) Zacharias (1:67-79)	Fact (2:21-24) Simeon (2:25-35) Anna (2:36-38)
Child's Growth				John (1:80)	Jesus (2:39-52)

An historical setting introduces each main character: **(a)** Zacharias, the Jewish priest, and his wife, Elizabeth from the daughters of Aaron, through Herod, the "King of the Jews;" **(b)** Mary through Nazareth of racially mixed Galilee; and **(c)** Joseph through the secular, international setting of Caesar Augustus, ruler of Rome, and Quirinius, governor of Syria:

> The placement of the characters is conspicuous: the one who cannot receive the message in Jerusalem, the one who can receive the message outside of Jerusalem, and the one to be the Savior of the world born under Roman rule.[13]

A life setting also describes significant characteristics of each main character. Zacharias and Elizabeth are "both righteous before God, walking blamelessly in all the commandments and requirements of the Lord" (Lk. 1:6), but they are without children and advanced in age (1:7). Mary is a virgin, engaged to Joseph (1:27); and Joseph is of royal lineage—of the descendants, house, and family of David (2:4-5; cf. 1:27).

Already differences and similarities are apparent between Zacharias and Mary; most of which are *explicitly* stated for Zacharias and *impliedly* apparent for Mary. He is old, advanced in days (προβεβηκότες ἐν ταῖς ἡμέραις αὐτῶν ἦσαν); she is young, at least by implication since she is a virgin and engaged to be married. Both are righteous. The term righteous (δίκαιοι) is explicitly used of Zacharias (and Elizabeth), and they are described as walking blamelessly (ἄμεμπτοι) in all the commandments and requirements of the Lord (ἐν πάσαις ταῖς ἐντολαῖς καὶ δικαιώμασιν τοῦ κυρίου). Mary is implicitly righteous in that she is a virgin (παρθένον) in her engaged state. Finally, both Zacharias and Elizabeth are

---

[13] Malick, "A Literary Approach to the Birth Narratives," 95.

without children. Elizabeth is explicitly described as barren (ἦν ἡ Ἐλισάβετ στεῖρα), and Mary is once again impliedly childless because she is a virgin.

The abundant, explicit descriptions of Zacharias as an older, married, righteous, priest set up a high expectation for the reader—perhaps higher than for a young, engaged, single woman from Nazareth. But there is one flaw in the fabric of Zacharias and Elizabeth's lives—they are without children. This might be felt as a personal disgrace for the couple (Lk. 1:25), but it was also an opportunity for God to show his powerful hand for the benefit of them and the nation of Israel.[14] Even though Mary is without children in the narrative, it is expected because she is a virgin. The giving of a child to the two couples will have an inverse effect—blessing for Zacharias and Elizabeth and potential cursing for Mary and Joseph because of Mary's unwed status. It is at this desolate intersection of Zacharias's forlorn dreams and Mary's unimaginable expectations that the Lord sends a messenger with direction. How these two righteous, but disparate, individuals respond to the message surprises the reader with new insight.

---

[14] Often in the Hebrew Scriptures the Lord worked to overcome bareness so that when a child finally was born there was no question that the Lord was the source of blessing, and the child was to be significant in the life of the nation. *See* Abraham and Sarah who gave birth to Isaac (Gen. 18:9-14; 21:1-3); Isaac and Rebekah who gave birth to Jacob (Gen. 25:20-21); Jacob and Rachel who gave birth to Joseph (Gen. 29:31; 30:1-8, 22-24), Judah and Tamar who gave birth to Perez (Gen. 38); Manoah and his wife who gave birth to Sampson (Judges 13:2-24); Boaz and Ruth who gave birth to Obed (Ruth 1:4-5; 4:13-17); Elkanah and Hannah who gave birth to Samuel (1 Sam. 1:2, 5, 11, 19-20); and Psalm 113:9.

Gabriel's announcements to Zacharias and Mary contain numerous, repetitive parallels which invite the reader to compare the characters:[15]

	ZACHARIAS	MARY
GABRIEL	**APPEARS** (vv. 11-12) • to him • in the holy place • Zacharias is afraid	**APPEARS** (vv. 26-28) • to her • in Nazareth • Mary is confused

	ANNOUNCES (vv. 13-17)
	• do not fear
	• your prayer is heard
	• you will have a son
	  o John
	  o great
	  o no wine; filled with the Holy Spirit
	  o prepare for the King
		ANNOUNCES (vv. 28-33)
		• do not fear
		• you have found favor
		• you will have a son
		  o Jesus
		  o great
		  o Son of the Most High
		  o King over Jacob

	AFFIRMS (vv. 19-20) • Source and nature of message • Mute	**AFFIRMS** (vv. 35-37) • Holy Spirit • Elizabeth • God's word

Comparisons in Gabriel's two appearances yield similarities and differences. Gabriel comes to Zacharias in the holy place of the temple, to the right of the altar of incense, in the holy city of Jerusalem (1:11). Gabriel shows himself to Mary in what may

---

[15] This table is adopted and adapted from Malick, "A Literary Approach to the Birth Narratives," 96-97. These announcements are very similar to Robert Alter's "annunciation type-scene" which "points to the weighty role in history for the child who is to be born, since only for such portentous figures is this sort of divine intervention in the natural order of conception required." *The Art of Biblical Narrative*. (New York, NY: Basic Books, Inc., 1981), 85. Alter sets forth the fixed pattern of the annunciation type-scene as including: "the barren wife's being vouchsafed an oracle, a prophecy from a man of God, or a promise from an angel, that she will be granted as son, sometimes with an explicit indication of the son's destiny, often with the invocation of the formula, 'At this season next year, you will be embracing a son.'" *Ibid*. There are permutations in the pattern in these announcements: the oracle is to Zacharias instead of Elizabeth; Mary is not barren but a virgin; and there is no formula setting forth the time of the birth. Nevertheless, the echoes of this pattern portend to the greatness of these children. *See* the announcements of the birth of Ishmael (Gen. 16:7-13); Isaac (Gen. 17:1-21; 18:1-15); Samson (Judg. 13:3-20); Samuel (1Sam. 1); *see also* Joseph A. Fitzmyer, *The Gospel According to Luke (I-IX): Introduction, Translation, and Notes*, The Anchor Bible (Garden City, NY: Doubleday & Company, Inc , 1979), 318, 335.

have been her home,[16] in the racially-mixed, northern region of Galilee, in the disdained city of Nazareth.[17] These contrasting locations (one holy, the other common) and contrasting recipients (a male priest; a young woman) capture the reader's curiosity. One might expect an angel to appear to a priest in the temple, but not to a woman at home in Nazareth of Galilee. Even though Gabriel's message will be good for each of the recipients, its effect will turn expectations upside down.

Gabriel's announcements to Zacharias and Mary have many similarities, with a progression of thought between them.[18] Each begins with a personal exhortation to stop being afraid (1:13, 30).[19] The quelling of their apprehension is then followed with a reason: for Zacharias, it is because (διότι) his petition (δέησίς) has been heard; for Mary it is because (γὰρ) she has found grace (χάριν) before God.[20] Each reason appears to be tied to God's presence in the individual's life situation. In the giving of a child, the Lord shows

---

[16] The text says, "and entering to her" (αἰ εἰσελθὼν πρὸς αὐτὴν) (Lk. 1:28). Kenneth R.R. Gros Louis astutely observes a significant distinction in the John and Jesus stories: "The events surrounding the birth of John, we notice, are heavily publicized; that is, many are involved—the multitude perplexed at the temple, the neighbors and kinfolk marveling at the circumcision, the countryside gossiping about 'what then will this child be?' By contrast, the events surrounding the birth of Jesus are private and isolated: Gabriel appears to Mary when she is alone, her news is shared only with Elizabeth and presumably with Joseph, the narrative takes Joseph and his family away from their home town, and therefore away from their neighbors and kinfolk, to be enrolled in Bethlehem; and even in that town, there is no room at the inn and the child must be born in a manger, out of sight, unnoticed by those who fill the inn." "The Jesus Birth Stories" in *Literary Interpretations of Biblical Narratives*, vol. II, ed. Kenneth R.R. Gros Louis (Nashville, TN: Abingdon 1982), 282-83. *See also* Bock, *Luke*, I:107 ("Luke contrasts the greatness of the setting of the announcement about John with the simplicity of the announcement about Jesus. The tone of the setting of Jesus' birth matches the tone of his ministry. The great God of heaven sends the gift of salvation to humans in a serene unadorned package of simplicity").

[17] As Nathanael said to Philip, "Can any good thing come out of Nazareth?" (Jn. 1:46). Frederick W. Danker observes: "That Gabriel, one of the eminent members of the heavenly council, should come to insignificant Nazareth and present himself before this undistinguished villager is a miracle of the New Age. This event presages the announcement of the Magnificat, that the mighty are brought low and the humble exalted. (v. 52.)." *Jesus and the New Age: A Commentary on St. Luke's Gospel.* Rev. and expanded (Philadelphia, PA: Fortress Press, 1988), 35. Although the Western manuscript (D) omits "which is named Nazareth," it is attested in the Alexandrian and Byzantine texts.

[18] As Fitzmyer describes it: "there is a step-parallelism at work, i.e. a parallelism with one-upmanship. The Jesus-side always comes off better." *Luke*, I:315.

[19] μὴ φοβοῦ, Ζαχαρία (v. 13); μὴ φοβοῦ, Μαριάμ (v. 30). The present imperative plus μή allows for the idea of cessation of activity in progress. As Dan Wallace states, "Here the idea is frequently progressive and the prohibition is of the 'cessation of some act that is already in progress.' It has the idea, *Stop continuing.* μὴ φοβοῦ is thus naturally used as the formula to quell someone's apprehensions." Daniel B. Wallace, *Greek Grammar: Beyond the Basics: An Exegetical Syntax of the New Testament* (Grand Rapids: Zondervan, 1996), 724.

[20] Many witnesses (including A C D Θ f^{13} 33 m latt sy bo^{mss}; Eus) add "blessed are you among women" (ευλογημενη συ εν γυναιξιν). However, it is probable that a copyist inserted these words from 1:42 where they originally appear from the mouth of Elizabeth. It is easier to see how these words were added, than to explain why they were removed. The shorter reading is supported by ℵ B L W Ψ f^1 565. 579. 700. 1241 *pc* co; Or^{lem} Epiph. *See* Bruce M. Metzger, *A Textual Commentary on the Greek New Testament.* 2d ed. (Stuttgart: Deutsch Biblgesellschaft, 1994), 108.

that he has heard Zacharias's prayer, and that Mary has found grace before him in this most unimaginable work.

Gabriel announces to each that they will have a son (1:13; 31).[21] Then the characteristics and ministries of the children are described with the younger, through Mary, being greater than the older through Zacharias (*see* 1:36).[22] Zacharias is to name the child John (1:13), and Mary is to name the child Jesus (1:31).[23] Both children are prophesized to be great (ἔσται μέγας)[24] (1:15, 32).[25] John will be separated unto the Lord (as a priest? Lev.

---

[21] The announcement in each case is given with respect to the woman baring a son. To Zacharias Gabriel states: "and your wife Elizabeth will bear a son to you" (καὶ ἡ γυνή σου Ἐλισάβετ γεννήσει υἱόν σοι), and to Mary Gabriel states: "And behold, you will conceive in *your* womb, and bear a son" (καὶ ἰδοὺ συλλήμψῃ ἐν γαστρὶ καὶ τέξῃ υἱόν).

[22] The theme that the younger will be greater than the older has its origins in Genesis where Abel was over Cain (Gen. 4), Shem was over Japheth (cf. Gen. 5:32; 7:5; 9:24; 10:21; 11:10); Abram was over his brothers (cf. Gen. 11:26, 32; 12:4); Isaac was over Ishmael (Gen. 16; 21:1-5, 12); Jacob was over Esau (Gen. 25:23); Rachel was loved over Leah (Gen. 29:21-26, 31); Joseph was over his brothers (Gen. 30:22-24; 37:5-11); Perez was over Zerah (Gen. 38:27-30); and Ephraim was over Manasseh (Gen. 48:8-19). For blessing to come through the younger was against the natural custom of life in favor of the progenitor. However, the Lord turns social custom upside down so that people will know that he is involved in the blessing. God can bless and use people from outside the paths of society's expectations. Even though John and Jesus are not from the same parents, the narrator is employing an intense comparison so that the reader will correlate them with one another and see that the younger (Jesus) is greater than the older (John). Even in the Genesis accounts the pattern of parentage is deviated from when Ishmael is born of Hagar, while Isaac is born of Sarah. Here there are two sets of parents, instead of only two mothers with Ishmael and Isaac, but the children are both from the Lord with an intensity placed upon the younger who, unlike John, is supernaturally begotten, and fulfills what John announces. God is turning social custom upside down in a climactic way through the birth of Jesus.

[23] These Hebrew names contribute to the message of the unit. John (Ἰωάννην/יְהוֹחָנָן) includes the sense of "grace;" Jesus (Ἰησοῦν/יֵשׁוּעַ) has the sense of "Yahweh is salvation." Zachariah (Ζαχαρία/זְכַרְיָה) means "Yahweh remembers," and Elizabeth (Ἐλισάβετ/אֱלִישֶׁבַע) means "covenant of God." The gracious God who remembers his covenant is now moving to save his people. *See* Malick, "A Literary Approach to the Birth Narratives," 105 n. 19. Commenting on the name "John" Fitzmyer contends: "Whether Gentile converts would have grasped the nuance may be missing the point; the implication is that God's grace or favor is now to come to humanity in a new form." *Luke*, I:318.

[24] John will be "great before the Lord" (μέγας ἐνώπιον [τοῦ] κυρίου) (1:15). Jesus is described as being great with no qualifier—"this one will be great" (οὗτος ἔσται μέγας) (1:32). As Fitzmyer observes: "Laurentin (*Structure*, 36) calls attention to the absolute use of *megas* "great," there and to the fact that in the LXX the absolute *megas* is an attribute of Yahweh himself (see Pss 48:2 = 145:3; 86:10; 135:5) whereas the adjective is qualified when it is used of human beings (see 2 Sam 19:33 LXX; Sir. 48:22). So it is here in the case of John. John's greatness (see Luke 7:28) is here measured in terms of *Kyrios*, who in this context is to be understood as Yahweh." *Luke*, I:325; *see also* Bock, *Luke*, I:84 ("So the unqualified description of Jesus with just this term in Luke 1:32 suggests Jesus' superiority to John and implies that Jesus is closer to Yahweh than is John.")

[25] An anomaly in the parallel structure is that before John is described as being great, Gabriel tells Zacharias that the child will bring him joy and gladness, and that many will rejoice at his birth (καὶ ἔσται χαρά σοι καὶ ἀγαλλίασις καὶ πολλοὶ ἐπὶ τῇ γενέσει αὐτοῦ χαρήσονται.) (1:14). The lack of perfect symmetry between the announcements to Zacharias and Mary does not invalidate the overall parallel structure. Charles H. Talbert notes well that perfect symmetry was not always valued in Greek and Ancient Near Eastern cultures. *Literary Patterns, Theological Themes, and the Genre of Luke-Acts*. (Missoula, MT: Society of Biblical Literature and Scholars Press, 1974), 78-79. Summarizing from his study in Luke-Acts, Talbert states: "Our survey of analogies has shown that symmetrophobia is at work in the composition of Israelite-

10:9; as a Nazirite? Num. 6:3, a prophet? 1 Sam. 1:11)²⁶ and filled with the Holy Spirit while still in his mother's womb (1:15).²⁷ On the other hand, Jesus will be called son of the Most High (υἱὸς ὑψίστου κληθήσεται) and the Lord God will give to him the Davidic throne (δώσει αὐτῷ κύριος ὁ θεὸς τὸν θρόνον Δαυὶδ τοῦ πατρὸς αὐτοῦ) (1:32; *cf*. Ps. 110:1). John will prepare the way for the King as the new Elijah (1:16-17; *cf*. Mal. 4:5-6), but Jesus will be the King who will rule over the people of Israel (the house of Jacob, οἶκον Ἰακώβ) forever (1:33). Clearly, the son of this woman from Galilee will be much greater than this older, magnificent son from Zacharias.

Jewish prose as well. Given the aversion to perfect symmetry in both classical and Near Eastern cultures, it is no surprise to find imperfections in the patterns of the early Christian writings of our survey and of Luke-Acts. They are to be expected in the midst of the most perfect symmetry." *Ibid.*, 79. Perhaps Luke's insertion about joy over the birth of John heightens the reader's expectation concerning Zacharias over Mary, but this is about to change with what follows in Gabriel's revelation to both parents.

[26] Darrell Bock comments that: "John lives a life of discipline. The restriction from wine represents special consecration. In the OT, such a restriction existed for the priests when they were performing their duties (Lev. 10:9). A more permanent restriction existed for the Nazirite, who could make a vow not to drink during his or her whole life (Judg. 13:4-5) or could vow to refrain for special periods (Num. 6:1-31). The strongest OT parallel to the wording here is 1 Sam. 1:11, an allusion to Samuel, who was presented as Israel's first prophet. By this parallel, John's office is implicitly affirmed." *Luke*, I:84-85.

[27] As Fitzmyer observes: "Yahweh's spirit will fill him instead of the drink from which he is to abstain." *Luke*, I:326.

The character and ministries of these children reverse the readers' expectations with an effect that the reader looks more closely at Mary in the response to Gabriel's message:[28]

	ZACHARIAH	ELIZABETH[29]	MARY
RESPONSE TO THE ANNOUNCEMENT	Troubled, fearful (1:12)		Confused, wondered what this would mean (1:29)
	"Prove it" (perhaps a spirit of suspicion or doubt due to old age and being hardened) (1:18) Is made mute (1:22) Went to the people (1:22) and to his home to Elizabeth (1:23)		Questioned how this could occur since she had not known a man; yet she agreed (1:38) Receives God's word Went to Elizabeth and rejoiced (1:39, 46-55)
	←————	Responded in a *quiet* way; kept herself in seclusion for five months (1:24) Responded in a *joyful* way (1:41-45)	————→
	God's Servant?		**God's Servant!**

Zacharias's response to this wonderful, joyful, fulfilling answer to prayer is to request proof: "According to what [how] will I know this (κατὰ τί γνώσομαι τοῦτο)" because we are old (1:18)?[30] Mary too asks a question in response to this incomprehensible announcement, but it is not for a sign, but for an explanation about how this is physically

---

[28] The following chart is adopted and adapted from Malick, "A Literary Approach to the Birth Narratives," 100.

[29] Elizabeth "is highlighted as both Zechariah and Mary travel to her. . . . Unlike Zechariah and Mary, Elizabeth only heard of the angel's visits; she had not seen the visions. Thus she stands in the place of the reader, who also is 'hearing' a report of what happened. In each case she was able to respond appropriately; she chose to be quiet with her husband (vv. 24-25) and to rejoice with Mary (vv. 41-45)." Ibid., 100-101

[30] Zacharias's question, "according to what [or how] shall I know?" is similar to Sarah's laughter after the Lord announced to Abraham that he would bare a son (Gen. 18:1-15). Sarah laughed because both she and Abraham were old (Gen. 18:12). Zacharias raises the very same issue—"for I am old and my wife is advance in her days" (Lk. 1:18). Just as the Lord addressed Sarah's laughter (Gen. 18:13-14), so does Gabriel address Zacharias request for proof so that he will know the truth of this message (Lk. 1:19). Of particular interest in the Lucan birth narratives is that the gender roles are reversed from the account in Genesis 18. In Genesis it was the woman who laughed, but in Luke it is the man who asks for proof.

possible for her as a virgin: "How is this since I do not know a man (πῶς ἔσται τοῦτο, ἐπεὶ ἄνδρα οὐ γινώσκω)" (1:34)?[31]

Gabriel's reply is *tailored* to each question, but *parallel in function*. Because of the many parallels between the announcements up to this point, it is logical to assume that Gabriel's reply to each party is functionally the same even if the content is necessarily different. The clear *affirmation* to Mary informs the reader of the function of Gabriel's words to Zacharias—they are to *affirm* him in the message that he is having difficulty believing, not simply to rebuke him.[32] For Mary who receives the word (1:38), the message is *affirmed* through an explanation and confirmation (1:35-17). For Zacharias who seeks proof of Gabriel's word, the message is *affirmed* through a confirmation that Gabriel brings this good news from God and a physical sign—his inability to speak (1:19-20).[33] Because of Mary's belief, she is told that the child will be supernaturally begotten (γεννώμενον) by the Holy Spirit (πνεῦμα ἅγιον), that her barren relative, Elizabeth, is in her sixth month of

---

[31] Bock notes: "In manuscript b of the Old Latin version, 1:34 is omitted and 1:38 appears leading some to suggest that 1:34 is not original to Luke's Gospel." Continuing he explains: "The possibility of an interpolation is to be rejected. First the textual evidence for the view is weak, limited to versions in the Western family. Second, the question's removal destroys the parallelism with the account of Zachariah, where he too responds to the announcement with a question. Third, the question's presence follows the standard form of birth announcements where the announcement often sparks a question or a request (Gen. 17:17; Judg. 13:8; R. Brown 1997: 307-308)." *Luke*, I:118-19.

[32] Contrary to many who view Zacharias' silence as punishment or discipline, *see* Witherington, *Women and the Genesis of Christianity*, ed. Ann Witherington (Cambridge: Cambridge University Press, 1990), 204; Bock, *Luke*, I:70, 74, 80, 91, **93**, 100; Danker: *Jesus and the New Age*, 32-33; Fitzmyer, *Luke*, I:328. However, I. Howard Marshall understands the sign to be both a punishment and "a confirmation of his prophecy." *The Gospel of Luke: A Commentary on the Greek Text*, The New International Greek Testament Commentary (Grand Rapids, MI: William B. Eerdmans Publishing Company, 1978), 60, 61 ("We should not, therefore, regard Zechariah's request simply as a punishment for unbelief. . . . These elements are certainly present (1:20), but in fact a sign is given, and it serves the deeper purpose of concealing the wonder of what was to happen until the due time.")

[33] Zacharias is first reminded that the angel is Gabriel who stands before God and was sent by God to speak this good news. This statement can be scanned as though it communicates outrage, but the words themselves place this understanding in question. If this is a rebuke to Zacharias for disregarding a message from an angel of such high rank and esteem, then why emphasize that he was sent by God (implied from the passive form of ἀπεστάλην), to communicate good news (εὐαγγελίσασθαί)? It is entirely possible that Gabriel's words are meant to answer Zacharias's question by confirming the source and nature of his message. Then as another affirmation of how Zacharias can know that these words are true, he will be silent and unable to speak until the time that these prophetic words come into being. In other words, he is not punished for his request for proof, but given evidence that he will comprehend (ἀνθ' ὧν οὐκ ἐπίστευσας τοῖς λόγοις μου) so that he will believe that the child is all that the angel has promised—the answer to his prayer for Elizabeth and himself and for the nation of Israel.

pregnancy, and that with God everything ([spoken word], ῥῆμα) is possible.³⁴ Therefore, Mary says, let it be to me according to your word (ῥῆμά).³⁵

The surprise for the reader is that even though Zacharias had all of the appearances of being the servant of the Lord as he ministered as an elder priest in the temple, in the Holy Place, and heard a message from an angel about a son who would prepare the way for the Davidic King, it is actually Mary who is the *servant of the Lord*, and this identity is placed upon her very lips: "behold, **the servant of the Lord**, may it be to me according to your word" (ἰδοὺ **ἡ δούλη κυρίου**· γένοιτό μοι κατὰ τὸ ῥῆμά σου).³⁶

That Mary was "greater than Zacharias" may be obvious, and even mundane, from the distance of history. However, from the narrative world of Luke's Gospel, from a first encounter of these characters, this outcome is shocking. Nevertheless, the narrative architecture of duality and balance constrains the reader to compare these accounts and arrive at this conclusion—it is not the male priest serving in the Temple who is the servant of the Lord even though he bares all of the outward appearances to that position, but it is the young women in Galilee who is the true servant of the Lord because she welcomes an incomprehensible word from the Lord.

This is but one example of where the narrative structure implicitly exalts a woman over a man—even one who is a leader in the community.

---

[34] Once again, this appears to be an echo from the Lord's word to Sarah: "Is anything too difficult for the Lord? (הֲיִפָּלֵא מֵיְהוָה דָּבָר)" (Gen. 18:14). The LXX translates the Hebrew μὴ ἀδυνατεῖ παρὰ τῷ θεῷ ῥῆμα. This Greek language is nearly identical in word choice to Gabriel's words in Luke 1:38: οὐκ ἀδυνατήσει παρὰ τοῦ θεοῦ πᾶν ῥῆμα. With Sarah this statement was placed as a question because she, like Zacharias, questioned the truth of the prophecy in their old age. However, with Mary it is stated as an affirmation confirming the most amazing message that she will conceive a child as a virgin outside of marriage.

[35] Unlike Zacharias who says "*According to* what (κατὰ τί) shall I know this?" (1:18), Mary says, "*according to* your word (κατὰ τὸ ῥῆμά σου) let it be to me" (1:38). Witherington correctly observes: "Mary's reaction to Gabriel's explanation is the classic expression of submission to God's word and will: 'Behold, I am the handmaid of the Lord; let it be to me according to your word' (1.38). The meaning of 1.38 is toned down by the translation 'handmaiden,' for the actual meaning is 'Behold the slave of the Lord.' Thus, Luke portrays Mary as binding herself totally to God's will, giving up her plans and desires for the future. Her response was one of submission in full recognition of what effect this act of God could have for her social position and relation to Joseph. We see the Evangelist presenting Mary as one who is willing to give up betrothal and reputation for God's purposes, the sort of self-sacrifice which, in Luke's Gospel, is the mark of a disciple." *Women and the Genesis of Christianity*, ed. Ann Witherington (Cambridge: Cambridge University Press, 1990), 205. As Bock summarizes: "There is risk in agreeing to go God's way, but as the Lord's servant, she willingly goes." *Luke*, I:127.

[36] "The servant of God is not determined by gender, age, position, function, or location, but by the one who can receive the Word of God." Malick, "A Literary Approach to the Birth Narratives," 101.

Jesus' Conversations with Nicodemus and the Woman at the Well
(John 3:1-12/21; 4:1-21)

As with Luke's accounts with Zacharias and Mary, John's accounts with Nicodemus and the Woman at the Well involve unique stories not included in the synoptic gospels. One difficulty in comparing Jesus' discussions with Nicodemus in John 3 and the Woman in John 4 is that there is an intervening narrative with John the Baptizer and his disciples in John 3:22-36.[37] Even though these two narratives are not immediately juxtaposed spatially, they are conceptually. Jesus has spoken to individuals in brief sentences previously in John (cf. Jn. 1:38, 39, 42, 47, 48, 50; 2:4, 8, 16, 19). These two discourses mark the first extended discussions Jesus has with individuals. Therefore, they invite the reader to compare the interactions of Jesus with a named man who is a religious leader in Jerusalem and an unnamed woman of difficult circumstances in Samaria. The parallels are primarily characterized by contrasts:[38]

---

[37] There may also be a narrative commentary on Jesus' discourse with Nicodemus in John 3:13-21. Rudolf Schnackenburg, *The Gospel According to St John: Volume One: Introduction and Commentary on Chapters 1—4* (New York, NY: Crossroad Publishing Company) 361-63 ("The dialogue with Nicodemus, as the evangelist wished to present it, comprises only vv. 1-12 . . . . Verses 13-21 do not form part of the Gospel narrative, but come from a kerygmatic exposition of the evangelist which was originally independent."); Talbert, *Reading John*, 100; Keener allows for the words to be Jesus' in 3:10-13, but then "the Johannine Jesus" through 3:21. *The Gospel of John: A Commentary*. Vol. 1 (Peabody, MA: Hendrickson Publishers, LLC), 558-59. D.A. Carson understands the discourse with Nicodemus to extend through 3:1-15, and views 3:17-21 as an extended comment. *The Gospel According to John*, The Pillar New Testament Commentary (Grand Rapids, MI: William B. Eerdmans Publishing Company 1991), 105, 185, 203-204 ("in vv. 1-21, the words of Jesus probably trail off at the end of v. 15, to be followed by the mediation of the Evangelist in vv. 16-21"). Raymond E. Brown argues for continuity in the discourse throughout 3:1-21. *The Gospel According To John (i-xii): Introduction, Translation, and Notes*. The Anchor Bible, vol. 29 (New York, NY: Doubleday 1966), 149.

[38] Brown identifies an implied contrast of faith between the account of Nicodemus and the Woman at the Well when he states: "We can scarcely believe that the evangelist did not mean for us to contrast the unsatisfactory faith of the Jews in ii 23-25 based on a superficial admiration of miracles with the deeper faith of the Samaritans based on the word of Jesus. Nicodemus, the rabbi of Jerusalem, could not understand Jesus' message that God had sent the Son into the world so that the world might be saved through him (iii 17); yet the peasants of Samaria readily come to know that Jesus is really the Savior of the World." *John*, I:185. Similarly, Keener writes: "Nicodemus's partial faith continues the theme of 2:23-25, but contrasts starkly with the fully reliable witness of John (3:21-26) and the responsiveness of the sinful Samaritan woman (4:1-42). . . . John invites his audience to contrast Nicodemus's slow response here to the ready response of the Samaritan woman in 4:7-29, who is able to overcome her misunderstanding in the course of that dialogue." *John*, 533. In his introduction to John 4:1-54, Keener also writes: "THE BULK OF THIS SECTION, which actually continues the general thought of 3:1-36, revolves around a sinful Samaritan woman and her response to Jesus. If the initial faith of the best representative from the Judean elite appears ambiguous (3:1-10), the faith of the socially worst representative from an unorthodox and ethnically mixed sect appears far more positive, even allowing her to bring her people as a whole to Jesus. . . . This extended narrative contrasts starkly with the Nicodemus narrative. There a religious teacher in Israel proved unable to understand Jesus' message (3:10); here a sinful Samaritan woman not only received the message (though starting with no less daunting social obstacles—cf πῶς in 3:4,9 and 4:9; perhaps πόθεν in 4:11), but brought it to her entire Samaritan town (4:28-29, 39-42). Here, as often, John employs ironic contrasts among

Nicodemus	The Samaritan Woman
A man	A woman
In Jerusalem	In Sycar
Ruler of the Jews	A Samaritan
Comes at night	Comes in the middle of the day
Is seeking out Jesus	Is sought out by Jesus
Knows who Jesus is	Does not know who Jesus is
Misperceives words with ambiguous meaning: "born again/above" (γεννηθῇ ἄνωθεν)	Misperceives words with ambiguous meaning: "living water" (ὕδωρ ζῶν)
Asks about spiritual; fixates on the natural	Asks about natural; receives the spiritual
Says little	Says much
Wonders if Jesus is Messiah	Learns directly that Jesus is Messiah
Rebuked by Jesus; response is not given	Response is favorable; publicly proclaims Jesus as Messiah

The beginning of each narrative introduces the minor characters in dialogue with Jesus, as a man (ἄνθρωπος)[39] and a woman (γυνὴ) (3:1; 4:7). Nicodemus is immediately set apart as a Pharisee (ἐκ τῶν Φαρισαίων) and a leader of the Jews (ἄρχων τῶν Ἰουδαίων) (3:1). Nicodemus is explicitly named (Νικόδημος ὄνομα αὐτῷ),[40] but the woman is anonymous and only described as coming "from Samaria" (ἐκ τῆς Σαμαρείας) (4:7). This location, Sycar, contrasts with Jerusalem where Nicodemus appears to meet Jesus during the Passover feast (2:23). At the threshold of each story, expectations are set for the reader when a known, eminently respectable, religious leader in Jerusalem and an unknown woman from Samaria begin a conversation with Jesus.

---

characters to convey his emphases. . . . The contrast between Nicodemus and the Samaritan woman (as well as some other characters) would frustrate a normal ancient Jewish reader's expectations (although John's own original audience already may be predisposed to suspect that the Judean elite is more hostile)." *Ibid.* at 584-85. Witherington likewise introduces his discussion of the Woman at the Well with the following comparison with Nicodemus: "Perhaps we see a contrast between Nicodemus of Jn 3, a teacher and representative of orthodox Judaism who fails to understand Jesus, and the common Samaritan woman who gains some insight into Jesus' true character." *Women in the Ministry of Jesus: A Study of Jesus' Attitudes to Woman and their Roles as Reflected in His Earthly Life* (New York, NY: Cambridge University Press, 1984), 57. Likewise, Carson writes: "John may intend a contrast between the woman of this narrative and Nicodemus of ch. 3. He was learned, powerful respected, orthodox, theologically trained; she was unschooled, without influence, despised, capable only of folk religion. He was a man, a Jew, a ruler; she was a woman, a Samaritan, a moral outcast. And both needed Jesus." *John*, 216.

[39] Perhaps the more generic word for "man" (ἄνθρωπος) is used in 3:1 because of the statement in the immediately preceding verse that Jesus "knew what was in man (ἐγίνωσκεν τί ἦν ἐν τῷ ἀνθρώπῳ)" (2:25); *see* Keener, *John*, I:535.

[40] As Keener observes: "What may be significant is that Nicodemus is named at all. Certainly many other figures in the Gospel, such as the woman in 4:7-42 or the men in 5:5-15 and 9:1-38, remain anonymous. They may remain anonymous unlike Nicodemus because John's tradition would be more apt to preserve the events of their encounter with Jesus than their names, whereas Nicodemus was of such a stratum of Jewish society that the tradition would preserve his name as well." Ibid. I:535-36.

However, the narratives quickly twist and turn to alert the reader that surprises lie on the horizon. Nicodemus is reported to have come to Jesus under cover of night (νυκτὸς) (4:2),[41] but the woman comes to draw water in the light of midday (ὥρα ἦν ὡς ἕκτη)[42] (4:6). And although it was Nicodemus who sought out Jesus (οὗτος ἦλθεν πρὸς αὐτὸν) and initiated the conversation (καὶ εἶπεν αὐτῷ) with a statement (3:2), it is Jesus who sought out the woman (Ἔδει[43] δὲ αὐτὸν διέρχεσθαι διὰ τῆς Σαμαρείας) (4:4), and initiated the conversation (λέγει αὐτῇ ὁ Ἰησοῦς) with a request (4:7). This additional information raises some questions for the reader about Nicodemus and focuses attention on the woman.

---

[41] As Brown notes: John consistently recalls this detail (xix 39) because of its symbolic import. Darkness and night symbolize the realm of evil, untruth, and ignorance (see ix 4, xi 10). In xiii 30 Judas leaves the light to go out into the night of Satan; Nicodemus, on the other hand comes out of the darkness into the light (vss. 19-21)." *John*, I:130. Likewise, Keener writes that even though Jewish teachers often studied at night, "[m]ore likely, he comes at night to avoid being seen (cf. 7:51-52; 12:42-43; 19:38); night was the time for secret (sometimes antisocial) deeds and whether one wished not to be known. Nicodemus remains a secret believer at this point, not a disciple. . . . in the story world, fear accounts for Nicodemus coming by night, but John probably also mentions 'night' on a more symbolic level for his audience (cf. 13:30), bracketing the narrative with Nicodemus coming 'by night' (3:2) and true believers leaving darkness to come to Jesus' light (3:21)." *John*, I:536; *see also* Carson, *John*, 186. Schnackenburg recognizes, but is more reserved about, the symbolic significance of "night" in this passage. *John*, I:365-66.

[42] If Jewish reckoning of time is employed, the sixth hour was noon. Frederick W. Danker, Walter A. Bauer, William Arndt, and F. W. Gingrich, *A Greek-English Lexicon of the New Testament and Other Early Christian Literature*, 3rd ed. (hereafter BDAG; Chicago: University of Chicago Press, 2000), s.v. "ἕκτος"; *see* Flavius Josephus and William Whiston, *The Works of Josephus:Complete and Unabridged*, Includes index., Life 1.279 (Peabody: Hendrickson, 1996, c1987). ("Upon his saying this, Justus came in and commended him for what he had said, and persuaded some of the people to be of his mind also. But the multitude were not pleased with what was said, and had certainly gone into a tumult, *unless the sixth hour, which was now come, had dissolved the assembly, at which hour our laws require us to go to dinner on Sabbath days*; so Jonathan and his colleagues put off their council till the next day, and went off without success.") (emphasis added); Harold W. Hoehner, *Chronological Aspects of the Life of Christ* (Grand Rapids, MI: Zondervan Publishing House, 1977), 86-89 (where he argues that the Gospel of John follows the Judean method of reckoning time used by the Sadducees). It is also significant that Jacob met Rachel seeking water about noon (Gen. 29:7) and Moses may have also met Zipporah at the well about noon (Ex. 2:15-17; cf. Josephus *Ant*. 2:257; *See* Keener, *John*, I:586, 593. Kenner emphasizes the contrast with Nicodemus: "A final possible reasons for mentioning Jesus' encounter with the woman at 'noon' is the narrative's contrast with Nicodemus who approached Jesus 'by night' (3:2; cf 3:19-21); in contrast to that encounter, this one is initiated by Jesus, who is not ashamed to be seen with with [sic] the person whom he meets." Ibid., 595.

[43] As W. Hall Harris writes: "Such a detour through Samaria was not **geographically necessary**. Although the main route from Judea to Galilee was through Samaria, Jesus, as many Jews did, could easily have gone up the Jordan valley into Galilee through the Bethshan gap, avoiding Samaria. Whenever John uses the impersonal verb Ἔδει the necessity involves **God's will or plan**: 3:7, 14, 30; 4:4, 20, 24; 9:4; 10:16; 12:34; and 20:9." *Commentary on the Gospel of John*, http://ww.netbible.com/docs/nt/books/joh/harris/gjohn-07.htm; *see also* Brown, *John*, I:169; *see also* Keener, "Given John's usage of δεῖ elsewhere (esp. in 3:14, 30; 9:4; 10:16; 12:34; 20:9), the 'necessity' that compels Jesus to take this route is probably his mission." *John*, I:590.

Nicodemus knows[44] who Jesus is (3:2), but the woman meets him for the first time when she comes to Jacob's well to draw water.[45] Nicodemus makes a statement to Jesus

---

[44] Regarding the statement, "Rabbi, we know that you have come from God" Schnackenburg observes: "It is a polite exaggeration when he [Nicodemus] affirms that the other doctors also share his opinion (οἴδαμεν). It is unlikely that they sent him to Jesus. He came on his own initiative. But the affirmation gives the dialogue a more universal import (cf. v. 11)." *John,* I:366.

[45] Whether this account meets the elements of a betrothal type-scene as described by Robert Alter, is debated. Alter sets out the following elements:
  The betrothal type-scene, then must take place with the future bridegroom, or his surrogate, having journeyed to a foreign land. There he encounters a girl—the term '*na'arah*' invariably occurs unless the maiden is identified as so-and-so's daughter—or girls at a well. Someone, either the man or the girl, then draws water from the well; afterward, the girl or girls rush to bring him the news of the stranger's arrival (the verbs 'hurry' and 'run' are given recurrent emphasis at this junction of the type-scene); finally, a betrothal is concluded between the stranger and the girl, in the majority of instances, only after he has been invited to a meal.
The Art of Biblical Narrative (New York: NY, Basic Books, Inc., Publishers 1981), 52. Although speaking in the context of Pauline literature, N.T. Wright states a principle about the narrative dimensions of thought that may be applicable here: "understanding how stories worked in the ancient world, and how a small allusion could and did summon up an entire implicit narrative, including narratives within which speaker and hearer believed themselves to be living, is a vital tool." *Paul In Fresh Perspective* (Minneapolis, MN: Fortress Press, 2005), 8. Therefore, Keener seems to be correct when he states: "This passage also evokes the rich biblical imagery and themes. Allusions to the cross gender well scenes of Gen 24, and secondarily to Gen 29 and Exod 2, are difficult to miss. That Jesus meets the woman at "Jacob's well" (4:6) plainly alludes to a different well in Mesopotamia where Jacob met the future matriarch Rachel and provided water for her (Gen 29:10), as Jesus provides this Samaritan woman living water. But this Jacob scene in Gen 29 recapitulates in some measure the scene in Gen 24, in which Abraham's steward finds a wife for Isaac." *John,* I:586
  Alter has no difficulty in applying the echo of a type-scene to the book of Ruth where that pattern does not completely match: "He [Boaz] enjoins her to follow his *ne'arot* who in the traditional type-scene would come out to draw water. Here, since it is a female protagonist who has come to the foreign land to find a spouse, the male counterparts of the maidens the *ne'arim*, take over the customary function of water-drawing." *The Art of Biblical Narrative,* 58-59. Continuing he unfolds the significance of the use of the betrothal type-scene in Ruth when he states: "The type-scene is not merely a way of formally recognizing a particular kind of narrative moment; it is also a means of attaching the moment to a larger pattern of historical and theological meaning. If Isaac and Rebekah, as the first man and wife born into the covenant God has made with Abraham and his seed, provide certain paradigmatic traits for the future historical destiny of Israel, any association of later figures with the crucial junctures of that first story—the betrothal, the life-threatening trial in the wilderness, the enunciation of the blessing—will imply some connection of meaning, some further working-out of the original covenant. . . . In this fashion, the alignment of Ruth's story with the Pentateuchal betrothal type-scene becomes an intimation of her portentous future as progenitrix of the divinely chosen house of David." *Ibid.* at 60.
  Applying a similar approach, R. Allan Culpepper suggests the significance of this narrative allusion in the meeting of Jesus with the woman at the well: "The encounter of the leading character with his future wife at a well is a conventional biblical type-scene (e.g., Abraham [?], Isaac, Jacob, and Moses). Allusions to the patriarch (4:5, 12) underline the scene's scriptural associations. The encounter takes place in a foreign land, the protagonist is expected to do or say something characteristic of his role in the story, one or the other of them will draw water, and the maiden will rush home and prepare for the man's coming to meet her father and eat with them. A wedding will follow. In John, however, conventional elements are treated unconventionally; Jesus asks for water but apparently receives none. Dialogue rather than action carries the scene. Living water, of which Jesus is the source, rather than well water, to which the Samaritan woman has

(3:2) and asks two explanatory questions (3:4, 9), speaking a total of 46 words. The woman first responds to Jesus' request for a drink (4:9), then questions Jesus' ability to provide water with nothing to draw from the deep well (4:11), then questions whether Jesus is greater than the patriarch Jacob (4:12), then asks for the water that Jesus is offering (4:15), then responds to Jesus' command to call her husband by explaining that she has no husband (4:17), then states that she perceives that Jesus is a prophet (4:19), then asks Jesus a question about the proper location for worship (4:20), then claims that when Messiah comes, he will declare all things to us (4:25), and then announces to the men in the city that she has met the Christ (4:29), speaking 120 words. The mere law of proportion emphasizes the woman's conversation over the conversation with Nicodemus.

Both Nicodemus and the woman misperceive words with ambiguous meanings.[46] When Jesus tells Nicodemus that unless one is "born *again*" he will not be able to see the kingdom of God, he uses an adverb in conjunction with the verb "to be born" (γεννάω) that could either mean "*again*" or "*from above*" (ἄνωθεν).[47] Nicodemus focuses on the repetitive, temporal sense.[48] When Jesus offers the woman "living water," (ὕδωρ ζῶν), she

---

access, becomes the central concern. And the woman is no marriageable maiden; she has had five husbands. Still, Jesus goes to her village, and she receives him as her Lord." *Anatomy of the Fourth Gospel: A Study in Literary Design* (Philadelphia, PA: Fortress Press, 1983), 136.

Perhaps this scene portends to a fulfillment of the betrothal type-scene imagery. This woman, who has known so much disruption in her married life and thirsts for resolution (4:16-18), meets the One at the well who will satisfy her thirst as her true, spiritual husband (*see* Jesus' words about the Spirit in 4:23-25). Then instead of returning home, she goes to the men (τοῖς ἀνθρώποις) of the town to tell them about the one she has met at the well (4:28-29). When she speaks to them, she specifically emphasizes the conversation with Jesus about her married life: "Come, see a man who said to me all things which I did." (4:29; *see* 4:16-18). Just as the character of Isaac, Jacob, and Moses is made manifest through the particulars of each type-scene, *see* Alter, *The Art of Biblical Narrative*, 52-58, so too Jesus' character is revealed in his conversation with the woman as a prophet and Messiah who truly understands the ways of people and God (Jn. 4:16-26). The metaphor of Christ's relation to the church as a husband to his bride will then be explicitly made by the Apostle Paul (Eph. 5:25-27), and the Apostle John (Rev. 19:7-8). Perhaps this expression of the type-scene is the narrative source of the later image.

[46] Keener observes, "Several of John's narratives involve the pattern of sign, misunderstanding, clarification and response." *John*, 535.

[47] BDAG, s.v. "ἄνωθεν;" John uses the word five (5) times; 3:3, 7, 3:31; 19:11, 23. In the last three usages, the context supports the sense of "from above." The primary meaning is "from above;" *see* Zane C. Hodges: Problem Passages in the Gospel of John Part 3: Water and Spirit—John 3:5" *Bibliotheca Sacra* 135:539 (July-September 1978): 213; Schnackenburg, *John*, I:367-68 ("According to the usage of ἄνωθεν elsewhere in John (3:31; 19:11, 23), and his doctrine of "birth from God" (1:13; 1 Jn 2:29; 3:9; 4:7; 5:1), the only justifiable translation is "from above").

[48] "Nicodemus concentrates on the demand for a 'birth' and, as was usual in the scholastic exercises of the rabbis, raises objections which are couched as paradoxically as possible. His two questions are meant to bring out the senseless nature of the doctrine (cf. 6:52) and force Jesus to admit to an absurdity (cf. Mk. 12:20-23 parr.)." Schnackenburg, *John*, I:368.

focuses on the sense of running, fresh, spring water[49] rather than the metaphorical reference to the Holy Spirit.[50]

Nicodemus begins his conversation with Jesus on a spiritual topic: "Rabbi, we know that You have come from God *as* a teacher; for no one can do these signs that You do unless God is with him" (3:2). However, Jesus begins his conversation with the woman on a physical topic: "Give me a drink" (4:7).

After Jesus responds to Nicodemus about the need to be born *again* (from above, ἄνωθεν), Nicodemus turns the conversation into a physical topic: "How can a man be born when he is old? He cannot enter a second time into his mother's womb and be born, can he?" On the contrary, the woman responds to Jesus' physical request, by asking a spiritual question regarding why he, a Jew, is speaking to her, a Samaritan woman (4:9); whereupon, Jesus responds with a spiritual statement: "If you knew the gift of God, and who it is who says to you, 'Give Me a drink,' you would have asked Him, and He would have given you living water." (4:10).[51]

---

[49] *Cf.* Gen. 26:19; Lev. 14:5, 6, 50, 51, 52; Ezk. 47:1-12.

[50] In the Gospel of John, Jesus often identifies the coming of the Spirit with "water." In John 3:5 he states, "Unless one is born of water and spirit ("wind") (ἐξ ὕδατος καὶ πνεύματος), he is not able to enter into the kingdom of God." Jesus continues to play off of words that have ambiguous meanings, namely water and spirit/wind (ἐξ ὕδατος καὶ πνεύματος) to emphasize the sense of "above" by the way these terms refer to the Spirit in Isaiah 44:3-5 and Ezek. 37:9-10. As Hodges writes: "it would certainly appear that the Savior's use of the words ἐξ ὕδατος καὶ πνεύματος – if taken in the sense "of water and wind" – can serve as a double metaphor for the work of the Holy Spirit as that work is reflected in the Old Testament Scriptures." "Problem Passages in the Gospel of John Part 3," 218. Jesus is describing the eschatological outpouring of the Spirit. Hodges also notes a connection with the word "water" in this discourse with the Woman at the Well: "In the very next chapter water is the prominent symbol employed in the discourse with the Samaritan woman (4:7-15) and there it seems plainly to stand for eternal life itself." *Ibid.*, 213-14. See also Brown, *John*, I:139-41; Talbert, *Reading John*, 98-99.

Jesus also identifies "water' with the giving of the Spirit in John 7:37-39. On the last day of the Feast of Tabernacles, Jesus exhorted all who were thirsty to come to him and drink (7:37-38). The narrator then explains: "He spoke of the Spirit, whom those who believed in Him were to receive; for the Spirit was not yet *given*, because Jesus was not yet glorified" (NASB). Leon Morris reports that the Feast of Tabernacles was celebrated with certain festival rituals, one of which was the procession each day from the temple to Gihon Spring where a priest filled a gold pitcher with water while the choir sang (Isaiah 12:3). Then they returned to the altar and poured out the water. *The Gospel According to John*. The International Commentary on the New Testament (Grand Rapids, MI: William B. Eerdmans Publishing Company, 1971), 420-21. Supposedly this ritual reminded Israel of "water" from the rock (Num 20) and the coming days of Messiah (Zech 14:8, 16-19). It is in this setting on the Feast's greatest, last day before a large gathering (Lev 23) that Jesus stood and pronounced his offer of spiritual salvation for the nation as Yahweh, the source of water. What he is offering is not physical water but the life-giving source of the Holy Spirit (7:39; *cf.* Isa. 12). Jesus is offering to satisfy their unsatisfied spiritual thirst. He makes the same offer to the woman at the well in John 4.

[51] Schnackenburg insightfully writes, "There is a masterly transition from the outward situation to the inner confrontation of man with the revealer. If the woman knew the 'gift of 'God' and the stranger who asks her for a drink of ordinary water, the roles would be exchanged. She (the σὺ is emphatic) would do the asking and become beneficiary. According to the chiastic structure of the sentence, which goes from the 'gift of God' to the person of the speaker, and from the speaker back to the 'living water', 'the gift of God'

Nicodemus is perplexed and appears to fixate on the physical explanation of birth even after Jesus offers an extensive explanation of the regenerative work of the Spirit (3:5-8) when he asks: "How can these things be?" (3:9).[52] The woman at first responds to Jesus' statement in a way similar to Nicodemus when she observes that Jesus does not have anything with which to draw physical water (4:11); but then she begins to open the door to a broader, spiritual discussion when she asks whether he is greater than the patriarch Jacob (4:12). This movement by the woman to open the conversation beyond his physical ability to draw from the well causes Jesus to explain more about the spiritual water that he is offering: "Everyone who drinks of this water will thirst again; but whoever drinks of the water that I will give him shall never thirst; but the water that I will give him will become in him a well of water springing up to eternal life" (4:13-14). The woman, not fully grasping the spiritual dimensions of Jesus' offer, nevertheless asks for the water Jesus is offering: "Sir, give me this water, so I will not be thirsty nor come here åto draw" (4:15).[53] Her response appears to prompt Jesus to then identify an area of spiritual thirst[54] in the woman's life that he has offered to satisfy when he states:

"Go, call your husband and come here."

The woman answered and said, "I have no husband."

Jesus said to her, "You have correctly said, 'I have no husband;' for you have had five husbands, and the one whom you now have is not your husband; this you have said truly."[55]

---

must be the 'living water' which Jesus can give, the true 'water of life' which is not a gift on the natural, earthly plane but a heavenly gift from God." *John*, I:426.

[52] Schnackenburg comments: "Nicodemus, however, continues to brood on the matter, and asks for a definite explanation of the "how", or the possibility (πῶς in the Semitic sense) of the miraculous event. He fails to see that in doing so he casts doubt on the power and wisdom of God and receives Jesus's words with incredulity, thereby reinforcing his own obtuseness (v. 4)." Ibid., I:374; *see also* Carson, *John*, 198.

[53] Although Schnackenburg discounts the woman's response, *John,* I:432, Culpepper seems to more correctly observe: "As the light of understanding begins to break, the Samaritan woman shows herself at each stage ready to receive it: 'Sir, give me this water' (4:15); 'Sir, I perceive that you are a prophet' (4:19); 'Come, see a man . . . the Christ?' (4:29). *Anatomy of the Fourth Gospel*, 137. Likewise, Witherington states: "the Samaritan woman wins the reader's admiration because of her openness to the revealing word of Jesus even when she does not understand. Her attitude is one of inquiry, not rejection, and it is this that makes her a suitable subject for faith." *Women in the Ministry of Jesus*, 59.

[54] That "thirst" describes more than physical thirst is evident on its face from the fact that the Spirit is being described as the "water" that quenches thirst. Jesus himself identified himself with the spiritual thirst of humankind when on the cross he stated: "I thirst (διψῶ)" (Jn. 19:28). This cry from the cross is only reported in the Gospel of John where twice Jesus claimed that he was the source of life-giving water that will satisfy thirst (Jn. 4:12; 7:37-39).

[55] Jesus' description of the woman's married life is usually interpreted to mean that she is an immoral person. *See* Keener, *John,* I:584, 595-96, 605-608; Witherington, *Women in the Ministry of Jesus*, 59-60; Schnackenburg, *St John*, I:432-433; Carson, *John*, 217, 218, 220-21, 228. However, Janeth Norfleete Day offers a different reconstruction of the woman's status as a person who is a victim of ancient, oppressive patriarchy rather than taken up in personal sin. *The Woman at the Well: Interpretation of John 4:1-42: in Retrospect and Prospect*. Interpretation Series 61 (Leiden/Boston: E.J. Brill, 2002), 169-75. Day surveys literature and art prior to the Reformation, and finds that it is not until the reformers that the woman is

(4:16-18).

The woman does not pursue a detour of personal defense or explanation, but directly engages in a spiritual conversation that results in Jesus identifying himself as Messiah (Jn. 4:19-26).[56] In other words, the conversation with the woman ends with a confirmation of Jesus' identity—the very thing that Nicodemus was seeking at the beginning of his encounter with Jesus (*see* 3:2). The woman received this revelation because she embraced the spiritual dimensions of Jesus' words, whereas Nicodemus resisted them.

Finally, at the end of the first conversation, Nicodemus is rebuked: "'Are you the teacher of Israel and do not understand these things?'" (3:10). However, at the end of the second conversation, the woman leaves her waterpot and goes into the city to testify to the people (τοῖς ἀνθρώποις) about Jesus as the Christ (4:29).[57] She appears to be the initial

---

portrayed as immoral. Accordingly, there may be room to reconsider presuppositions about the character of the woman. Rather than assuming from the gaps in the narrative that the woman has been the initiator of an immoral lifestyle, it is possible that she has been outlived by her husbands, or was divorced by men due to no particular fault of her own (such as the inability to bear children—since no children are mentioned). Day notes that Jewish thought allowed a maximum of three marriages for a woman; the fact that she had been married five times indicates that her life had been especially difficult, and probably meant that she was an object of either pity or ridicule, perhaps both. *Ibid.* at 70. The fact that she is now living with a man who is not her husband may not be a matter of choice so much as of cultural necessity in order to have the protection of a man and a place to live. She may be advanced in age (5 marriages); she may not be able to support herself, so the man may have been her only means of survival culturally. The man may be unwilling, or unable financially, to marry her, but willing to extend to her the protection of his household. Perhaps the man was a relative in the kinsman-redeemer tradition but unwilling, or unable, to raise-up children (like Judah with Tamar in Gen. 38). There are numerous ways to understand the gaps in this Scripture. The response from the people whom she tells about Jesus raises a question about whether they saw her as sinful. If so, they more than likely would have laughed and ridiculed her for her testimony; but they respond readily with no resistance; the people appear to be eager to believe her testimony.

[56] As Schnackenburg observes: "The Samaritan, who must have been astonished at the stranger's knowledge of her hidden past, concludes that he is a prophet (cf. Lk. 7:39)." *John*, I:433. In John 4:19-26 the dialogue unfolds:

"The woman said to Him, 'Sir, I perceive that You are a prophet. Our fathers worshiped in this mountain, and you *people* say that in Jerusalem is the place where men ought to worship.'

Jesus said to her, 'Woman, believe Me, an hour is coming when neither in this mountain nor in Jerusalem will you worship the Father. You worship what you do not know; we worship what we know, for salvation is from the Jews. But an hour is coming, and now is, when the true worshipers will worship the Father in spirit and truth; for such people the Father seeks to be His worshipers. God is spirit, and those who worship Him must worship in spirit and truth.'

The woman said to Him, 'I know that Messiah is coming (He who is called Christ); when that One comes, He will declare all things to us.'

Jesus said to her, 'I who speak to you am *He*'"

(NASB).

[57] Of significance is that her testimony is about her own personal life, which Jesus highlighted in their conversation: "Come, see a man who told me all the things which I did; is this one not the Christ?" (4:29; see also 4:39). In other words, she appears to testify to the One who can satisfy her personal, spiritual

evangelist of Jesus to the Samaritans, and the disciples will follow in her footsteps as they bring in the harvest that she has planted. (4:30, 35-42).[58]

Clearly, Jesus' conversation with the woman is greater than his conversation with Nicodemus—in length, content, and result. The unnamed, troubled woman from Samaria is not only more engaged and more receptive to Jesus' words than the esteemed teacher of the Jews, but she becomes Jesus' emissary leading the way for the disciples in the evangelization of the Samaritans, while Nicodemus lies silent under Jesus' criticism for being spiritually dull.[59] This outcome surprises the reader as the author uses the technique

---

thirst for life. Perhaps this is an implied significance of her leaving behind her waterpot. She now has spiritual, living water, and not the physical water she initially sought.

[58] The elevation of the woman over the disciples is also hinted at in the placement of the disciples' suspicious attitude toward her against her departure to tell the Samaritans about Jesus: "At this point His disciples came, and they were amazed that He had been speaking with a woman, yet no one said, 'What do You seek?' or, 'Why do You speak with her?' So the woman left her waterpot, and went into the city and said to the men, 'Come, see a man who told me all the things that I *have* done; this is not the Christ, is it?'" (NASB) (Jn. 4:27-29). While the Twelve are concerned that Jesus would be talking to this woman, she is proclaiming the good news about Jesus to the Samaritans. Then as the Samaritans are coming to see Jesus, Jesus is instructing his disciples "to reap that for which others have labored" perhaps having a direct reference to bringing the coming Samaritans to faith in Jesus (Jn. 4:31-38). *See* Keener, *John*, 626 ("In the most immediate context, Jesus may refer to himself and the Samaritan woman (hence the plural ἄλλοι), who brought the town to him (4:29-30, 39)"); likewise Witherington, *Women in the Ministry of Jesus*, 61 ("Who then are the ἄλλοι of verse 38? Perhaps the most likely answer is, Jesus and the Samaritan woman. Jesus has sown the Word in her and, in turn, she has sown the word in the other Samaritans"). As Culpepper observes: "She precedes the disciples, laboring where they are sent. They will enter into her work (4:38). True to her traditional name, therefore, the 'Samaritan woman' is a model of the female disciple and possibly a model of Samaritan believers also." *Anatomy of the Fourth Gospel*, 137. As Keener observes, "The narrative thus places her on a par with Jesus' other disciples who brought his message to the world (cf. 17:20)." Continuing he describes John's pattern of women's testimony, concluding. "The women disciples may, indeed, prove more faithful in their discipleship than 'the Twelve' (6:70-71); cf. 16:32; 19:25-27." *John*, 622, 623. Likewise, Witherington states: "The Evangelist makes clear that this woman's witness was fruitful -- Ἐκ δὲ τῆς πόλεως ἐκείνης πολλοὶ ἐπίστευσαν εἰς αὐτὸν τῶν Σαμαριτῶν διὰ τὸν λόγον τῆς γυναικὸς μαρτυρούσης. This should be compared to Jesus' prayer -- περὶ τῶν πιστευόντων διὰ τοῦ λόγου αὐτῶν εἰς ἐμέ (Jn. 17:20). This woman is presented as one of Jesus' witnesses, through whom others are led to Him." *Women in the Ministry of Jesus*, 61. Continuing, Witherington also observes: "On the level of the Evangelist's intentions we may note the following: (1) If Jn 4.31—4 and 35—8 is an insertion from a traditional source, then it is the Evangelist who is portraying this woman as a 'sower' and the disciples as somewhat less spiritually perceptive and active in their faith than she. The Samaritans believed because of this woman's witness. With typical irony, the Evangelist paints a contrast between the disciples who bring Jesus physical food that does not satisfy, while a woman brings Jesus His true spiritual food by helping Him to complete God's work. Once again, the pattern of reversal of expectation and of expected male-female roles becomes apparent." Ibid. at 62.

[59] Culpepper writes:
The scene culminates in a critical judgment on Nicodemus. Any expectations the reader may have had of the authority and enlightenment of a Jewish leader are overturned. Nicodemus is a teacher of Israel, but he cannot understand even earthly things. Having temporarily fulfilled his role, he fades from the narrative.

When Nicodemus reappears in 7:50 and 19:39, he is reintroduced by allusion to the earlier scene. He concretizes and personalizes the division among the Jews which develops

of duality and balance to elevate the spiritual sensitivity and ministry of a woman over a man—even a Pharisaic teacher of Israel.

---

through chapter 7. He also brings to the surface the irony of the Pharisees' response to the crowd in 7:47-48 – 'Are you led astray, you also? Have any of the authorities or of the Pharisees believed in him?' Yet, Nicodemus is 'one of them' (7:50) a Ruler and a Pharisee. He does not confess belief in Jesus, but asks for due process under their Law. This ruler of the Jews, like Pilate, is attracted to Jesus. reluctant to confess faith but desirous of protecting Jesus, and rebuffed by the Jewish leaders. In the end he comes forward to bury Jesus (19:39-42). He expresses his grief by bringing expensive spices, but finds no life in Jesus' death. His association with Joseph of Arimathea provides evidence for regarding Nicodemus as another of the 'secret disciples' who feared the Jews (19:38). Nicodemus and Joseph of Arimathea represent those who believe but refuse to confess lest they be put out of the synagogue (12:42).

Anatomy of the Fourth Gospel, 135-36.

Peter's Healing of Aeneas and Tabitha
(Acts 9:32-42)

Some commentators have not found much use for these unique Lucan narratives beyond affirming Peter's ministry and providing a geographical progress from Samaria to Caesarea.[60] However, there are numerous textual parallels between Aeneas and Tabitha that invite the reader to compare the two narratives:

Persons	Aeneas (9:32-36)	Tabitha (9:37-42)
Opening	"Now it came about ..." (9:32)	"And it came about ..." (9:37)
The City	Lydda (9:32)	Joppa (9:36)
Identification	"A certain man–Aeneas"[61] [a Man] (9:33)	"A certain disciple–Tabitha" [a Woman] (9:36)
Condition	Bedridden & Paralyzed (9:33)	Sick & Died (9:40)
Peter's Words	"Arise"[62] (9:34)	"Arise" (9:40)
Response	"He arose" (9:34)	"She sat up" (9:40)
The Result	Many "turned to the Lord" (9:35)	"many believed in the Lord" (9:42)

---

[60] C.K. Barrett sees little, Lucan function in the healing of Aeneas: "It is hard to see any motive that Luke could have had in telling the story beyond the following: (1) It provided a further example (cf. 5.15, 16) of the power of Jesus working through Peter; (2) it was connected in tradition with Lydda and thus served to bring Peter on the way to Caesarea (ch. 10)." *The Acts Of The Apostles,* The International Critical Commentary on the Holy Scriptures of the Old and New Testaments, vol. 1 (New York, NY: T&T Clark, 1994), 477. Haenchen does not find much use for these miracles beyond this geographical progress and affirming Peter's ministry. *The Acts of The Apostles: A Commentary* (Philadelphia, PA: The Westminster Press, 1971), 340-41; Luke Timothy Johnson writes, "These two miracle stories therefore serve as something of a narrative transition. Geographically, they draw Peter from Jerusalem to the costal city of Joppa, and therefore closer in the reader's imagination to the wider world of the Gentiles, which boundary will be crossed in the story of Cornelius' conversion." *The Acts of the Apostles.* Sacra Pagina, vol. 5, ed. Daniel J. Harrington, (Collegeville, Minnesota: The Liturgical Press, 1994), 179; *see also* Charles H. Talbert, *Reading Act: A Literary and Theological Commentary on the Acts of the Apostles* (New York, NY: A Crossroad Book, 1997), 104.

[61] As Josep Ruis-Camps and Jenny Read-Heimerdinger state, "Aeneas is a representative character ('a certain', τινάν) . . ., and man (ἄνθρωπος), which establishes him as a universal character (as opposed to ἀνήρ, one with a specific function)." They also identify this sense with the use of τὶς with the introduction of Tabitha (9:36), Simon the Tanner (9:43), and Cornelius (10:1). *The Message of Acts,* 209, 212, 216, 244. Regarding the use of characters as types in narratives, Robert Scholes and Robert Kellogg affirm: "In every case, whenever we consider a character as a type, we are moving away from considering him as an individual character and moving toward considering him as part of some larger framework. This framework may be moral, theological, referable to some essentially extra-literary scheme; or it may be referable to a part of the narrative situation itself. When we consider characters . . . we are thinking of them not as characters in themselves but as elements which contribute to the whole, as part of the plot or meaning of a work" Robert Scholes, James Phelan, and Robert Kellogg, *The Nature of Narrative.* Fortieth Anniversary Edition, Revised and Expanded. (New York, NY: Oxford University Press, 2006), 204.

[62] The term used in each case is an imperative form of ἀνίστημι, namely ἀνάστηθι (cf. 9:34, 40; 10:26); Although Ben Witherington, does note the use of the term, "to rise," in the two miracles, he does not connect it to the Cornelius account. *Acts,* 328.

There is also an intensification with the second miracle. The healing of Aeneas consists of four verses and 62 words (Acts 9:32-35); the healing of Tabitha consists of seven verses and 151 words (Acts 9:36-42). The law of proportion emphasizes the Tabitha narrative over the Aeneas narrative by giving more than double the amount of space to her account.

In addition, the magnitude of the miraculous increases across the narratives. Aeneas's healing is significant. He is paralyzed and has been bedridden for eight years (9:33). Peter's words enable him to rise and immediately engage in making his bed (9:34). But Tabitha has died (9:37). Peter's words bring her back to life (9:40-41).

The narrator tells us little about Aeneas, focusing on his malady. But the narrator abounds with additional information about Tabitha.[63] It is hard to know for sure the origin of the name, Aneas (Αἰνέας); it may be Greek,[64] but Craig Keener argues for it being Jewish.[65] The name of his city, Lydda, is Greek for *Lod*,[66] a Jewish town[67] approximately 25 miles northwest of Jerusalem on the road to Joppa.[68] The Jewish-Gentile nature of this account is implicit in the Aeneas narrative. However, the ethnic mixture is made more explicit with the Tabitha account. Her Aramaic name, Tabitha (Ταβιθά, טְבִיתָא), is explicitly given a Greek equivalent, Dorcas (Δορκάς) (9:36).[69] And her city, Joppa, was far more

---

[63] Her name in Greek was Dorcas (Δορκάς) (9:36); she was full of good works (ἔργων ἀγαθῶν) and charitable giving (ἐλεημοσυνῶν) (9:36); her body was washed and laid in an upper room (9:37); the widows were weeping (9:39); the widows showed Peter all the tunics and garments that Dorcas made (9:39).

[64] BDAG, s.v. "Αἰνέας;" Ruis-Camps & Read-Heimerdinger are of the opinion that "His name is Greek, indicating he was a Hellenist, possibly one of those who had to flee from Hierosoluma (8.4). *The Message of Acts*, 2:209-10.

[65] "Some scholars think that Aeneas was a Gentile because of his name. The name "Aeneas" could be Jewish, however; it appeared among Palestinian Jews as early as the time of Hyrcanus I (Jos. *Ant.* 14.248) and continued through the Judean-Roman war (*War* 5.326-28) and as late as the fourth century (*CIJ* 2.1209) and (less surprisingly) in the Diaspora (*CPJ* 1.24.23). Indeed before Acts 10, a Gentile in Peter's ministry is extremely unlikely (Acts 10:28), and Aeneas would have warranted specific mention as such if he had been one." Craig S. Keener, *Acts: An Exegetical Commentary 3:1—14:28*. Vol. 2 (Grand Rapids: Baker Academic, 2013), 1706.

[66] לֹד, *cf.* 1 Chron. 8:12; Ezra 2:33; Neh. 7:37 *cf.* 11:35.

[67] Keener notes: "It was Sharon plain's most significant Jewish city, added to Judea from Samaria (1 Macc 11:34 [cf. 10:30; 11:28]; Jos. *Ant.* 13.127). It had long been a Jewish city (1 Macc 11:34) whose men attended Jerusalem's feasts (Jos. *War* 2.515)." *Acts*, II:1705.

[68] Bock writes: "It was the center of toparchy, one of ten administrative districts in Judea (Josephus, *J.W.* 3.3.5§§52-56; Johnson 1992:177). It was a predominantly Jewish town of mixed population." *Acts*, Baker Exegetical Commentary on the New Testament (Grand Rapids, MI: Baker Academic, 2007), 376. Likewise F.F. Bruce explains: "it was the capital of a Jewish toparchy." *The Acts of the Apostles: Greek Text with Introduction and Commentary*, 3d rev. and enlarged ed. (Grand Rapids, MI: William B. Eerdmans Publishing Company, 1990), 247.

[69] Ruis-Camps and Read-Heimerdinger correlate the two names given for this woman (Tabitha/Dorcas) as symbolizing the Hebrew-Greek nature of this community when they write, "The fact that her name is given in Aramaic indicates that she was not of Hellenistic origin but the translation of her name and the use of it a second time (cf. 9.39) would imply that the community of believers included Greek as well as Aramaic speakers." Continuing they write, "'The reference to the gazelle in this context occurs

Gentile in its makeup than Lydda.⁷⁰ This movement of Peter from Lydda to Joppa is part of Luke's narrative trajectory to bring Peter into a Gentile region.

We are not told anything about the character of Aeneas.⁷¹ On the other hand, Tabitha's character is explicitly set forth. She was full of good works and charitable giving (9:36), and made tunics and garments (9:39). Perhaps the making of clothing was a particular expression of her good works and mercy. In addition, because her Greek name, Dorcas, is used with the description of the clothing she made (9:39), it may be implied that she made these items for Gentiles in her community. She was apparently loved by the widows who were weeping over her death (9:39), and her body was honored by being washed and placed in the upper room (9:37). This expansion of the Tabitha narrative enhances her in the reader's eye by elevating her into the realm of a three-dimensional character over two-dimensional Aeneas.

In addition, one of the character descriptions given to Tabitha is later attributed to Cornelius, the Gentile who is the focus of this larger unit. Just as Tabitha abounded in *charitable giving* (ἐλεημοσύνη, 9:36) to the Gentiles, so too Cornelius gave many *alms* (ἐλεημοσύνη)⁷² to the Jewish people (τῷ λαῷ, Acts 10:2). From both sides of a cultural divide, these characters are performing acts of mercy, Tabitha toward the Gentiles, and Cornelius towards the Jews. The lead word for "alms" (ἐλεημοσύνη) is a textual clue that draws the Cornelius narrative alongside the Aeneas and Tabitha accounts. Together, the miracle narratives function as stepping stones to confirm, prepare, and bring Peter to Cornelius.

---

three times in the course of the reformed laws in the book of Deuteronomy, and could be a way of indicating here that Tabitha represented a community of both Hebrews (clean) and Hellenists (unclean); the use of her name in Greek suggests as much." *The Message of Acts*, 212.

⁷⁰ Bock notes: "The region was partly Gentile, as Sharon comprised the costal plain extending from Joppa to Carmel and to Caesarea. Joppa was a far more Gentile city than Lydda (Barrett 1994:482) and was involved in battles during the Maccabean war (Joseph, *Ant.* 13.5.10§180; 13.6.4§202; 13.6.7§215)." *Acts*, 377. Keener argues that Joppa was Jewish but clearly identifies its Hellenization: "Once a Philistine city, it was later Hellenized and used by Ptolemies and Seleucids." *Acts:* II:1714. Further he writes: "Its inscriptions are 90 percent Greek, about 12 percent more than in Rome or Beth She'arim and 55 percent more than in Jerusalem (Levine, *Hellenism*, 182)." Ibid., 1714 n. 95.

⁷¹ Perhaps an implication can be made that Aeneas was a believer from the fact that Peter came to the saints (πρὸς τοὺς ἁγίους) who lived in Lydda (9:32). Because the term "saints" was used for believers in Jerusalem (9:13), Aeneas may be considered to be a Christian, but this is a conclusion by implication, at best.

⁷² Both individuals are described by the same Greek term, ἐλεημοσύνη, describing alms, or charitable giving. BDAG, s.v. "ἐλεημοσύνη." Interestingly, this same term is also used to describe the lame man in Acts 3:2. Even though Bock identifies the use of the term with Tabitha and Cornelius, he does not connect the two figures any further. *Acts* 386; *see also* Ruis-Camps and Read-Heimerdinger, *The Message of Acts*, 2:212.

Therefore, it is not surprising that the textual parallels from the two miracles extend into the Cornelius account: [73]

Two Miracles by Peter & the Cornelius' Conversion			
Persons	**Aeneas** (9:32-36)	**Tabitha** (9:37-42)	**Cornelius** (9:43–10:48)
Opening	"Now it came about ..." (9:32)	"And it came about ..." (9:37)	"And it came about ..." (9:43)
The City	Lydda (9:32)	Joppa (9:36)	Caesarea (10:1)
Identification	"A certain man–Aeneas" [a Man] (9:33)	"A certain disciple–Tabitha" [a Woman] (9:36)	"A certain man–Cornelius [a Man] (10:1)
Condition	Bedridden & Paralyzed (9:33)	Sick & Died (9:40)	(*Like Aeneas he goes nowhere; like Tabitha he needs new life*)
Peter's Words	"Arise" (9:34)	"Arise" (9:40)	"Arise" (10:26)
Response	"He arose" (9:34)	"She sat up" (9:40)	"The Holy Spirit fell upon those who were listening" (10:44)
The Result	Many "turned to the Lord" (9:35)	"many believed in the Lord" (9:42)	"They were hearing them speaking with tongues and exalting God" (10:46)

Peter is being prepared in the physical realm through the healings of Aeneas and Tabatha for the spiritual need of Cornelius (a Gentile), and sovereignly brought[74] to Cornelius through the physical need of Aeneas and Tabatha.[75] Together, the narrative

---

[73] Barrett sees many of the parallels between Aeneas and Tabitha, but he does not continue the correlations to Cornelius. *The Acts*, I:477.

[74] Peter was traveling through the region and found Aeneas in Lydda (9:32-33); then he was called by the people of Joppa to quickly come for Tabitha (9:37-38). Then Cornelius (at God's command) called Peter to Caesarea (10:3-8). Peter appears to be an actor on the stage, but he is in fact just a pawn in God's hand. Alter describes this dual aspect well in his discussion of Hebrew Scriptures' narrative when he states that, "The Hebrew Bible is animated by an untiring, shrewdly perceptive fascination with the theater of human behavior in the textual foreground, seen against a background of forces that can be neither grasped nor controlled by humankind." *The World of Biblical Literature* (New York, NY: BasicBooks, 1992), 22.

[75] Johnson writes, "Notice that Peter tells both Aeneas and Tabitha to 'rise up' (anaththi), using the word associated so frequently with the resurrection of Jesus. The reader is given an early signal that the conversion of the Gentiles that Luke will now relate is to be understood similarly as coming from the 'Holy

healings picture Cornelius as one who does good works but is spiritually dead, unable to walk with God, and in need of God's miraculous deliverance. The Lord is going to bring Cornelius to spiritual life,[76] just as He brought Tabitha to physical life,[77] and He is going to enable Cornelius to walk[78] with Him spiritually, just as He enabled Aeneas to physically conduct his life.[79] Through a permutation of the sign-sermon structure (where here there are two signs, not just one, prior to the sermon with Cornelius), Luke has provided physical foreshadows to Cornelius's spiritual condition that begin to open Peter, and the reader, to God's outreach to the Gentiles.[80]

Spirit," that is the power of the resurrected one, and also as itself an extension of the 'resurrection/rebuilding' of Israel (Acts 15:16-17)." *Acts*, 180.

[76] Another link between the Tabitha/Cornelius stories may be found with the "upper room" as Ruis-Camps and Read-Heimerdinger affirm: "The location of the upper room will set up a further parallel with the next episode as it is told in the text of Codex Bezae (Acts 10.9 d05, *in cenaculum*) for it is again in an 'upper room' that Peter receives his vision of the ritually unclean animals (cf. 'rooftop', AT)." *The Message of Acts*, 2:213. Likewise, the transitional nature of these narratives extends to Peter staying with a certain Simon the Tanner: "Peter has clearly learnt something from the practical experience of Tabitha's death, and yet has still to discover the full extent of the teaching that the distinction clean/unclean no longer has any force. This will follow while he is staying with Simon the Tanner, with whom Peter's affinity is indicated by the shared name." Ibid., 2:216.

[77] Barrett does not understand the raising of Tabitha to have much usefulness in the narrative: "The latter story, as a resurrection, is even more striking and is told more fully, but it seems to acquire no additional motivation and to have been intended to teach no further truth." *Acts*, I:477-78.

[78] Luke employed the image of "walking" (πορεύομαι) in 9:31 to describe the conduct of the church in Judea, Galilee, and Samaria. As Ruis-Camps and Read-Heimerdinger state, "The verb πορεύομαι, 'walk', expresses the typically Lukan concept of the walking in the paths of the Lord (cf. Lk. 8.14; 9.57; 10.38; 13.33 *et al*; Acts 8.36, 39) as distinct from the way of Judaism (21.21, cf. v. 24 D05) or the Gentiles (14.16)." *The Message of Acts*, 2:209 n. 120. In addition, to "walk" is wisdom imagery from the Hebrew Scriptures depicting close fellowship (cf. Gen 5:24; Ps 1:1).

[79] Zane C. Hodges, class notes of student. This spiritual focus is also hinted in the fact that the miracles had an evangelistic effect (*cf.* Acts 9:35, 42); *see* Witherington, *Acts*, 330. But even more foundational is Jesus' healing of the paralytic in Mark 2:1-12 (= Matt. 9:1-8 = Luke 5:17-26), where a man is physically healed to demonstrate that Jesus has authority to forgive sins. *See* Bruce, *Acts*, 216; Ruis-Camps and Read-Heimerdinger also identify the physical paralysis as symbolic of a "spiritual rigidity" and correctly identify echoes in the terms to describe Aeneas with those in the Gospel's account of the healing of the paralytic: κατακείμενον, cf. Lk. 5.25 B03; ἦν παραλελυμένος 5.18, 24 B03 (παραλυτικος D05, cf. 5.19 D05), ἐπὶ κραβαττον is found in the Bezan text of Luke's Gospel (Lk. 5.19 D05, 24 D05) and in Mark's parallel account (Mk. 2.4, 9, 11, 12) whereas Luke according to B03 uses κλινίδιόν (Lk. 5.19.24)," but wrongly connect it with the state of the church in Lydda rather than with Cornelius. *The Message of Acts*, 2:210 n. 124.

[80] Peter will be explicitly shown to be reluctant to move in God's direction toward the Gentiles in the next section (Acts 10:14-16). Ruis-Camps and Read-Heimerdinger write: "Taking into account the symbolical significance of Tabitha's death as the death of Jewish attitudes to Gentiles (9.37a above), Peter's uncertainty can be linked to the situation he finds himself confronted with concerning the Jewish Law – as he sees the old mentality being challenged, he struggles to explore new territory, feeling his way step by step." *The Message of Acts*, 2:215.

Geographically, the two miracles move Peter in the direction of Caesarea. This is the city where the narrator left Philip (Acts 8:40)[81] after his involvement with one who might have been a Gentile (the Ethiopian Eunuch). It is also the city from which Saul, the future apostle to the Gentiles, was sent to Tarsus (9:30).[82] Luke uses this common city[83] to bring into fruition the earlier foreshadows of Gentile inclusion.[84]

The Tabatha narrative is the tipping point in the flow of the gospel story. This might have been accomplished through another narrative involving a man, but that was not Luke's choice. Instead, he places a narrative involving a woman at the center of two outer narratives involving men. There is something about her femaleness that contributes to the progression of Luke's larger story. The Tabitha narrative is greatly expanded over the Aeneas narrative to show the progression of the gospel. Luke chooses the story about Tabitha to emphasize her shared giving of alms with Cornelius, and to foreshadow the new life about to be given to Cornelius through Peter's mediation. More than Aeneas, it is Tabatha who is the half-way house to the Gentiles. Her name is given in *Aramaic and Greek*, and she is identified as a female disciple (μαθήτρια). She appears to be a physical emblem of Luke's expanding Gospel. She is *not* a Jew (Acts 1—7); she is *not* a Samaritan (Acts 8); she is *not* a Hellenistic Jew (Aeneas); and she is *not* a Gentile (Cornelius); but she is a woman, *a female disciple* (μαθήτρια) showing mercy to Gentiles. The gospel is radically crossing ethnic and racial barriers, and the breakdown of the male, gender preference, in the Tabatha narrative, pictures how expansive this transition is becoming. In Tabitha, Luke shows the reader that the gospel is also reaching into the lives of women who are deeply loved, and who serve those outside of their own community with good works and charitable giving. For the reader, the question arises, how far, then, will this gospel

---

[81] "But Philip found himself at Azotus, and as he passed through he kept preaching the gospel to all the cities until he came to Caesarea." (NASB).

[82] "But when the brethren learned *of it*, they brought him down to Caesarea and sent him away to Tarsus." (NASB).

[83] Leland Ryken identifies this literary device as the functional use of geography to communicate a message in the Gospel of Mark: "Sometimes the geography is used for structural purposes. The Gospel of Mark, for example, is structured on a grand contrast between Galilee, place of acceptance, and Jerusalem, which symbolizes rejection of Jesus." Leland Ryken, *Words of Life: A Literary Introduction to the New Testament* (Grand Rapids, MI: Baker Book House, 1987), 33.

[84] Witherington also argues for a movement toward the Gentile mission due to the Greek nature of these cities and peoples in these transitional narratives when he states: "Peter was traveling in increasingly more Hellenized territory, and so we should not be surprised that it was in this sort of locale that the question of Gentiles and the Christian faith seems to first have arisen in a significant way." Witherington *Acts*, 330. F. F. Bruce also observes: "Since much of this territory was semi-Gentile in population, a further widening of the range of the saving message is implied." F. F. Bruce, *The Book of Acts*, rev. ed. The New International Commentary on the New Testament (Grand Rapids, MI: William B. Eerdmans Publishing Company, 1988), 198, see also 201. In other words, the ethnic nature of the people in these two miracles also foreshadows a movement to the Gentiles in the Cornelius narrative. Ironically, Caesarea will also be the place where the antagonist to Peter and the gospel, Herod, will be sovereignly slain (Acts 12:19-23). God will vindicate Peter, and the expansion of the movement, through the events which are played out around Caesarea.

expansion go? The answer is revealed as the gospel reaches Cornelius, a Gentile brought to new life.

Conclusion

This study is not based on a feminist hermeneutic, but a literary sensitivity to narratives involving men and women that have intentional structures already embedded in the text.

Reading, like listening, is a linear progression that cannot be comprehended if interrupted. A visual medium enables the viewer to see the whole all at once, but the whole must be constructed, piece-by-piece, when words are employed. This study has been an attempt to visually display the whole to the reader without interruptions by traditional barriers like changes in subject matter, chapter divisions, and assumptions about the text. As in all literature, ideas are often *covered up* in a work. However, once a reader shows what is there, it appears to subsequent readers that it has always been there; and it has—because the writer put it there. What has been presented here is part of what is already present in Luke, John, and Acts, even if it has sometimes escaped the reader's attention.

These readings do not resolve the larger, biblical question regarding the relationship of men and women, but do provide pictures which show the prominence of women – even over a male priest named Zacharias, a male teacher in Israel named Nicodemus, and a healed man named Aeneas. In other words, these narratives provide an additional weight of evidence in biblical gender studies as they unveil the significant contributions of Mary, the Woman at the Well, and Tabatha that may have been *covered up* in the biblical narratives.

All these stories touch on the mission of God in salvation setting forth a mirror image in the plan of God. Just as one woman played a part in taking the first step away from God, so is it that these women take first steps back to God—Mary in receiving the revelation and the Son, the Woman at the Well in receiving and communicating Jesus as Messiah to the Samaritans, and Tabitha in preparing the way for the Gentiles.[85] These great reversals only honor God.

---

[85] I am grateful to my good friend, Drew Gentile, of Cru for bringing this final observation to my attention.

CHAPTER II

SIMON'S MOTHER-IN-LAW AS A MINOR CHARACTER IN THE GOSPEL OF MARK:
A NARRATIVE ANALYSIS[1]

Introduction

Legend has it that Ernest Hemmingway, known for his concise language, once won a wager that he could tell a story in just six words. He then wrote on a napkin: "For sale. Baby shoes. Never worn." Whenever I share this story, invariably the audience fills in the gaps by positing a backstory which includes the baby's death. One thing is clear—, the story did not start at the beginning; it was told out of chronological order.

Narratives do not simply record what happened; they are selective arrangements of material.[2] For instance, the call of Simon is presented differently in the Gospel of Mark than it is in the Gospel of Luke. In Mark the call is concise and *precedes* the healing of Simon's mother-in-law (Mk. 1:16-18, cf. 1:29-31), while in Luke the call is more developed and *follows* the healing of Simon's mother-in-law (cf. Lk. 5:1-11 with 4:38-39). As Abraham Kuruvilla is fond of saying, an interpreter must ask: "What is the author, *doing* with what he is *saying*?"[3]

Narratives often have two aspects, or a two-storied architecture. Following French structuralists, Seymour Chatman categorizes the two tiers as "story" and "discourse."[4] "Story" consists of the *what* of the narrative including events, plot, and existents (character and setting); "discourse" is the *way* of the narrative, or the "means

---

[1] This article first appeared in *Priscilla Papers* Vol. 31, No. 2 (Spring 2017).

[2] Tsvetan Todorov, "Primitive Narrative," in *The Poetics of Prose*, trans. Richard Howard (Cornell Univ Press, 1977), 55 ("there is no 'primitive narrative.' No narrative is natural; a choice and a construction will always preside over its appearance; narrative is a discourse, not a series of events.").

[3] Abraham Kuruvilla, *Mark: A Theological Commentary for Preachers* (Eugene, Or: Cascade Books, 2012), x; *Privilege the Text!: A Theological Hermeneutic for Preaching*, New Edition edition. (Moody Publishers, 2013), 89–150; "David v. Goliath (1 Samuel 17): What Is the Author Doing with What He Is Saying?," *J. Evang. Theol. Soc.*, 3/58 (2015): 490. Kuruvilla also set forth this memorable metaphor: "Mark must be read as story, rather than primarily as history. It is not a *plain-glass window* through which we only see what happened; it is a *stained-glass window* that, in addition, tells a story itself—the theology of the text." *Mark*, xiv.

[4] Seymour Chatman, *Story and Discourse: Narrative Structure in Fiction and Film* (Ithaca, N.Y.: Cornell University Press, 1980), 9.

through which the story is transmitted."[5] Russian formalists have a similar, dualist model distinguishing *fabula* (story/tale, the sequence of events referred to in a narrative in their causal, chronological order) from *sjužet* (discourse, the sequence of events in the order in which they appear in the narrative).[6]

Within these categories, the analysis of character is often discussed under the category of "story."[7] However, because characterization looks at *how* characters are developed in a narrative, it seems more appropriate to identify characterization with "discourse" than with "story."[8] While character may be described, in the abstract, as a

---

[5] Ibid. This writer will use Chatman's categories of "story" and "discourse" in this discussion.

[6] Boris Viktorovich Tomashevsky, "Thematics," in *Russian Formalist Criticism: Four Essays*, trans. Lee T. Lemon and Marion J. Reis (Lincoln: University of Nebraska Press, 1965), 66–68 ("In brief, the story is 'the action itself,' the plot, 'how the reader learns of the action.'" 67 n.5); James L. Resseguie, *Narrative Criticism of the New Testament: An Introduction* (Grand Rapids, Mich: Baker Academic, 2005). David M. Rhoads and Donald Michie, *Mark as Story: An Introduction to the Narrative of a Gospel* (Philadelphia: Fortress Press, 1982), 9. Tzvetan Todorov distinguishes between '*histoire*' (story—a reality of events that would have passed—events reported) and '*discours*' (the manner in which the narrator makes events known to us) "The Categories of Literary Narrative," trans. Joseph Kestner, *Pap. Lang. Lit.* 50, no. 3/4 (2014): 383–384. Mieke Ball follows a three-layer distinction of narrative text (a finite, structured whole composed of language signs that tells a story), story (the sequence of events), and *fabula* (a series of logically and chronologically related events that are caused or experienced by actors—the way in which events are presented). *Narratology: Introduction to the Theory of Narrative*, 2 edition. (University of Toronto Press, 1997), 5–6. Shlomith Rimmon-Kenan, *Narrative Fiction: Contemporary Poetics*, 2 edition. (Routledge, 2003).

[7] Chatman, *Story and Discourse*, 107–138. Rhoads and Michie, *Mark as Story*, 101–136. R. Alan Culpepper, *Anatomy of the Fourth Gospel*, 1st edition. (Philadelphia: Fortress Press, 1983). Jack Dean Kingsbury, *Conflict in Mark: Jesus, Authorities, Disciples* (Minneapolis: Fortress Press, 1989), 9–30. Todorov, "The Categories of Literary Narrative," 393–402; Bal, *Narratology*, 114–131.

[8] As Moore wrote: "when we come to read or analyze a concrete narrative text, for example, Mark, everything in that text is encountered as discourse-rhetoric." Stephen D. Moore, *Literary Criticism and the Gospels: The Theoretical Challenge* (New Haven: Yale Univ Pr, 1989), 61. Rimmon-Kenan also observes that in the text: "the events do not necessarily appear in chronological order, the characteristics of the participants are dispersed throughout, and all the items of the narrative content are filtered through some prism or perspective ('focalizer')." Rimmon-Kenan, *Narrative Fiction*, 5. Moore continues: "the notion of form encompasses everything in the presentation of the contentual set of events to which the given gospel refers. Such presentational strategies include plotting, characterization, the filtering of story events through theocentric, Christocentric, and other perspective, and the rearrangement of chronological sequence, the use of literary patterns and techniques, and so on." Moore, *Literary Criticism and the Gospels*, 61. Berlin seems to approach characterization as discourse when she states: "The reader reconstructs a character from the information provided to him in the discourse." Adele Berlin, *Poetics and Interpretation of Biblical Narrative* (Winona Lake, Ind.: Eisenbrauns, 1994), 33–42. More broadly, Henry James commented on the interface of story and discourse long ago: "This sense of the story being the idea, the starting-point, of the novel is the only one that I see in which it can be spoken of as something different from its organic whole; and since,

compilation of motifs, or a cluster of traits of someone in the narrative, and in that sense fall under the umbrella of "story," characterization is built from *how* the account is told—the author's presentation as found in the discourse of the work.[9]

One means of developing character within the discourse is through comparisons and contrasts, providing the reader opportunities to fill in gaps by implication.[10] This means of characterization causes traits to stand out: "Even if a characterization is implicit in the words or deeds of a character, it stands out more clearly if it is contrasted with its opposite,

---

in proportion as the work is successful, the idea permeates and penetrates it, informs and animates it, so that every word and every punctuation-point contribute directly to the expression, in that proportion do we lose our sense of the story being a blade which may be drawn more or less out of its sheath. The story and the novel, the idea and the form, are the needle and thread, and I never heard of a guild of tailors who recommended the use of the thread without the needle or the needle without the thread." Henry James, "The Art of Fiction," *Longman's Magazine*, September 1884.

[9] Tomashevesky describes characterization as a function of discourse when he explains the distinction between direct and indirect characterization: "In *direct characterization* the author may characterize the figure directly by a straightforward report; he may have other characters discuss the person in question; or he may have the character tell about himself in, say, a confession of some sort. *Indirect characterization* also occurs frequently; the character in such a case betrays himself in his actions or conduct." Tomashevsky, "Thematics," 88. Both direct and indirect characterization look to how the author presents the character in the narrative. See also Rimmon-Kenan, *Narrative Fiction*. ("in the story character is a construct, put together by the reader from various indications dispersed throughout the text."). Thompson argues that: "Rather than mining the text for the specific virtues and traits possessed by a particular character, they mine the text for its rhetorical and literary strategies in presenting characters. Thus the emphasis falls not so much on *what* a character is (e.g. honest, virtuous, brave, pious, etc), but on *how* the character is constructed by the reader (i.e. through actions, speech, description, etc.) and *how* these elements of characterization are progressively coordinated by the reader." Thompson Marianne Meye, "'God's Voice You Have Never Heard, God's Form You Have Never Seen': The Characterization of God in the Gospel of John," in *Characterization in Biblical Literature*, ed. Elizabeth Struthers Malbon and Adele Berlin, Semeia 63 (Society of Biblical Literature, 1993), 180.

[10] Berlin focuses on the term, "contrast," noting that characterization is developed through "three types of contrast: 1) contrast with another character, 2) contrast with an earlier action of the same character, and 3) contrast with the expected norm." Berlin, *Poetics and Interpretation of Biblical Narrative*, 40. Alice Bach provides a good example of comparing and contrasting an earlier presentation of Bathsheba as an object in 2 Samuel 11—12 with the later transformation of Bathsheba as queen mother in 1 Kings 1—2. "Signs of the Flesh: Observations on Characterization in the Bible," in *Characterization in Biblical Literature*, ed. Elizabeth Struthers Malbon and Adele Berlin, Semeia 63 (Society of Biblical Literature, 1993), 70–77. Laura Donaldson also provides a good example of comparison between Joseph and Potiphar's wife to show that Potiphar's wife "uses her sexuality as a weapon to prevent the household's passing from man to man (from Potiphar to Joseph) rather than from man to woman (from Potiphar to Potiphar's wife)." "Cyborgs, Ciphers, and Sexuality; Re-Theorizing Literary and Biblical Characters," in *Characterization in Biblical Literature*, ed. Elizabeth Struthers Malbon and Adele Berlin, Semeia 63 (Society of Biblical Literature, 1993), 90. See also Joel F. Williams, *Other Followers of Jesus: Minor Characters as Major Figures in Mark's Gospel*, Journal for the study of the New Testament (Sheffield: JSOT Pr, 1994), 65–66.

e.g. Nabal and Abigail, Esau and Jacob."[11] Often it is through comparison that the reader discovers the contrast. Furthermore, it is through comparison that a character is often developed throughout a narrative.[12] Accordingly, characters are not so much individuals as "interdividuals" in that they are seen, compared, and contrasted, in relationship to others.[13]

Various women are among the minor characters in the Gospel of Mark.[14] This study will examine an especially minor character in Mark who is not named, not given significant space in the narrative,[15] and rarely discussed in scholarship—Simon's mother-in-law (Mk. 1:29-31). When her narrative is read within the narrative structure and logic of Mark's Gospel (the story's discourse), it makes significant contributions to the message of Mark, and more broadly, to Mark's biblical theology of discipleship.

---

[11] Berlin, *Poetics and Interpretation of Biblical Narrative*, 40.

[12] Marianne Thompson argues that characters are presented and developed in biblical narratives. "'God's Voice You Have Never Heard," 179. See also Robert Scholes, James Phelan, and Robert Kellogg, *The Nature of Narrative: Revised and Expanded*, 40th anniversary edition. (Oxford ; New York: Oxford University Press, 2006), 169.

[13] David McCraken, "Character in the Boundary: Bakhtin's Interdividuality in Biblical Narratives," in *Characterization in Biblical Literature*, ed. Elizabeth Struthers Malbon and Adele Berlin, Semeia 63 (Society of Biblical Literature, 1993), 36.

[14] Malbon provides a helpful definition of minor characters: "For my purposes a 'minor' character is one who lacks a continuing or recurrent presence in the story as narrated. For the most part minor characters appear only once." Elizabeth Struthers Malbon, "The Major Importance of the Minor Characters in Mark," in *New Literary Criticism and the New Testament* (Sheffield, Eng: Sheffield Academic Pr, 1994), 60. See also Susan Miller, "Women Characters in Mark's Gospel," in *Character Studies and The Gospel of Mark*, ed. Christopher W. Skinner and Matthew Ryan Hauge, 1st ed., Library of New Testament Studies 483 (New York: Bloomsbury T&T Clark, 2014), 175; Williams, *Other Followers of Jesus;* Malbon, "Fallible Followers : Women and Men in the Gospel of Mark," *Semeia*, no. 28 (1983): 29–48.

[15] Some women in Mark are central to larger narrative sections, namely intercalations, that comprise more space in the narrative. See David E. Malick, "An Examination of Jesus's View of Women through Three Intercalations in the Gospel of Mark," *Priscilla Pap.* 27, no. 3 (2013): 4–15.

The Healing of Simon's Mother-in-law
(Mark 1:29-31)

Performance criticism (analysis based on an oral-aural presentation of the text) focuses on the progressive nature of the narrative as presented from beginning to end for the first-time, reader or hearer, rather than on the final form of the narrative which is only discerned upon second, third, and other subsequent readings.[16] The argument is that texts were originally heard in their progressive development and not with an understanding of the whole. Certainly, a first reading, or hearing, differs from a subsequent reading or hearing; however, it does not seem necessary to limit the interpretation of a text to only one approach. Those who originally presented the Gospel may have memorized it, or at least read it multiple times before performing it aloud. Therefore, the presenters had a sense of the whole, and their presentations may have emphasized significant themes for the first-time listener.[17] Furthermore, a text may have been read aloud more than once to an audience. Accordingly, a strict dichotomy between first and subsequent readings may be an overemphasis. Mark's account of the healing of Simon's mother-in-law occurs early in the narrative; therefore, we will examine it from both the perspective of a first-time reading and then from the perspective of a subsequent reading.

A First Reading of the Narrative

The Gospel of Mark opens with a prologue that foreshadows many themes that will be developed in the book including geographical themes (wilderness, Galilee,

---

[16] See Moore, *Literary Criticism and the Gospels*, 84–88. See also Jouette M. Bassler, "The Parable of the Loaves," *J. Relig.* 66, no. 2 (1986): 157–72; David Rhoads, Joanna Dewey, and Donald Michie, *Mark As Story: An Introduction to the Narrative of a Gospel*, 3 edition. (Minneapolis: Fortress Press, 2012), ("Recent New Testament research has recognized that first-century Mediterranean societies were predominantly oral/ aural cultures in which probably no more than three to five percent of the people were able to read or write."), Kindle location 177; by contrast, see Robert Tannehill, *The Narrative Unity of Luke-Acts: A Literary Interpretation, Vol. 1: The Gospel According to Luke*, vol. 1: The Gospel according to Luke, 1st edition. (Philadelphia: Fortress Press, 1986), 6.("the discussion that follows is not simply an expanded reading; it is commentary. It represents part of what might be said after reading a second, third, or fourth time. It is not confined to what is happening when reading for the first time, with much of the text still unknown.")

[17] "Ancient storytellers brought out the dynamics of the story in their telling, putting their stamp on the story, and shaping it to each particular audience. The performer used voice, volume, pace, gestures, facial expressions, and bodily movement to express an interpretation of the story and to engender certain impacts on different audiences. The performance would stimulate the audience's imagination and bring out the emotion, the humor, and the irony of the story." Rhoads, Dewey, and Michie, *Mark As Story*, Kindle location 191.

Jerusalem, the way); the centrality of Jesus through the multiple witnesses of Isaiah, John the Baptizer, the Father, and the Spirit; the identity of Jesus as the Son of God; and a story that is characterized by an authoritative revelation of Jesus in the midst of an ambiguous human response.[18] While it is true that many of these themes are only fully discerned upon a subsequent reading/hearing of the gospel, they still express themselves in the first exposure to the text. As the account continues, the listener will be able to identify the echoes of earlier voices.[19]

The wilderness focus of the prologue (cf. ἔρημος in 1:3, 4, 12) transitions to Jesus' activity in Galilee.[20] Each time Jesus calls disciples, he is reported to be near the sea of Galilee.[21] Four disciples are explicitly named in 1:16-20 (Simon, Andrew, James, and John). They will reappear by name in our brief narrative. Jesus then begins to demonstrate who he is through a sequence of cures, the last of which involves a conflict (1:21—2:12).[22]

---

[18] See Mary Ann Tolbert, *Sowing the Gospel: Mark's World in Literary-Historical Perspective* (Minneapolis: Fortress Press, 1989), 108–113, 316-17.

[19] In a more modern sense, one might liken these foreshadows in the prologue to the overture of a musical. The first time one hears an overture, all of the music is unfamiliar. However, it sets up themes that are revisited later in the show. Then, upon subsequent listening, the overture is filled with meaning from the fullness of the musical. Present-day audiences more easily comprehend literary theory expressed through the mediums of auditory and visual expression. The foreshadows of the prologue will resonate with the reader/hearer upon a virginal reading, and then become more explicitly meaningful upon subsequent readings.

[20] Jesus came into Galilee (εἰς τὴν Γαλιλαίαν) 1:14.

[21] The call of Simon and Andrew and James and John in 1:16-20 ("and going by the sea of Gailiee," Καὶ παράγων παρὰ τὴν θάλασσαν τῆς Γαλιλαίας); the call of Levi in 2:13-14 ("and he went out again by the sea," Καὶ ἐξῆλθεν πάλιν παρὰ τὴν θάλασσαν); the call of the Twelve in 3:7-19 ("And Jesus with his disciples withdrew to the sea," Καὶ ὁ Ἰησοῦς μετὰ τῶν μαθητῶν αὐτοῦ ἀνεχώρησεν πρὸς τὴν θάλασσαν).

[22] C. S. Mann, ed., *Mark: A New Translation with Introduction and Commentary*, 1st ed., The Anchor Bible v. 27 (Garden City, N.Y: Doubleday, 1986), 180–81. The overall structure of this section is construed differently by others who group the controversies as a unit in 2:1—3:6. See Wilfrid Harrington, *New Testament Message: A Biblical-Theological Commentary*, New Testament Message Volume 4 (Dublin: Veritas Pubns, Dublin, 1979), 24–25; P. Mourlon Beernaert, "Jésus Controversé. Structure Et Théologie de Marc 2, 1–3, 6," *Nouv. Rev. Théologique* 95, no. 2 (1973): 129–49. Joanna Dewey groups the controversies as a unit. *Markan Public Debate: Literary Technique, Concentric Structure, and Theology in Mark 2:1-3:6* (Scholars Pr, 1980), 110. However, it seems to this writer that some of Dewey's parallels are strained. For instance, Dewey combines the call of Levi with the pericope about Jesus eating with sinners in 2:13-17. This grouping enables her to see a pattern in 2:13-17 and 2:23-27 where the activity begins out of doors and then continues indoors. Ibid., 113-14. However, this arrangement of the text appears to have overlooked the textual clues that structure the narrative around Jesus going by the sea to call the four disciples (1:16-20),

These cures have an alternating pattern between the spiritual and the physical:

    A (spiritual): casting out a demon (1:21-28)

    B (physical): healing Simon's mother-in law (1:29-31)

    B'/A' (physical/spiritual): healing many with diseases & casting out many demons (1:32-39)

    B'' (physical): healing man with leprosy (1:40-45)

    A''/B''' (spiritual/physical): forgiveness of sins/healing the paralytic (2:1-12)

There is also an interchange between healing individuals (A, B, A'', B'''), and healing the multitude (B'/A'). Simon's mother-in-law is the first individual physically healed in 1:29-31:

> And immediately after going out of the synagogue, they came into the house of Simon and Andrew with James and John. And Simon's mother-in-law was lying down with a fever, and immediately they spoke with him concerning her. And coming, he raised her up taking hold of her hand, and the fever left her, and she served them.

Many interpret the "serving" response of Simon's mother-in-law merely as a verification of her healing.[23] However, even in a first reading/hearing of the Gospel, the

---

Levi (2:13-14), and the Twelve (3:7-19). With these textual clues in view, it seems better to break the narrative into an alternating pattern:

    A Call of four disciples (1:16-20)
        B Jesus demonstrates who he is through a sequence of cures, the last involving a conflict (1:21—2:12),
    A' Call of Levi (2:13-14),
        B' Jesus demonstrates who he is through a sequence of conflicts, the last involving a cure (2:15—3:6), and
    A'' Choice of the Twelve (3:7-10).

This is not to say that correlations do not exist between 2:1-12 and 3:1-6, but these correlations do not seem to be significant enough to move 2:1-2 from the narrative logic of the units that precede it in 1:21-45.

[23] Kathleen E. Corley, *Private Women, Public Meals: Social Conflict in the Synoptic Tradition* (Peabody, Mass: Hendrickson Pubs, 1993), 88 ("Mark does nothing to emphasize her activity, and the woman does not join the men for their meal. In this context, the service of Peter's mother-in-law merely verifies her healing."); Williams, *Other Followers of Jesus*, 94 ("At this point in the narrative, the service of the woman seems to function simply as evidence that she is completely healed of her affliction"); D. E. Nineham, *Saint Mark* (Penguin Books, 1973), 81 ("The words show both the completeness of the cure (cf. Introduction, p. 24) and also its miraculous speed"); William L. Lane, *The Gospel according to Mark: The English Text With Introduction, Exposition, and Notes* (Wm. B. Eerdmans Publishing, 1974), 78 ("The

word describing her service (διακονέω) was already used in close proximity of angels who served, or ministered, to Jesus after his temptation in the wilderness (1:13).[24] Therefore, whatever Simon's mother-in-law is doing in response to Jesus' healing is similar to what angels did for Jesus after his temptation. This similarity would not be lost on the reader or listener in Greek.

In addition, every miracle in this broader section of the narrative (1:21—2:12) includes a *response*, and the action of Simon's mother-in-law is the only *positive* response in the entire section:

> **A** (spiritual): casting out a demon (1:21-28)
> *[An improper response of a demon (24-26)]*
> **B** (physical): healing Simon's mother-in law (1:29-31)
> *[A proper response of Simon's mother-in law (31)]*
> **B'/A'** (physical/spiritual): healing many with diseases & casting out many demons (1:32-39)
> *[An improper response of the disciples, corrected, (35-39)]*
> **B''** (physical): healing man with leprosy (1:40-45)
> *[An improper response of a healed man, magnified (44-45)]*
> **A''/B'''** (spiritual/physical): forgiveness of sins/healing the paralytic (2:1-12)
> *[An improper response of scribes, controversy (2:7)]*[25]

---

notice that the woman 'ministered to them' confirms the mercy and compassion extended toward her by Jesus and indicates that the figures in the background of the gospel narrative are affected by the power of this mysterious Galilean."); R. T. France, *The Gospel of Mark* (Wm. B. Eerdmans Publishing Co., 2002), 108 ("The completeness of the cure is emphasized by the clause καὶ διηκόνει αὐτοῖς. no period of convalescence was needed. While διακονέω has a wide range of meaning, in this context its basic sense of domestic provision seems most likely; she fulfilled what would have been the expected role of the mother-in-law in the family home, by serving up refreshments"). Some others interpret the woman's activity as a proclamation that she is free from Sabbath restrictions. Augustine Stock, *The Method and the Message of Mark* (Wilmington, Del: Michael Glazier, 1989), 80 ("She seems to have come to the conclusion that if Jesus was free to heal her on the Sabbath, then she was free from the Sabbath restrictions preventing her from serving and helping others."); Bas M. van Iersel, *Mark* (London ; New York: Bloomsbury T&T Clark, 2005), 138–139 (Here begins—for the reader, not for the characters—the conflict over the question of whether the sabbath regulations are still valid.").

[24] "And the angels served, or ministered, to him," (καὶ οἱ ἄγγελοι **διηκόνουν** αὐτῷ). See also Tolbert, *Sowing the Gospel*, 137-38 n. 20.

[25] It may be argued that the onlookers appear to have a positive response to the healing of the lame man when the narrator states that "all were amazed and glorified God saying that we have never seen this" (ἐξίστασθαι πάντας καὶ δοξάζειν τὸν θεὸν λέγοντας ὅτι οὕτως οὐδέποτε εἴδομεν). However, it is questionable whether the term for "amazed" (ἐξίστημι) is explicitly positive. It is used in the LXX for astonishment mingled with fear (Gen. 43:33; Ruth 3:8; 1 Sam. 14:15). The term in Mark is used elsewhere

The first-time reader/hearer would notice this responsive contrast in the progression of the narrative once again magnifying the *service* of Simon's mother-in-law.[26]

Moreover, the use of names in the response to Jesus' healing of the multitude highlights a contrast between Simon and his mother-in-law. As set forth above, the names of all four of the disciples called in 1:16-20 are repeated in 1:29: "And immediately after going out of the synagogue, they came into the house of Simon and Andrew with James and John." However, in the response to Jesus' healing of the multitude, Jesus goes away to a secluded place (ἔρημος τόπον) to pray.[27] Only Simon is specifically identified among those searching for him: "and Simon and those with him hunted for him" (1:36).[28] The diffusion of those with Simon, and the highlighting of Simon once again reminds the reader of the anonymous woman earlier identified as "*Simon's* mother-in-law" (πενθερὰ *Σίμωνος*) in 1:29. This linking of names sets-up an implied comparison between the woman and the disciple. In response to Jesus' personal healing, Simon's mother-in-law served them (διηκόνει αὐτοῖς). However, in response to Jesus' healing of the multitude, Simon hunted, or tracked, Jesus down (κατεδίωξεν, third person singular). This term is used elsewhere to describe the pursuit of someone in a hostile sense.[29] Then Simon and his companions say: "All are seeking you" (πάντες ζητοῦσίν σε) 1:37. These words appear to be a rebuke, or correction, of Jesus for secluding himself.[30] Then Jesus redirects their attention away from

---

with the same sense (Mk. 5:42; 6:51; see also Acts 2:7, 12). Nevertheless, the onlookers do glorify God (δοξάζειν τὸν θεὸν). Therefore, one might say that this is a mixed response by the people, but the response of the religious leaders is clearly negative (Mk. 2:6-7), and it is the focus of the unit—the reason for the healing.

[26] As Elizabeth Struthers Malbon has stated: "[N]ot only must attention to characterization be integrated with analysis of plot, settings, rhetoric, etc., but also all the characters—'minor' as well as 'major'—must be observed in relation with each other if we are to be competent and sensitive readers of biblical narratives. "The Major Importance of the Minor Characters in Mark," 59. Continuing, she explains: I read Mark's Gospel as not only the story of Jesus as the Christ, the Son of God, but also the story of others' response to him in that role. For some time I have been investigating the characters around the Markan Jesus, especially the religious leaders and the disciples or followers. Here I wish to show how the minor characters extend the continuum of responses to Jesus that these major characters present." Ibid., 63–64.

[27] Because there is not a "wilderness" per se in Galilee, the use of the term ἔρημος may echo the spiritual testing of the temptation (cf. 1:12-13).

[28] καὶ κατεδίωξεν αὐτὸν Σίμων καὶ οἱ μετ' αὐτοῦ

[29] See LXX of Psalms of Solomon 15:8, "for they will flee from the holy ones like those *pursued* in battle;" see also BDAG, s.v. "καταδιώκω."

[30] The disciples are "craving for self-enhancement. They want to be known, respected, honored, obeyed, and generally held in high repute as the greatest and the first." But Jesus strives to suppress his reputation. "Understanding the disciples' desire for glory and renown as a foil to Jesus' actions suggests a

the multitudes to his purpose of proclaiming his message in other rural towns ("κωμόπολις," 1:38). Jesus' correction of Simon's response is the first indication in the Gospel that these eager followers may not be perfectly aligned with what Jesus is doing. It is a flag for the initial reader who has identified with the followers, and places in stark relief the unique response of Simon's mother-in-law who alone offers to *serve* them.[31]

The first-time reader/hearer of Mark is given many contextual clues through the repetition of terms and the contrasting responses to Jesus' healing to suspect that the serving response of Simon's mother-in-law was not only uniquely proper, but as significant as the service of angels after Jesus' temptation. After subsequent readings of the Gospel, these heuristic guesses will be fully validated.

Subsequent Readings of the Narrative

Westerners tend to be more adept at interpreting visual media than written media. Upon a first-time viewing of the movie, *The Sixth Sense*, most audiences were stunned to realize at the end of the show that the child psychologist, Dr. Malcolm Crowe (played by Bruce Willis) was actually dead. And the reason the troubled boy, Cole Sear (played by Haley Joel Osment), was able to talk with Dr. Crowe was because he sees "dead people." Upon a re-viewing of the movie, the careful observer discovers clues throughout the show that pointed to Dr. Crowe being dead—his conversations with his wife and Cole's mother are one-sided; the color red prominently appears when the dead are near (red concrete, red clothes, a red door knob, red hats, red fingernails, a red balloon); Dr. Crowe mostly wears the same clothes he was wearing when he was shot; and rooms become cold whenever the dead are near. Then when Dr. Crowe's wife drops his wedding ring, he suddenly realizes he has not been wearing it, and the past and the present meet in an awareness that he is in fact dead. There are also parallels in the show—the former patient who shot Dr. Crowe also

---

different construction for secrecy: Jesus' commands for silence and his attempts to stay hidden define his steadfast rejection of personal renown and glory. Closely related to this rejection is his attempt to avoid drawing crowds. . . . [T]he first four healings in the Gospel (1:21—2:12) all ended in reports of Jesus' fame spreading, crowds growing, and his constant efforts to stem that tide. His consistent point is to keep from becoming known (1:34; 3:12; 5:43; 7:24)." Tolbert, *Sowing the Gospel*, 226–27.

[31] As Malbon observes: "Only minor characters, never major characters such as the disciples or the religious leaders, are healed by Jesus in the Markan narrative, and the minor characters whom he has healed exemplify faith in Jesus' power and authority. Their stories of faith and healing are absolutely essential to Mark's story of Jesus as the Christ. Their responses of exemplary faith extend the Markan response continuum: from enemies to fallible followers to exemplars." "The Major Importance of the Minor Characters in Mark," 65. Clearly Simon's mother-in-law is being shown to be an "exemplar" in her service while Simon is showing himself to be a "fallible follower" early in the narrative as he attempts to redirect Jesus' activity.

saw "dead people;" so by helping Cole, who now sees ghosts, Dr. Crowe is able to correct a fatal flaw in his care for an earlier patient. These subsequent viewings make the movie even more fascinating for the viewer as the patterns, which were always there, become more transparent. Similar insights, depths, and delights are present for subsequent readers and hearers of the Gospel of Mark. Since earlier audiences were more familiar with the written/oral presentation of story, they may have made the connections sooner than modern Western readers.

As noted above, even though the four male disciples who were explicitly called to follow Jesus in 1:16-20 are named (Simon, Andrew, James, and John) in the unit describing the healing of Simon's mother-in-law (1:29), she is anonymous. Often in Mark's Gospel, the unnamed are exemplary followers of Christ who express faith: the Gerasene demoniac (Mk. 5:1-20); the woman with the flow of blood (Mk. 5:25-34); the Syrophoenician woman (Mk. 7:24-30); the widow who gives at the temple (Mk. 12:41-44); the woman who anoints Jesus for his death (Mk. 14:3-9); and the many women who came up with Jesus from Galilee to Jerusalem (Mk. 15:41). Therefore, in the overarching pattern of the Gospel, Simon's mother-in-law is the first of a group of faithful followers who are anonymous.[32]

In addition, the service (διακονέω) of Simon's mother-in-law adumbrates the major theme of "service" in Mark. In the central section of Mark, Jesus emphasizes the need for the disciples to serve:

> Calling them to Himself, Jesus said to them, "You know that those who are recognized as rulers of the Gentiles lord it over (κατακυριεύουσιν) them; and their great men exercise authority over (κατεξουσιάζουσιν) them. "But it is not this way among you, but whoever wishes to become great among you shall be your servant (διάκονος); and whoever wishes to be first among you shall be slave (δοῦλος) of all. "For even the Son of Man did not come to be served (διακονηθῆναι), but to serve (διακονῆσαι), and to give His life a ransom for many.
>
> (Mk. 10:42-45, NASB).

---

[32] Tolbert identifies the anonymous followers as examples of the good soil who also are aligned with Jesus. See *Sowing the Gospel*, 226-27 ("Not only is this drive [by the disciples for self-enhancement] the antithesis of that embodied by the anonymous, faithful ones who are healed, it also stands in stark contrast to the depiction of Jesus himself, who throughout Division One actively strives to suppress his reputation and keep his name from becoming known. . . . Jesus' commands for silence and his attempts to stay hidden define his steadfast rejection of personal renown and glory. Closely related to this rejection is his attempt to avoid drawing crowds.").

Some might object that the statement in 1:31 only says: "and the fever left her and she served them (διηκόνει αὐτοῖς); this clearly has the sense that she provided them "table service"[33] and is not parallel to the service described in Mark 10:42-45. However, a similar discussion of "service" in the central section of the Gospel clarifies that the service Jesus has in view includes "table service:"

> Sitting down, He called the twelve and said to them, "If anyone wants to be first, he shall be last of all *and servant (διάκονος) of all.*" Taking a child, He set him before them, and taking him in His arms, He said to them, "Whoever receives one child like this in My name receives Me; and whoever receives Me does not receive Me, but Him who sent Me."
>
> John said to Him, "Teacher, we saw someone casting out demons in Your name, and we tried to prevent him because he was not following us."
>
> But Jesus said, "Do not hinder him, for there is no one who will perform a miracle in My name, and be able soon afterward to speak evil of Me. "For he who is not against us is for us. *For whoever gives you a cup of water to drink because of your name as followers of Christ, truly I say to you, he will not lose his reward.*"

(Mark 9:35-41, emphasis added, NASB). In other words, serving children and serving water are the kind of activities for which disciples will be rewarded.

Finally, the only other place in the Gospel of Mark where the verb for service (διακονέω) is used for people in the company of Jesus is in the description of the women who provided for Jesus' needs from Galilee to Jerusalem:

> There were also *some* women looking on from a distance, among whom *were* Mary Magdalene, and Mary the mother of James the Less and Joses, and Salome. When He was in Galilee, they used to follow Him and minister to Him (διηκόνουν αὐτῷ); and *there were* many other women who came up with Him to Jerusalem.

Mark 15:40-41 NASB).[34] Here Mark describes women who have been a part of the story all along but have not been brought to the narrative's foreground. Even though four women

---

[33] Corley, *Private Women, Public Meals*, 87.

[34] Iersel, *Mark*, 117 ("After the cure the woman may seem to drop out of the picture. That she does not is something that the reader does not discover until the last page of the book, where the narrator mentions several women who ministered to Jesus when he was in Galilee (15.40-41). As it is, this information is anticipated in the first part of the book by the mention of at least one woman who ministered to Jesus and his companions in Galilee (1.31). These are the only two places in Mark where the verb διακονέω ('minister to') is used for people in Jesus' company.")

are explicitly named in verse 40, they have functioned in the story as the ultimate expression of the anonymous in that their presence was active but unknown to the reader. And the essence of their activity was serving, or ministering (διακονέω) to Jesus—whatever that entailed. In their *service,* they have multiplied and magnified the initial response of Simon's mother-in-law to her healing.

Service is the pattern of discipleship that Jesus is showing his followers, and the example he will give in Jerusalem—not by leading, *per se,* but by giving up his own life for them. The very first example of a person who follows in this pattern of service is Simon's mother-in-law, whose response to being healed was to *serve* them—even if what she provided was "table service."[35] To separate "table service" from the service of discipleship is to make a distinction without a difference—especially from the perspective of subsequent readings of the Gospel of Mark.

---

[35] Others have reservedly correlated the response of Simon's mother-in-law to discipleship. Lane, *The Gospel according to Mark*, 78 n. 128 ("Yet in Chs. 9:33-37 and 10:43-45 the essence of discipleship is described in terms of service, and this may be anticipated in the present narrative."); Joanna Dewey, "Women in the Gospel of Mark," *Word World* 26, no. 1 (2006): 22–23 ("Service becomes an important Markan theme describing ideal discipleship, which in retrospect may apply in this passage. Peter's mother-in-law is ministering to the disciples"); Malbon, "Fallible Followers," 34–35 (""[I]t is not clear at this early point in the narrative whether her service, her ministry, shares—and foreshadows—the theological connotations that the ministry of Mary Magdalene, Mary the mother of James and Joses, and Salome manifests later (διηκόνουν, 15:41);" see also Iersel, *Mark*, 117, 138 n. 33 (quoted above). More recently, Abraham Kuruvilla has positively asserted: "It is no doubt significant that there are only two instance of διακονέω (*diakoneō*, "serve") with humans as subjects in Mark's Gospel (1:31 and 15:41), and both times the subjects are women. A subtle jab! The narrator is pointing an appreciative finger at the example of this mother-in-law, a woman who does the male disciples one better! She is already doing what Jesus himself will later model for his disciples. The same verb διακονέω is found in the statement on the essence of Jesus' mission: The Son of man did not come to be served, but to *serve* (10:45). The narrator is implying that this woman is a true disciple, serving after the fashion of her Lord. Simon's mother-in-law is thus a foil to both crowds and disciples, indeed, to all who might follow Jesus for the wrong reasons." *Mark,* 38–39.

Conclusion

The concept of *service* is hard for many of us—the educated, the academe, the professional. As "servant-leaders," we more readily identify with "leadership" than with "servanthood." As Henri Nouwen, Roman Catholic priest and former faculty member at Harvard and Yale, once said as he prepared to serve the mentally disabled at L'Arche in France:

> I feel a deep resistance against this way. Somehow I have come to think about eating, drinking, washing, and dressing as so many necessary preconditions for reading, speaking, teaching, or writing. Somehow the pure word was the real thing for me. Time spent with "material" things was necessary but needed to be kept to a minimum. But at L'Arche, that is where all the attention goes. At L'Arche the body is the place where the word is met. It is in relationship to the wounded body of the handicapped person that I must learn to discover God.
>
> This is very hard for me. I still find a long meal in the middle of the day a waste of time. I still think that I have more important things to do than to set the table, eat slowly, wash the dishes, and set the table again. I think, "Surely we must eat, but the work which comes after is what counts." But L'Arche cannot be endured with this mind set.
>
> I wonder when and how I will learn to fully live the Incarnation. I suppose that only the handicapped people themselves will be able to show me the way. I must trust that God will send me the teachers I need.[36]

It is entirely possible that our "deep resistance against this way" of service is one reason why the response of Simon's mother-in-law has historically been exegetically minimized. But for a careful first and subsequent reader/hearer of the Gospel of Mark, the service of Simon's mother-in-law is a first sounding of a growing chorus about the essence of following Jesus who came not to be served, but to serve. Like the disciples, we tend to focus on content, direction, opportunities, objectives, building, creating a movement—our activities. But like Simon's mother-in-law, we are exhorted to focus on need, helping, providing, and restoring—the care of others. The response of Simon's mother-in-law is the first explicit example of discipleship in the Gospel of Mark.

---

[36] Henri Nouwen, *The Road to Daybreak: A Spiritual Journey* (New York: Image, 1990), 151.

CHAPTER III

AN EXAMINATION OF JESUS' VIEW OF WOMEN
THROUGH THREE INTERCALATIONS IN THE GOSPEL OF MARK[1]

Introduction

A basic tenet in the hermeneutics of theology is to build a doctrine upon the clearer, or less disputed, passages and then interpret the more difficult passages in light of the clearer passages.[2] However, in gender studies, the ground is often first broken in the rough terrain of 1 Timothy 2, 1 Corinthians 11 and 14, or with the household codes of Ephesians 5—6; Colossians 3; and 1 Peter 2—3. This study will examine three passages involving women in Mark's gospel in Mark 3, 5, and 14, all of which are undisputed in terms of significant lexicography, grammar, or relevant gender theology. As clearer passages, they form part of a greater foundation to the theology of gender studies.

---

[1] A shorter version of this article first appeared in *Priscilla Papers* 27.3 (2013): 4–15.

[2] It must be granted that a statement that there are "clearer" or "less disputed" passages is an assumption that could be questioned because of the multitudinous challenges to interpreting Scripture. Nevertheless, there are some passages that pose greater interpretive issues than others. It is the passages with less interpretive issues that are referred to here, and that are often used to form a foundation for a particular doctrine. "In the case of difficult or obscure passages, the interpreter should give precedence to biblical passages where the doctrine is clear." Jim Wilhoit and Leland Ryken, *"Effective Bible Teaching* (Grand Rapids: Baker Academic, 1998), 126. Under the category of "the analogy of scripture" Grant R. Osborne explained, "Milton Terry's dictum still stands: 'No single statement or obscure passage of one book can be allowed to set aside a doctrine which is clearly established by many passages" (1890: 578). I would strengthen this by adding that doctrines should not be built on a single passage but rather should summarize all that Scripture says on that topic " *The Hermeneutical Spiral: A Comprehensive Introduction to Biblical Interpretation* Revised and Expanded 2d ed. (Downers Grove: InterVarsity Press, 2006), 28. Millard J. Erickson set forth his method of theology in part under the subcategory of "unification of the biblical materials" as follows: "This means we are proceeding on the assumption that there are a unity and a consistency among these several books and authors. We will, then, emphasize the points of agreement among the Synoptic Gospels and interpret the rest in that light. We will treat any apparent discrepancies as differing and complementary interpretations rather than contradictions." *Christian Theology*, 2d ed. (Grand Rapids: Baker Academic, 1998), 73. Erickson applies this method to the issue of perseverance of the saints by harmonizing Hebrews 6 with what he considers to be the clear teaching of John 10:27-30. Ibid. at 1003-1005; An example of Wayne Grudem's use of this approach may be found in his chapter on "perseverance of the saints" where after discussing the emphasis of Hebrews 3:14 he states: "Attention to the context of Hebrews 3:14 will keep us from using this and other similar passages in a pastorally inappropriate way. We must remember that there are other evidences elsewhere in Scripture that give Christians assurance of salvation, so *we should not think that assurance that we belong to Christ is impossible until we die."* *Systematic Theology: An Introduction to Biblical Doctrine* (Grand Rapids: Zondervan, 1994), 793 (emphasis in original). This study suggests that there may be numerous, clearer passages that set forth points of agreement regarding women that must be used to interpret the more difficult passages of 1 Timothy 2 and 1 Corinthians 11 and 14.

The message of these passages is amplified through the literary technique know as intercalation[3] where a first story is begun, then interrupted by a second, inner, story which is told to its conclusion,[4] whereupon the first story resumes and is told to its completion.[5] This method of story telling invites the reader to compare and contrast the outer and inner stories[6] resulting in a new story outcome that includes, but also transcends, the component

---

[3] "[I]ntercalation has gone by a number of names in scholarly debate over the Gospel of Mark, including interpolation, framing, bracketing, "sandwiching," and intercalation." Tom Shepherd, "Markan Sandwich Stories: Narration, Definition, and Function." Andrews University Doctoral Dissertation Series, Vol. 18 (Andrews University Press: 1993), 4. Shepherd provides eight characteristics that occur in each intercalation: "1. apart from initial focalization, the outer story is the temporal border of the inner story. 2. There is a unique pattern of focalization and defocalization of the two stories which includes incomplete defocalization of the outer story at the point where breakaway occurs to the inner story. This creates a 'gap' for the outer story across the inner story. 3. A new character or newly named character is noted at the reentry into the outer story. 4. Active character crossover does not occur between the two stories, except for Jesus. 5. Parallel actions are done by contrasting groups or contrasting actions are done by parallel groups in the two stories. 6. The outer story has an elliptical action which crosses the inner story and contrasts with the actions of the inner story. 7. The plots of the two stories interlink following a turn—return pattern. 8. An ellipsis of the outer story occurs across the inner story. Ibid. 327.

[4] James Edwards is of the opinion that *"The middle story nearly always provides the key to the theological purpose* of the sandwich. The insertion interprets the flanking halves. To use the language of medicine, the transplanted organ enlivens the host material." James R. Edwards, "Markan Sandwiches: The Significance of Interpolations in Markan Narratives." *Novum Testamentum* xxxi:3 (1989) 196.

[5] Tom Shepherd, "The Narrative Function of Markan Intercalation," *New Test. Stud.* 41 (1995) 522. F. Gerald Downing has sought out literary parallels among the Hellenistic and Roman histories, lives, theatrical comedies, and romances yielding only a few examples, none of which are completely analogous. "Markan Intercalation in Cultural Context" in *Narrativity Biblical and Related Texts*, ed. G.J. Brooke and J.-D. Kaestli (Leuven Belgium: Leuven University Press 2000), 105-117. Edwards suggests examples from the Hebrew Scriptures in Hosea 1—3 (Hosea-God-Gomer) and 2 Samuel 11—12 (David-Nathan-Bathsheba), but notes a significant distinction when he states that: "[t]hese stories differ from Mark's sandwiches in one important respect: their B-episodes are intentional commentaries on the flanking A-episodes, whereas in Mark the B-episode is (with exception of 4:1-20) always an independent narrative." "Markan Sandwiches," 201-203. Perhaps Mark is employing a technique observed in Genesis 37, 38, and 39, where the Joseph story is interrupted by the story of Judah. Time extends in the inner story through Judah's "grandchildren" before the Joseph story picks up again from exactly the point where it terminated—as he was taken down to Egypt (*cf.* Gen. 37:36 with Gen. 39:1). Through this literary device, the writer in Genesis has created a dramatic irony for the reader who compares Judah with Joseph and sees that "God's design for Joseph's prominence could not be set aside as easily as Judah thought. In his own family, and despite his own indifference to Tamar, Judah saw the strange outworking of the plan whereby the younger gained priority in the family. The next chapter of Genesis, then present Joseph alive, and prospering in Egypt." Allen P. Ross, *Creation and Blessing: A Guide to the Study and Exposition of the Book of Genesis.* (Grand Rapids: Baker Book House, 1988), 612; *See also* Gordon J. Wenham, *Genesis 16—50*, Word Biblical Commentary, vol. 2 (Nashville: Thomas Nelson, 2000), 363-65.

[6] As Rhoads and Michie write, "The related stories illuminate and enrich each other, commenting on and clarifying the meaning, one of the other. This is sometimes done by comparison. . . . At other times, the framing provides commentary by contrast. . . . Details of these comparisons and contrasts highlight major themes of the gospel." *Mark as Story: An Introduction to the Narrative of a Gospel* (Philadelphia: Fortress Press, 1982), 51; Frank Kermode, notes our tendency not to give intercalations interpretive attention: "We tend not to give them the kind of attention we would think appropriate to the interpolated sequences of an epyllion, whether Alexandrian or in the imitations of Catullus or the Elizabethan erotic poets. There we see an invitation to interpret, here [Mark 14:53-72] the word "homiletic" dismisses the

stories.⁷ A key to interpreting an intercalation is to recognize the way in which the writer has brought the two stories together and yet holds them apart to produce an interpretation of the stories.⁸ The three Marcan intercalations we will examine involve women, two of whom are anonymous, in the outer and/or inner stories, namely, Jesus' mother (Mark 3), the woman with the hemorrhage of blood and Jairus' daughter (Mark 5), and the woman who anoints Jesus for his burial (Mark 14).⁹

Because Jesus did not set forth a didactic discourse on the topic of women, we must discern his view of women in the same way that we discern other issues in the gospels. Narratives do not explicitly tell us, but show us, their theology.¹⁰ For instance, in a Pauline epistle the Apostle explicitly states that Adam was a type (τύπος) of Christ (Rom. 5:14), but the Gospel of Luke shows us that Jesus is the new Adam by running his genealogy back to Adam, and then rearranging the order of the temptation account from that in Matthew,

---

case." *The Genesis of Secrecy on the Interpretation of Narrative* (Cambridge: Harvard University Press, 1979), 114-15.

⁷ Shepherd, "The Narrative Function of Markan Intercalation," 523. Fowler writes: "The intercalations exhibit a hermeneutical function for duality. The intercalated episodes are sharply opposed to each other, but at the same time they frequently contain so many verbal echoes of each other that the reader can scarcely fail to take up the implicit invitation to read the framed episode in the light of the frame episode and vice versa. The frame episode and the framed episode are thus placed on a par with each other, with neither having priority, either logically or chronologically. Intercalation is narrative sleight of hand, a crafty manipulation of the discourse level that creates the illusion that the two episodes are taking place simultaneously. In an intercalation neither episode has begun until both have begun, and neither is concluded until both are concluded." *Let the Reader Understand: Reader-Response Criticism and the Gospel of Mark* (Minneapolis: Fortress, 1991) 143-44. Shepherd explains the new story outcome as a function of dramatic irony: "We see the two stories juxtaposed, intertwined, yet we realize that they are still separate enough to comment one on the other. The one story becomes the ironic contrast to the other informing the reader of a new plot, a new sense of direction in the Gospel." Shepherd, "The Narrative Function of Markan Intercalation," 539. Picking up on dramatic irony in intercalations, Downing writes, "There is then a dramatic irony evoked, for the author and the hearer obviously understand more than the protagonists can, unable as the latter are to share in comparing and contrasting the stories which both link and separate them." "Markan Intercalation in Cultural Context," 107. Edwards argues that the literary technique has a theological purpose: "the sandwiches emphasize the major motifs of the Gospel, especially the meaning of faith, discipleship, bearing witness, and the dangers of apostasy." "Markan Sandwiches," 196.

⁸ Shepherd, "The Narrative Function of Markan Intercalation," 523.

⁹ The number of intercalations in the Gospel of Mark is disputed. Shepherd sets forth a table in the appendix to his dissertation compiling a list of twenty intercalations identified by nineteen scholars. He works extensively with six passages that most scholars identify as intercalations. Among the six, the three examined in this paper are largely agreed upon. Shepherd, "Markan Sandwich Stories," 388-92; *see also* Geert Van Oyen, "Intercalation and Irony in the Gospel of Mark" in *Four Gospels 1992: Festschrift Frans Neirynck*, eds. Frans van Segbroeck, C.M. Tuckett, vol. 2 (Leuven Belgium: Peeters ,1992), 949, 951.

¹⁰ As Leland Ryken states: "To begin, literature is experiential. This means that the subject matter of literature is human experience. The approach to human experience, moreover, is concrete rather than abstract. Literature does not, for example, discourse about virtue but instead shows a virtuous person acting. We might say that literature does not tell *about* characters and actions and concepts but *presents* characters in action." *The Literature of The Bible* (Grand Rapids: Zondervan Publishing House, 1974), 13. An example of narrative that was later explicitly explained in didactic literature is Abram's encounter with Melchizedek (*cf.* Genesis 14:18-20 with Hebrews 7:1-10). The narrative in Genesis showed what the writer of Hebrews later told.

to match the temptation of Adam and Eve in the garden.[11] Luke shows us what Paul tells us.

So too when we read the narratives in Mark, we should look to how the narrative shows its theology of women rather than for explicit, didactic statements about women. We need to ask questions like: How does Jesus interact with women when he encounters them? What is the writer doing with the material to communicate his theological message? Is the arrangement of the material significant to its message? How the writer communicates his message is as much a part of the message as what the writer says.[12]

For instance, the sermon-sign structure in Mark 7 sets forth Jesus' proposition that it is not that which goes into a person that makes a person unclean but that which comes out of a person's heart that defiles a person. (Mk. 7:14-23) This teaching (sermon) section is then followed by three[13] narrative pictures (signs) that specifically demonstrate the truth of the sermon as Jesus goes among people whom Israel considered to be unclean including: (a) the Syrophoenician woman (7:24-30); (b) the deaf mute in the Decapolis area whom he touched (put his fingers into his ears, and touching his tongue) (Mk. 7:31-37); and (c) the 4,000, who were probably Gentiles (Mk. 8:1-9). At the head of this symbolic trio is Jesus' encounter with a Gentile woman of the Syrophoenician race (Mk. 7:26). Unlike the disciples in the immediately preceding sermon who did not understand what Jesus said when he spoke in a parable (Mk. 7:14-18), she not only understands the metaphor Jesus spoke to her, but immediately adapts it to persuade him to provide her with the overflow of his blessings to Israel: "Yes, Lord, but even the dogs under the table feed on the children's crumbs" (Mk. 7:28). Accordingly, Jesus tells the woman her request has been granted: "Because of this answer go your way; the demon has gone out of your daughter" (Mk. 7:29). The structure of the sermon-sign contributes to the meaning of the text by showing the significance of what Jesus has just taught—a person is not unclean because of what a person eats. Moreover, the details of the encounter show that this Gentile woman is unique in Mark's gospel because she understands Jesus' parables, engages with his words beyond the Twelve, and thereby sets forth the significant theology that Gentiles may share in the blessings to Israel. Mark shows his theology through the literary device of sermon-signs.

---

[11] *See* S. Craig Glickman, "The Temptation Account in Matthew and Luke," Ph.D. diss. University of Basel, (1983): 407-24; *Knowing Christ: Life-changing Glimpses of Our Lord* (Chicago: Moody Press, 1980), 49-60; *see also* Darrell L. Bock, *Luke 1:1—9:50*, Baker Exegetical Commentary on the New Testament (Grand Rapids: Baker Books, 1994): 349, 360, 383.

[12] As Adele Berlin has stated, "And we must look not only for *what* the text says, but also *how* it says it." *Poetics and Interpretation of Biblical Narrative*, Bible and Literature Series. JSOTSup 9 (Sheffield: Almond Press, 1983), 20.

[13] In their discussion of "episodes in a series of three" in the Gospel of Mark, Rhoads and Michie note that "a threefold series is no mere repetition of similar events, but involves a progressive development. Each incident uncovers more about the characters or the conflicts, and the third episode fully reveals the dynamic of the entire series. . . . [W]hen the series unfolds, the reader then looks back from the perspective of the third scene and understands more clearly the issues involved in the first and second scenes." *Mark as Story*, 55.

Furthermore, his view of women is clarified through an encounter with one whose understanding exceeds that of the Twelve.

It is possible that Jesus, as a First Century "man," never thought of appointing a woman as one of the Twelve because it was not a situation that culturally presented itself to him. However, when a situation involving a woman did cross his path, he stepped up to meet it. In his day, no one would have thought to ask him a question about women in leadership, so he did not address it directly. Nevertheless, he showed some of how he thought on this issue by how he related to women in his world—often interacting with them in ways which taught, corrected, and rebuked the Twelve. Many of these insights are particularly set forth by the literary use of intercalations where outer and inner stories are juxtaposed to one another so that the reader will compare them and draw conclusions beyond those found in either individual story.

Jesus' Relatives and the Beelzebul Controversy (Mk. 3:20-35)
(Outer Story 3:20-21; Inner Story 3:22-30; Outer Story 3:31-35)

Some have argued that the most anyone can say about Jesus' treatment of women is that he was positive toward them in that he spoke with them (Mk. 7:24-30; Lk. 10:38-42; Jn. 4:1-42), was sensitive to those in need (Mk. 1:29-31; 5:21-43), and let those who were unclean touch him (Matt. 9:18-26; Lk. 8:40-56), but he did not affirm them by appointing them leaders in his community.[14] Some in the Roman Catholic Church have gone so far as to say that Jesus' treatment of his mother, Mary, demonstrates his unwillingness to promote women into leadership since she was a very special person, but did not baptize him and was not a priest. Accordingly, the argument goes that If Mary was not chosen by Jesus for these leadership positions, no woman should be in church leadership.

One need not resolve this apparent impasse with the questionable arguments of Elaine Pagels who asserts that the apocryphal gospels give women freedom that cannot be found in the canonical Gospels.[15] The unified church, under Constantine, put away all of the apocryphal works, like the Gospel of Thomas, that allowed for a wide variety of beliefs.

---

[14] "Only a baptized man (*vir*) validly receives sacred ordination." [n. 66, CIC, can. 1024.] The Lord Jesus chose men (*ver*) to form the college of the twelve apostles, and the apostles did the same when they chose collaborators to succeed them in their ministry [n. 67, Cf. *Mk* 3:14-19; *Lk* 6:12-16; *1 Tim* 3:1-13; *2 Tim* 1:6; *Titus* 1:5-9; St. Clement of Rome, *Ad Cor.* 42,4; 44,3:PG 1.292-293; 300]. The college of bishops, with whom the priests are united in the priesthood, makes the college of the twelve an ever-present and ever-active reality until Christ's return. The Church recognizes herself to be bound by this choice made by the Lord himself. For this reason the ordination of women is not possible [n. 68, Cf. John Paul II, MD 26-27; CDF, declaration, *Inter insigniores*: AAS 69 (1977) 98-116]." *Catechism of the Catholic Church: Second Edition*, Part Two; Section Two: The Seven Sacraments of the Church; Chapter Three: The Sacraments at the Service of Communion; Article 6: The Sacrament of Holy Orders; VI: Who Can Receive This Sacrament; Par. 1577.

[15] Elaine Pagels, *Beyond Belief: The Secret Gospel of Thomas*, Reprint edition. (Vintage, 2004).

On the contrary, a canonical response within the Gospel of Mark may provide at least one reason why Mary was not part of the leadership during the time of Jesus – she was resistant to how Jesus was presenting himself.[16] From a distance, we often assume that with all of the special revelation Mary received surrounding the birth of Jesus, she was completely compliant and in agreement with the ways in which he ministered and demonstrated who he was. But she, like the rest of us who read the synoptic gospels, was building her theology one brick at a time. When the shepherds came to the stable and reported what the Angel had said to them, Luke states that "Mary treasured up all of these things (ῥήματα) pondering (συμβάλλουσα) them in her heart" (Lk. 2:19).[17] This does not mean that she completely understood and integrated her Christology at this time.

The first hint we have of Mary's confusion over Jesus' actions is seen when at the age of twelve, Jesus, without explanation, stays behind at the Passover feast in Jerusalem to be among those of his Father. Mary is the one who questioned Jesus asking, "Son, why have you treated us this way? Behold, your father and I have been anxiously looking for you" (Lk. 2:48). And upon Jesus' answer, the narrator states that his parents "did not understand the statement which he had made to them" (Lk. 2:50).

Likewise when the wine ran dry at the wedding of Cana, it was Mary who came to Jesus to resolve the dilemma, and Jesus responded with a phrase that demons often used to question Jesus' authority[18] when he said literally, "What with me and with you, woman?

---

[16] This brief discussion of Mary is not unaware of the differences that exist between a Protestant and Catholic view of Mary. See *Journeys of Faith: Evangelicalism, Eastern Orthodoxy, Catholicism, and Anglicanism*; ed. Robert L. Plummer (Grand Rapids: Zondervan, 2012), 121-122, 239. Without attempting to address the significant theological differences, or even daring to propose a *via media*, this essay attempts to focus solely upon the Scriptural witness to Mary, especially in the intercalation of Mark 3:20-35. It is not being argued that Mary "sinned" in any way, but that she wrestled with her imperfect, and growing understanding of who Jesus was and what he was doing. She, like all of us, had to build her Christology one brick at a time, from the ground-up. Accordingly, Catholicism's view of Mary need not turn this intercalation into a less clear, or disputed, passage.

[17] "When Luke combines the idea of keeping the words in the heart with *symballein*, the idea may be that Mary has preserved in her heart the mysterious words and events that surrounded Jesus' birth (or his finding in the Temple) *trying to interpret them*. This would mean that Mary did not grasp immediately all that she had heard but listened willingly, letting the events sink into her memory and seeking to work out their meaning." *Mary in the New Testament: A Collaborative Assessment by Protestant and Roman Catholic Scholars*, ed. Raymond Brown, *et al.* (Philadelphia: Fortress Press, 1978), 150-51. *See also* Joseph Fitzmeyer discussion of the verb συνετήρει in the LXX of Genesis 37:11 and Daniel 4:28 where he concludes: "Both the Genesis and Daniel passages show a person puzzled by what he has heard, keeping the words in mind in an effort to fathom their meaning. This too would be the picture of Mary here." *The Gospel According to Luke (I-IX): Introduction, Translation, and Notes*. The Anchor Bible. (Garden City: Doubleday & Company, Inc., 1981), 413. Bock also observes: "It is debated whether this term [συμβάλλουσα] suggests that Mary did put the events completely together. In light of passages like Mark 3:20-35, it seems unlikely she figured them all out in these early days." *Luke*, I:222-23.

[18] In Mark 5:7 the demonized man from the tombs ran up to Jesus and cried in a great voice saying: "τί ἐμοὶ καὶ σοί;" *cf.* Luke 8:28; *see also* Mk. 1:24 (λέγων· τί ἡμῖν καὶ σοί, Ἰησοῦ Ναζαρηνέ; ἦλθες ἀπολέσαι ἡμᾶς) *cf.* Lk. 4:34.). This may be a Semitism from the Hebrew Scriptures, *see A Greek-English Lexicon of the New Testament and Other Early Christian Literature*, William Arndt, Frederick W. Danker, and Walter

(τί ἐμοὶ καὶ σοί, γύναι)" which is glossed in the NASB as "Woman, what do I have to do with you?" Then Jesus adds, "My hour has not yet come" (οὔπω ἥκει ἡ ὥρα μου). This may well imply that Mary wanted Jesus to make a public demonstration of who he was, but he did not think it to be the right time yet; when Jesus went public with his identity, he was soon killed.[19] Therefore, he did what she asked him to do, privately, and she complied instructing the servants to do whatever he says to them (Jn. 2:5).[20]

So too, when we come to the intercalation in Mark 3:20-21, Mary appears to be out of alignment with what Jesus is doing at the beginning of his ministry. We are told in the outer story that Jesus returned home,[21] and a multitude of people gathered to the extent that Jesus and his disciples could not even eat a meal. When his "own people" (οἱ παρ' αὐτοῦ)[22] heard of this, they went out to take custody[23] of him saying that "he has lost his senses," or

---

A Bauer. 3rd ed. (Chicago: University of Chicago Press, 2000), s.v. "ἐγώ." "When someone is asked to get involved in something which he feels is no business of his, he may use the phrase, meaning: 'That is your business; how am I involved?' Examples are 2 Kgs. 3:13; Hos. 14:8. . . . Thus, at least what Mary is asking for, or the aspect under which she is speaking to Jesus, does not belong to Jesus' understanding of the work his Father has given him to do." *Mary in the New Testament*, 191.

[19] As Keener states: "[T]he primary reason for the rebuff must be that his mother does not understand what this sign will cost Jesus: It starts him on the road to his hour, the cross. Thus John speaks of the 'beginning' of Jesus' signs (2:11), referring to the 'beginning' of a public ministry (6:64; 8:25; 15:27; 16:4) destined to culminate in his final 'hour.'" *The Gospel of John: A Commentary, Volume I* (Peabody, Mass.: Hendrickson Publishers, 2003), 506.

[20] "In this passage Jesus' mother continues with the 'holy chutzpah' demonstrated in 2:3; in 2:5 she bids the servants to do whatever Jesus says, thus both recognizing Jesus' authority and demonstrating her expectation that he is going to do something to change the situation." Keener, *The Gospel of John*, 509.

[21] There is an actual reference to a "house" where Jesus is located in Mark 3:20 (Καὶ ἔρχεται εἰς οἶκον·). The term, "house," will be played upon as a *Lietwort* throughout the intercalation with reference to the "house divided" and the "house of the strong man" in the inner story (Mk. 3:26-27), and the physical house in the outer story, and Jesus' metaphorical "house" standing outside (his relatives). *See* Shepherd, "Markan Sandwich Stories, 114, 135.

[22] The Western witnesses (D, W, *it*) move the focus away from Jesus' family to the scribes and others (περι αυτου οι γραμματεις και οι λοιποι). However, when the outer story is picked up again in 3:31, it is clear that this cryptic phrase refers to Jesus' mother and brothers (ἡ μήτηρ αὐτοῦ καὶ οἱ ἀδελφοὶ αὐτοῦ) (*cf.* Matt. 12:46; Lk. 8:19). Bruce M. Metzger writes, "The original reading οἱ παρ' αὐτοῦ ("his friends" or his relatives") apparently proved to be so embarrassing that D W *al* altered it to read, "When *the scribes and the others* had heard about him, they went out to seize him, for they said, "He is beside himself." *A Textual Commentary on the Greek New Testament*, (2d ed., 1994), 70; *see also* Ben Witherington, III, *Women in the Ministry of Jesus*, (Cambridge University Press, 1984), 86 ("It is likely that Mark intended οἱ παρ' αὐτοῦ to be explained in verse 31 (ἡ μήτηρ αὐτοῦ καὶ οἱ ἀδελφοὶ αὐτοῦ)"); *Mary in the New Testament*, 55-57 ("The comparison of the two scenes makes it likely that for Mark the 'mother and brothers' of 3:31 who arrive (at the house in Capernaum) asking for Jesus are the same as the 'his own' of 3:21 who set out (from Nazareth) to seize him.")

[23] "The phrases about Jesus' family are strong and definite: they set out to *take charge* (Greek *kratêsai*)—a verb used several times in Mark 6 and 14 with the meaning "to arrest." Furthermore the expression *people were saying* in its Greek form (*elegon*) could equally well include members of his family." C.S. Mann, *Mark; A New Translation with Introduction and Commentary*. The Anchor Bible (New York: Doubleday) 252.

is out of his mind (ἐξέστη).²⁴ This section, unique to Mark, is clarified in Mark 3:30 where his "own people" are identified as his mother and his brothers (ἡ μήτηρ αὐτοῦ καὶ οἱ ἀδελφοὶ αὐτοῦ).²⁵

This alignment of Mary with Jesus' brothers may be significant because of the hostile dialogue between Jesus and his brothers prior to the Feast of Booths in John 7:1-9 where we learn that they did not believe in him (οὐδὲ γὰρ οἱ ἀδελφοὶ αὐτοῦ ἐπίστευον εἰς αὐτόν). As in John 2 where Jesus addressed Mary's request for a public display of who he was, Jesus again says to his brothers that he will not go publically to the Feast of Booths in Jerusalem because his time has not yet fully come (Jn. 7:8). Now, in Mark's outer story, Jesus' mother and brothers join forces to abduct him because they think he has lost his mind.

The outer story breaks off prior to its completion, and an inner story commences describing a conflict between Jesus and the Jerusalem scribes who accuse him, not of being out of his mind, but being possessed by Beelzebul, and of casting out demons by the power of the ruler of demons. (Mk. 3:22).²⁶ Jesus confronts the scribes' accusation stating that Satan cannot cast out Satan because a divided kingdom cannot stand (Mk. 3:23-24).²⁷

When the outer and inner stories are read together, Jesus' parabolic proclamation in the inner story appears to be problematic—if a house divided cannot stand, how can his house stand since his own family appears to be divided with his mother and brothers waiting to take him away. While the scribes in the inner story make a spiritual charge against his character that he is demon possessed (based upon his activity of casting out demons), Jesus' family makes a psychological charge against his character that he is out of his mind (based

---

²⁴ "Paul uses the same verb in 2 Cor. 5:13, speaking of himself in contrast to his correspondents." Mann, *Mark*, 252. Citing to Wisd. Sol. 5:1-5, William Lane notes: "The entire incident calls to mind passages in which the man of God is despised by family and contemporaries who mistake his zeal for God as 'madness.'" *The Gospel According to Mark: The English Text with Introduction, Exposition, and Notes* (Grand Rapids: William B. Eerdmans Publishing Company, 1974), 139.

²⁵ In Mark 3:32 "sisters" are included (καὶ αἱ ἀδελφαί σου) in A D Γ 700 *pm* it vg^mss sy^hmg, but this reading is disputed even though Jesus does add "sister" in 3:35 (οὗτος ἀδελφός μου καὶ ἀδελφὴ). See Metzger, *A Textual Commentary*, 70.

²⁶ Discourse time appears to continue between the two stories. As Shepherd observes: "Story time thus continues straight through the intercalation. The spatial markers make this clear. In Mark 3:20 Jesus enters a house. The result of his active ministry is lack of time to eat. This report comes to his relatives who set out to seize him, with the cry, 'He's crazy!' The inner story begins at this point and the accusation of the scribes is met by Jesus *summoning* them. This spatial indicator illustrates that the time relationship has continued straight from 3:20 through this point in 3:23. The local has not changed (the house), as is made clear later in the return to the outer story where the relatives of Jesus wait *outside* to talk to him (3:31). Thus, story time in the Mark 3 intercalation continues straight through both stories." Shepherd, "The Narrative Function of Markan Intercalation," 525-26; "Markan Sandwich Stories," 130-33.

²⁷ Even though Lane does not acknowledge the actual structure of an intercalation stating that this is a "self contained unit," he cannot help but hear the echo of the outer stories where Jesus states that a house divided cannot stand, writing in a footnote: "Is there a reference here to the division in Jesus' own household, which is illustrated by Ch. 3:20f, 31-35?" *The Gospel According to Mark*, 143 n. 90.

upon his activity of ministering without eating).[28] Moreover, in the context leading up to this intercalation, Jesus' closest followers are identified in the call of the Twelve (Mk. 3:13-19). In the last verse of the unit, just before the story dealing with Jesus' family, one of the Twelve is identified as "Judas Iscariot, who also betrayed him" (Mk. 3:19). Every manifestation of Jesus' house appears to be divided—from the Twelve, to his biological family. The reader is left with the question presented by Jesus himself—how can Jesus' house stand?

The answer is given when the outer story is resumed in Mark 3:31-35.[29] So often we tend to read Jesus' words outside of the crucible of this context and they appear to be the musing of one in a daze:

"Who are my mother and my brothers?" And looking about on those who were sitting around Him, he said, "Behold, my mother and my brothers! For whoever does the will of God, he is my brother and sister and mother."

(Mk. 3:31-35, NASB). These words, are not those spoken by someone in a spiritual trance, but make explicit the truth that Jesus' family consist of those who obey his Father, even if one of the Twelve will betray him, and his own mother and brothers think he has lost his mind.[30] In other words, Jesus' house may appear to be divided but it is not, because his house does not consist of those who are called as part of the Twelve, or of those who are

---

[28] Shepherd keenly observes: "Interesting parallels exist between these two diverse groups, the relatives of Jesus (his 'friends') and the scribes from Jerusalem (his enemies). Both groups bring charges against Jesus based upon some activity he has been doing. The judgment of each party makes some statement about Jesus' interior state. They contend that the activity he carries on reflects negatively on his character. Jesus, on the other hand, indicates the fallacy of each of these groups by means of authoritative statements. The two groups, who never meet, are nevertheless drawn together by the juxtaposition of the two stories and by the intertwining of the charges and rebuttals which link their individual stories. What is so interesting is that the two *opposite* groups, relatives (friends of Jesus) and scribes (enemies of Jesus), actually act in *similar* ways against Jesus and are countered by his authoritative word. "The Narrative Function of Markan Intercalation," 529; see also "Markan Sandwich Stories," 121-22.

[29] "A Chiasm is present in both the outer and inner stories in regards to the actors as speakers or action makers. In the outer story, the pattern is Jesus, crowd, relatives, relatives, crowd, Jesus. In the inner story, the pattern is scribes, Jesus, scribes. Thus Jesus as actor is at both ends of the intercalation and at the center." Shepherd, "Markan Sandwich Stories," 125.

[30] Shepherd writes: "Two themes which arise in this intercalation are Christology and discipleship. The challenge of Jesus' sanity and the accusation about the source of his power are challenges to the claim of Messiahship. The responses by Jesus are therefore a teaching on his Christological role. He is on the side of God. He has the Holy Spirit and his true family do the will of God. On the level of discipleship (presented from the standpoint of family relation), the true disciple cannot oppose the mission of Jesus even though the mission appears 'crazy' from a human viewpoint." "Markan Sandwich Stories," 129.

biologically related to him. Rather, his house consists of those who obey his Father—they comprise his true family.[31] Therefore, Jesus' house will stand.[32]

Narrative Intercalation
Mark 3:20-35

The Outer Story
- **Continuity**: we meet Jesus' relatives
- **Spatial setting**: A house
- **Temporal setting**: continues
- **Charge:** Relatives make psychological charge against his character based on his activity—Is Jesus crazy?
- **Jesus counters** with authoritative statement
- **Implied question**: Is Jesus' house divided?
- **Jesus redefines his family** along moral lines—implication—his house is not divided.

The Inner Story
- **Discontinuity**: we never meet Jesus' relatives
- **Spatial setting**: Jerusalem
- **Temporal setting**: continues
- **Charge:** Enemies make spiritual charge against his character based on his activity—Is Jesus demon possessed?
- **Jesus counters** with authoritative statement
- **Statement**: A divided house is unable to stand!

This theological theme rises again in the narrative picture of Mary and the disciple whom Jesus loved standing at the foot of the cross in John's gospel:

> When Jesus then saw His mother, and the disciple whom He loved standing nearby, He said to His mother, "Woman, behold, your son!" Then He said to the disciple, "Behold, your mother!" From that hour the disciple took her into his own *household*.

(Jn. 19:26-27). These words again appear to be odd when placed in a vacuum. Mary is not John's mother, and John is not Jesus' brother,[33] but as they identify with him at his

---

[31] Jesus transforms the social understanding of family into a moral understanding. This transformation is fitting as the social accusation that he is crazy in 3:21 shifted to a moral accusation in 3:22 that he had Beelzebul. *See* Shepherd, "Markan Sandwich Stories," 113-14 n. 1, 117.

[32] Shepherd summarizes the dramatic irony in this intercalation as follows: "Jesus' family goes out to 'save' him and in the process ally themselves with his enemies. Jesus argues that a divided house cannot stand, yet his relatives are divided from him. However, they are not his true relatives." "The Narrative Function of Markan Intercalation," 539.

[33] As a matter of fact, Mary has other children according to John 7:1-10. Therefore, it is unlikely that the point of this narrative is "to report simply that after Jesus died his mother went to live in the home of a favorite disciple. To interpret John thus would be to misinterpret the way the evangelist uses symbols, as well as the significance he attributes to the beloved disciple. Moreover, all the other Johannine crucifixion episodes have clear symbolic and theological significance, and by analogy that should be true of 19:25-27

crucifixion, they become part of Jesus' true family—those who do the will of God.[34] Therefore, they are to care for each other as family henceforth.

One contribution of this Markan intercalation is that it shows the humanity of Mary. Yes, she received the word of God through the angel, Gabriel, before her miraculous conception. Yes, her very words before Elizabeth became part of Scripture as she echoed themes proclaimed hundred of years earlier by Hannah. Yes, she heard the words of the shepherds, and of Simeon and Anna in the temple at Jesus' dedication. But Jesus' ministry did not develop as she expected, and she appeared to find herself at odds with him on numerous occasions even to the point of thinking he had lost his mind. This activity may well account for one significant reason why Mary was not given a leadership role by Jesus.[35]

---

as well." *Mary in the New Testament,* 201-02, n. 465, *see also* Raymond E. Brown, *The Gospel According to John (XIII-XX1): Introduction, Translation, and Notes.* The Anchor Bible (New York: Doubleday, 1970), 923 (who sees Mary as Lady Zion and the new Eve); Keener appears to disagree seeing Jesus as literally entrusting Mary to the believing community. Craig S. Keener, *The Gospel of John,* 1144-45; *likewise,* Leon Morris, *The Gospel According to John: The English Text with Introduction, Exposition and Notes* (Grand Rapids: Wm. B. Eerdmans Publishing Co., 1971), 811-12.

[34] "[T]he new mother-son relationship proclaimed by Jesus in John 19:26-27 reflects the replacement of his natural family by a new family of disciples, the eschatological family we spoke of in reference to Mark 3:31-35. We saw that in Mark's view the physical family members were not among those whom Jesus pointed to as his eschatological family of disciples, i.e., those of whom he says, 'Behold my mother and my brothers!' . . . but at the foot of the cross Jesus gives his physical mother a spiritual role as mother of the disciple par excellence, and the disciple a role as her son. Thus there remerges a familial relationship in terms of discipleship." *Mary in the New Testament,* 212-13, 218, 288. As R.V.G. Tasker states: "Beneath the cross Christian fellowship is born, a fellowship wholly different from all purely human fellowship based on natural kinship, mutual sympathy, or a common outlook upon human affairs. The great and distinctive characteristic of this new fellowship is that all who enjoy it are drawn to one another by the consciousness that they are all brothers for whom Christ died." *The Gospel According to St. John.* Tyndale New Testament Commentaries (Grand Rapids: Wm. B. Eerdmans Publishing Company, 1960), 211.

[35] There is some merit to an argument that the Twelve are portrayed throughout the Gospel of Mark negatively—as lacking understanding, hard in heart, and influenced by Herod and the Pharisees (*See* Mark 8:14-21). As a matter of fact, Peter's resistance to Jesus' impending suffering is rebuked as a temptation from Satan (Mk. 8:31-33). Therefore, it might be argued that it does not follow that Mary may not have been given a leadership role in Jesus' earthly ministry because of her resistance to Jesus when the Twelve do have a leadership role in spite of their resistance. However, a contextual reading of the narrative may shed light on this apparent quandary. First, the narrative regarding Mary and Jesus occurs in the early, Galilean portion of Mark's gospel where the disciples are not portrayed as resisting Jesus' ministry. Up to this point, only the demons (Mk. 1:24, 34; 3:11-12), the religious leaders (Mk. 2:6-7, 16, 24; 3:2-6), and the Herodians (Mk. 3:6) are critical of Jesus (and perhaps the disciples of John in Mk. 2:18, but this may be merely a question of clarification). Those who will make up the Twelve "immediately" follow after him (Mk. 1:16-20; 2:14), and the multitudes enthusiastically seek him out (Mk. 1:32-34, 37, 45; 2:1-4, 12, 13, 3:7-10). It is in this immediate context that Mark sets forth Mary and Jesus' brothers as resisting him, and their resistance is parallel with the resistance of the religious leaders. Although the narrator never explicitly states where the Twelve are in this intercalation, it may not be too much, in view of the broader context, and especially Jesus' calling of the Twelve in the immediately adjacent pericope (Mk. 3:13-19) to suppose that they are in the house with the multitude whom Jesus is addressing, while Jesus' family and the religious leaders are outside of the house. Therefore, in the narrative world of Mark, it appears that Mary and Jesus' brothers are distinct from the Twelve—especially at this point in the narrative. The only one of the Twelve who might be likened to them is Judas who was foreshadowed in Mark 3:19 as the one who betrayed him,

Mary is not even named among the women in Luke 8:1-3 who play an essential part in his itinerate ministry. Therefore, Mary's position is not controlling in a discussion about women in leadership. But in the end, she grows in her understanding and stands in solidarity with Jesus at the foot of the cross, thereby entering into the true family of God.[36]

Jairus' Daughter and The Woman with a Hemorrhage (5:21-43)
(Outer Story 5:21-24; Inner Story 5:25-34; Outer Story 5:35-43)

This material is set forth as an intercalation in all three synoptic gospels (*cf.* Matt. 9:18-26 and Lk. 8:40-56). Time seems to run as a continuous thread throughout the two stories, and thus becomes the constant that highlights the contrast.[37] Other than Jesus, the only named person in these stories is Jairus,[38] and he is identified as an important man, one of the rulers of the synagogues. He also comes with a matter of extreme urgency announcing

---

and then specifically aligned himself with the religious leaders against Jesus in Mark 14:10-11. (For more on Judas, see the discussion below on the intercalation in Mark 14:1-11.) By the end of Mark's gospel, everyone appears to have forsaken Jesus—even the women (Mk. 16:1-8). The only one left as a witness to Jesus is the reader. *See* Mary Ann Tolbert, *Sowing the Gospel: Mark's World in Literary – Historical Perspective* (Minneapolis: Fortress Press, 1989), 295-99; Geert Van Oyen, "Intercalation and Irony in the Gospel of Mark," 961. However, this synthetic reading of the Gospel need not override the contextual distinctions set forth in the progression of the narrative where Jesus' mother and brothers are distinct from the disciples, and even the multitude, and more closely aligned with the religious leaders as they make accusations against Jesus. Therefore, Mary's resistance to Jesus may have been one reason why she was not given a leadership role with the Twelve.

[36] Of course, Mary is also found in the upper room with the eleven apostles, the women, and Jesus' brothers in Acts 1:14. In placing her here, Luke is identifying her with the believing community as a disciple. As one author stated emphasizing the unity in Luke's writings: "Mary's first response to the good news was: 'Behold the handmaid of the Lord. Let it be to me according to your word.' The real import of Acts 1:14 is to remind the reader that she had not changed her mind." *Mary in the New Testament*, 177. One might wonder why Mary was not included among the leadership after the resurrection since she is now included with the believing community, or why other women who were not resistant to Jesus' ministry were not resistant to Jesus' ministry were not included in leadership. These questions exceed the scope of this study, but if there was a cultural discomfort with women in leadership, it may not have entered the leaderships' mind after Pentecost to place women in leadership, or to raise it as an issue at the time. This may be similar to Paul's dealing with slavery in the house tables of Ephesians and Colossians. He does not resist the Roman culture that prominently makes use of slaves, but undoes its ethical moorings by addressing the responsibility of masters to slaves, and by his discussion of Onesimus in Philemon.

[37] Shepherd notes: "Story time continues across the entire intercalation. . . . When the woman's story ends, the story of Jairus picks up again, but not where it left off. The woman's story has 'consumed time' or taken time in the Jairus story, thus the two stories are temporally interlinked." "Markan Sandwich Stories," 140.

[38] The name Jairus is absent from several Western witnesses (D *it*). *See* Metzger, *A Textual Commentary*, 73-74, for arguments for the inclusion of the name where it is concluded: "[F]rom a text-critical point of view it is more probable that the name Jairus was accidently dropped during the transmission of part of the Western text (represented by one Greek manuscript and several Old Latin witnesses) than that it was added, at the same point in the narrative, in all the other textual groups." The name in Hebrew means "he who enlightens" (יָאִיר) *see BDAG*, s.v. "Ἰάϊρος," p. 103.

that his dear daughter (θυγάτριον)[39] is near death, and asking Jesus to come and lay hands on her so that she might be made well (σῴζω) and live (ζάω).

However, as Jesus goes with Jairus, he is interrupted by an unclean woman in the crowd who touches Jesus' garment and unintentionally stops the rescue mission as Jesus turns to ask the crowd, "Who touched my garments?" Although Jairus says nothing, Jesus' disciples are indignant:[40] "You see the crowd pressing around you, and yet you say, "Who touched me?" But Jesus continues to search to find the one who had done this.

It is at this crossroad, as the clock continues to click for Jairus and his daughter, that the tension in the two stories rises, contrasts multiply, and we are once again given a glimpse into Jesus' view of women.

Jairus is obviously a male, and the woman with the hemorrhage is obviously female. Jairus is named, but the woman is anonymous. Jairus is a leader of a synagogue, but the woman may not have gone to synagogue because her constant bleeding would have made her ritually impure according to Leviticus 15:25-27.[41] Jairus is a father with an ailing

---

[39] The diminutive (θυγάτριον) is probably used as a term of affection or endearment. *See* Mk. 7:25; BDAG, s.v. "θυγάτριον" p. 461; Mann, *Mark,* 284.

[40] Rather than criticize the disciples, Shepherd sees the humor in the scene that results in our identification with the disciples: "It is really very funny that Jesus says, 'Who touched me?' Jesus is the comedian in this scene. The disciples come across as the typical 'straight man' in their response, 'You see the crowd pressing upon you and you say "Who touched me?"' We have to laugh at the disciples, because we know who did touch Jesus and that it was a very meaningful touch. The point is, that in a straight man we do not usually see someone we disparage, but rather in all too common depiction of real life that the comedian lampoons. Seeing from the angle of omniscience we catch a glimpse of the comical nature of our own lives. Thus, we might actually see identification with the disciples here via the comedy." "Markan Sandwich Stories, 148 n. 1. Even if one has questions about the strength of an analogy between Jesus and Jerry Lewis, there is dramatic irony taking place for the reader that magnifies the distance between the understanding of Jesus and his disciples. As Lane states: "Their impatience with the Lord reflects an awareness that their immediate mission was to assist a girl who was dying, and delay could be fatal. It also betrays that they had no understanding of what had taken place." *The Gospel According to Mark,* 193.

[41] Mark does not comment on this, but those aware of the purity laws in Leviticus, the implied reader, would have understood this implication. Regarding Leviticus 15:26-27 Baruch A. Levine notes: "This is the primary symptom: irregularity of blood discharges, which either persist beyond the regular menstrual period or are unconnected with it altogether. A woman who has discharges of blood not due to her menstruation bears the same impurity as a menstruating woman for as long as the discharges last." *Leviticus* ויקרא*: The Traditional Hebrew Text and the New JPS Translation Commentary.* The JPS Torah Commentary (Philadelphia: The Jewish Publication Society, 1989), 98. Accordingly, in discussing the earlier passage in Lev. 15:19, Levine states: "[a]nyone who has contact with a woman during her menstrual period is impure until evening" and "whatever the woman sits on or lies on becomes impure, and whoever touches such objects becomes impure in turn." *Id.* at 97. Leviticus 15:31 emphasizes that the uncleanness separated the person from God's sanctuary. As Allen P. Ross explains concerning a woman with a chronic discharge of blood: "Such infections are very personal. Naturally, a woman did not make this kind of condition known outside the home. In all probability, some may have feigned purity for the sake of participation in worship services or in society. But devout believers who walked in faith and good conscience before God realized that they could not go to the sanctuary until this chronic disorder cleared up and they had gone through the prescribed ritual." *Holiness to the Lord: A Guide to the Exposition of the Book of Leviticus* (Grand Rapids: Baker Academic, 2002), 309. Even though the synagogue was not the

daughter, but the woman has no family to speak of.[42] Jairus has asked Jesus publically to heal his daughter, but the woman sought Jesus secretly.[43] The looming question at this nexus is whether Jesus will arrive in time to heal Jairus' daughter. This delay for an unknown, unclean woman may cause the death of Jairus' daughter. Maybe that is one reason why the disciples were so impatient with his question.

Nothing in these stories disparages Jairus, but everything coalesces to focus on the obscure woman.[44] Jesus will bring this vital rescue mission for a prominent, religious leader to a stand-still to exalt her faith. The narrator has allowed us to know her musings before she is publically identified:[45] "If I touch even his garments, I shall be made well." And her thoughts are realized when she touches his garments, "and immediately the hemorrhage ceased; and she felt in her body that she was healed from the suffering, or torment (ἀπὸ τῆς μάστιγος)."

Jesus does not allow her faith and healing to remain private. He asks, "Who touched my garments?" and looked around to see who had done it.[46] She alone knows the answer to his question, and humbly comes to him in fear and trembling, telling all the truth. That truth includes the information the narrator has already shared with the reader about her long period of uncleanness, her suffering (παθοῦσα) at the hands of many physicians who only

---

sanctuary, by attending, she would at least risk spreading her impurity to others; therefore, she probably did not go to synagogue.

[42] Shepherd suggests that "If she had been married she was probably divorced since she could not have had sexual intercourse with her husband. Cf. Lev 15:25-7." Shepherd, "The Narrative Function of Markan Intercalation," 529 n. 21. More accurately, she could have sexual relations with her husband, but every encounter would render him impure for seven days. *See* Lev. 15:24. Of course, Mark does not directly address any of this.

[43] Perhaps she comes secretly because of her ritual impurity. As Edwards observes: "Whereas Jairus approaches Jesus face-to-face, she approaches Jesus unaware and from behind. . . . Despite her embarrassing condition she pushes through the crowd, even past the disciples, hoping only to touch the back of Jesus' garment." Edwards, "Markan Sandwiches," 204.

[44] Discussing the spatial boarders of the intercalation, Shepherd observes: "Spatial borders for the outer story become progressively narrower and narrower (the seaside, the way, the house, the room). In the inner story all occurs 'in the crowd' which could seem to suggest no change in spatial borders. However, the change in the woman's relation to Jesus, from secrecy to a confession at his feet, would suggest a change in spatial borders, one might say from 'behind Jesus' to 'in front of Jesus.' Accompanying this is a movement from the woman knowing the healing alone (except for Jesus) to the entire crowd knowing. So the spatial borders for the inner story ever expand." Shepherd, "Markan Sandwich Stories," 141.

[45] Shepherd correctly observes: "The introduction of the woman is an extended anachrony (in this case an analepsis the placement of an event from the story time past within the discourse of the present), but her 'present' is with Jesus in the crowd." "The Narrative Function of Markan Intercalation," 526.

[46] The Greek text suggests that Jesus may already know who touched his garment by the use of the feminine form of the interrogative, τίς , twice in Mark 5:30-31, and the feminine article, τὴν, followed by the feminine singular accusative aorist participle, ποιήσασαν, in 5:32 (**τίς** μου ἥψατο τῶν ἱματίων. . . . καὶ λέγεις· **τίς** μου ἥψατο; . . . καὶ περιεβλέπετο ἰδεῖν **τὴν** τοῦτο **ποιήσασαν** (emphasis added). As Shepherd observes, "When Jesus looked 'to see who it was that did this' do we have Jesus' inner knowledge, or a slight intrusion of the narrator who has already revealed to the reader who it was in 5:25-9?" "The Narrative Function of Markan Intercalation," 534 n. 28. As in other parts of Scripture, when God asks questions, it is not to find out answers, but to reveal something to the characters (*cf.* Gen. 3:9-13).

made her condition worse, and her poverty because she "had spent all that she had" for treatment. When Jesus stops an emergency run for the leader of a synagogue for this woman, he emphasizes just how important she is in his eyes. And then he emphasizes her faith: "Daughter, your faith (πίστις)[47] has made you well; go in peace, and be healed of your suffering (ἀπὸ τῆς μάστιγός σου)."

At this point, the first story resumes with the hard announcement from those that came from the house of the "ruler of the synagogue" (ἔρχονται ἀπὸ τοῦ ἀρχισυναγώγου)[48] that his daughter is dead.[49] But the echo and example of the woman from the inner story becomes the lesson that Jesus must give to "the ruler of the synagogue" (τῷ ἀρχισυναγώγῳ): "Stop being afraid, only believe" (μὴ φοβοῦ, μόνον πίστευε).[50] This unknown, unclean woman who suffered for twelve years believed that Jesus could save her. Jairus is told to emulate her faith as he hears that his twelve-year-old daughter has died.[51] Not only did Jesus show his interest in the unknown woman by stopping to make public her faith, but it is her faith that is now used to instruct the ruler of the synagogue. These

---

[47] Jesus saw the woman's faith, not her ritual uncleanness. M.J. Selvidge "Mark 5:25-34 and Leviticus 15:19-20: A Reaction to Restrictive Purity Regulations," *Journal of Biblical Literature* 103 (4, 1984) 619-23. Mann further explains her faith stating: "Faith (Greek *pistis*) in the New Testament is not a name for an inner experience, but describes primarily a committal of trust to God, which in its turn is made effective by God's response to that trust." *Mark*, 286.

[48] Jairus is only identified by name once in this narrative (Mk. 5:23). Every other reference to him is by his title, "ruler of the synagogue" (ἀρχισυνάγωγος) (Mk. 5:35, 36, 38) emphasizing his high social status.

[49] In story time, the healing of the woman and the death of Jairus' daughter are simultaneous and show the impact of one story upon the other in this intercalation. "This bringing together of death and life is epitomized at the juncture of the two stories by the simultaneous benediction of peace (5:34) and the report of the child's death (5:35). Even as the woman's healing preceded this benediction, so the child's death preceded the report." Shepherd, "Markan Sandwich Stories," 157-58.

[50] The present imperative plus μή allows for the idea of cessation of activity in progress. As Dan Wallace states, "Here the idea is frequently progressive and the prohibition is of the 'cessation of some act that is already in progress.' It has the idea, *Stop continuing*. μὴ φοβοῦ is thus naturally used as the formula to quell someone's apprehensions." Daniel B. Wallace, *Greek Grammar: Beyond the Basics: An Exegetical Syntax of the New Testament* (Grand Rapids: Zondervan, 1996), 724. Perhaps there is a correlation between the fear (φοβηθεῖσα Mk. 5:33) of the woman and the fear (φοβοῦ Mk. 5:36) of Jairus in the two stories. The woman may have been fearful to publically proclaim her previous unclean life when she told "all the truth," and now Jairus was fearful of his life without his daughter. It is almost as if the fear of the woman has transferred itself to Jairus, even though its content is distinct, so he must be told to stop being afraid. It is the faith of each in Jesus that delivers them from their suffering lives. As Edwards states: "Jairus and the woman share only one thing in common: They both are victims of desperate circumstances, and apart from Jesus they have no hope." "Markan Sandwiches," 204.

[51] Edwards writes: "It is as though Mark were asking his readers, 'Is there any hope for Jairus now?' And his answer—coming from the mouth of Jesus—is a resounding 'Yes,' If Jairus does 'Not fear, but believe' (v 36). But what kind of belief must Jairus have in a situation in which all human hopes are exhausted? The answer is given in Jesus' command to believe (*pisteuein*, v 36): Jairus must have the kind of faith (*pistis*, v. 34) the woman had!" James R. Edwards, "Markan Sandwiches," 204. Continuing he concludes: "The woman's faith forms the center of the sandwich and is the key to its interpretation. Though her Mark shows how faith in Jesus can transform fear and despair into hope and salvation. It is a powerful lesson for Jairus, as well as for Mark's readers." Ibid. at 205.

narrative encounters of Jesus with women are not only stories about what happened, but of what happens; they are theological pictures that demonstrate that value of women to teach others, even male leaders in the community.

The narrative chords between Jairus' daughter and the woman who was healed sympathetically resonate for the benefit of Jairus and the reader.[52] Both Jairus' daughter and the woman are called "daughter" (θυγάτηρ in Mk. 5:34, 35, and θυγάτριον in 5:23).[53] These emotional titles express the endearment of family that Jesus feels toward the suffering woman, as Jairus feels for his daughter. No doubt, when Jesus called the woman, "daughter," that word resonated deep within Jairus as he thought about his dear, sick girl. Just as Jairus' daughter needed to be healed, or saved (σῴζω, Mk. 5:23), so too was the woman healed, or saved, from her illness (σῴζω, Mk. 5:29, 34). Now that Jairus' daughter has died, the need for salvation is even greater, and it will result in a resurrection (ἀνίστημι, Mk. 5:42). Furthermore, it is only at the end of the first story that we learn that Jairus' daughter was twelve years old (Mk. 5:42).[54] Obviously, Jairus knew this all along, but now the reader is brought under the umbrella revealing that the length of the woman's suffering, and the age of the suffering daughter were the same (Mk. 5:25, 42). This woman's faith after twelve years of suffering was directly applicable to Jairus whose twelve-year old daughter had just died. And just as Jesus made an unclean woman who touched him instantly clean, he was able to make an unclean daughter who had died[55] instantly clean by

---

[52] Shepherd argues that correlation between major characters "is perhaps the most important method the Evangelist uses to invite the reader to compare the two stories." "The Narrative Function of Markan Intercalation," 529, and insists that the linkages between Jairus and the woman, and the woman and Jairus' daughter "force the reader to compare the various characters. Although they do not enter one another's story, they themselves serve as links between the accounts. On the whole Jairus is the contrast to the woman, while the little girl is parallel to the woman." Ibid. at 530.

[53] The term for Jairus' daughter is actually a diminutive. All but one of the words used for Jairus' daughter are diminutives: "little daughter," "daughter," "little child," "Talitha," (diminutive of "lamb" "טַלְיְתָא") and "little girl." As Shepherd observes: "It is not until almost the end of the story that we learn her true age. The use of the diminutives illustrates how much she was loved, not her age." "Markan Sandwich Stories," 150.

[54] As Kermode observes: "Yet in matters of this kind there is really no such thing as nonsignificant coincidence, and we are entitled to consider that this coincidence signifies a narrative relation of some kind between the woman and the girl." *The Genesis of Secrecy*, 132. However, the significance of the correlation is not always obvious or agreed upon. Kermode argues for sexual innuendo. Ibid. 132-33. Tolbert provocatively writes: "In the case of the twelve-year-old child and the woman with a twelve-year illness, it is very tempting to note that the only use of twelve prior to their appearance is related to the disciples, the Twelve. That those twelve turn out to be rocky ground, while these two healed ones demonstrate the fruitfulness of faith raises the possibility of seeing this use of twelve as a subtle clue to the identity of Jesus' true family." *Sowing the Gospel*, 168 n. 58. Edwards also suggests that "Twelve, moreover, may signify Israel to Mark's readers, indeed, Israel coming to faith in Jesus." "Markan Sandwiches," 204-05 n.34.

[55] Setting forth arguments that Jairus' daughter actually died, Shepherd uncovers another parallel between the outer and inner stories: "The ironic character in which Jesus' remark in 5:39 ['Why make a commotion and weep? The child has not died, but is asleep.'] is parallel to the ironic question in the inner story 'Who touched me?' (5:30) suggests that Jesus' central statements in the inner and outer story carry a truth beyond their surface expression." "Markan Sandwich Stories," 156 n. 6 ¶ 4.

touching her and telling her to rise.[56] The first healing happened in secret but was made public by having the woman confess in public, while the second healing occurred before others, Peter, James, John, and her parents, but was then sworn to secrecy,[57] emphasizing that the point of the miracles may not have been the healings themselves, but the interaction between the faith of the woman and the needed faith of Jairus in Jesus.

The structure of this intercalation is evident in the following table:

Narrative Intercalation Mark 5:21-43

The Outer Stories	The Inner Story
• **Continuity**: Journey to save Jairus' daughter	• **Discontinuity**: we never meet Jairus' daughter
• **Spatial setting**: A plea to come heal Jairus' daughter	• **Spatial setting**: Woman with a hemorrhage
• **Temporal setting**: continues	• **Temporal setting**: continues
• **Contrasts:** Jairus is male, leader of synagogue, father, asks Jesus publicly to heal daughter, receives miracle in private, sworn to secrecy.	• **Contrasts:** Woman is female, has no name, excluded from synagogue (Lev), no family mentioned, touches Jesus secretly, receives miracle secretly, confesses in public
• **Continuity:** female, 12 years old, unclean (dead), is touched by Jesus, delay in healing	• **Continuity:** female, sick for 12 years, unclean (hemorrhage), touches Jesus, healed instantly
• **Gap:** Will Jesus arrive in time to heal the little girl? Delay for woman may cause girl's death.	• **Resolution:** The girl has died / hope / resurrection!

Through this confluence of two stories, Jesus is not only seen to be interested in women, even at the distress of a prominent, male, religious leader, but to provide an essential lesson to that leader in the face of his terror by the faith of a woman in the midst of her suffering.

---

[56] Kermode states: "The text seems to be continually interested in providing instance of a generalized opposition between clean and unclean, and we ought not to dispose of this fact by some historical discourse about Jewish Law. The woman, in the present instance, is ritually unclean so long as her hemorrhage continues; but she is at once, by an exercise of power, *dunamis*, relieved of this disability. The girl, dead or supposed dead, is also unclean, or supposed unclean; she is restored by an exercise of power which is, in antithetical contrast, explicit and willed." *The Genesis of Secrecy*, 133.

[57] Shepherd identifies the dramatic irony in this intercalation as follows: "A little girl dies before the healer arrives because a woman 'snatches' a healing incognito. The healer takes a long time looking for who got healed. But the tragedy ends in joy when he little girl is raised. Openness goes to silence (Jairus), secrets become public knowledge (the woman)." "The Narrative Function of Markan Intercalation," 539. Elsewhere he also states: "Jairus' spaces move from openness to "closedness", the woman's spaces move from closedness to openness." "Markan Sandwich Stories," 141.

The Death Plot of the Leaders and the Anointing at Bethany (14:1-11)
(Outer Story 14:1-2; Inner Story 14:3-9; Outer Story 14:10-11)

This Markan intercalation is also employed by Matthew (Matt. 26:1-16), but Luke only includes the outer story (Lk. 22:1-6). The inner story appears to stand on its own in John (Jn. 12:1-8).

The outer story begins two days before the Passover and the Feast of Unleavened Bread with a plot by the Jewish, religious leaders (the chief priests and the scribes) to secretly apprehend Jesus and kill him (Mk. 14:1-2).[58] In light of Jesus' popularity with the people, the dilemma before the leaders is how they can secretly[59] arrest him:

[T]he chief priests and the scribes were seeking[60] how to seize Him by stealth and kill *Him;* for they were saying, "Not during the festival, otherwise there might be a riot of the people."

The theme of Jesus' impending death crosses into the next story where Jesus is anointed for his burial. Again, the unspoken question arises—"How is the death of Jesus going to happen?" Furthermore, the second narrative takes place at a different location--in Bethany at the house of Simon the leper (Mk. 14:3). The irony is apparent—in the setting of the holy feast of Passover and Unleavened Bread, the religious leaders are plotting Jesus' murder, while Jesus is just outside of the holy city in the home of an unclean leper. The reader may wonder, "Who are the upright?" Appearances may be deceptive. This irony will only increase as the stories unfold.

The inner story develops as an anonymous woman breaks an alabaster jar of nard and pours it down upon Jesus' head (Mk. 14:3).[61] The value of the oil is amplified by the

---

[58] The two stories have contrasting moral backgrounds: "In the outer story, the moral background centers on the issues of deceit, killing, betrayal. In the inner story, the moral background has to do with stewardship, the proper handling of resources (is it a waste or is it good to anoint Jesus?). While the woman shows care and concern for Jesus, Judas betrays him into the hands of his enemies." Shepherd, "Markan Sandwich Stories," 243.

[59] A question arises as to whether "in secret" and "not in the feast" are temporal or spatial descriptions. Shepherd argues for spatial with the following support: "Do the rulers intend to wait until after the Passover season to arrest Jesus, or do they not want to seize him in a public place? The later is probably the correct interpretation since the γάρ of 14:2 indicates that the statement of 14:2 is a reason for some gap opened in 14:1. In 14:1 the plot of the rulers is presented, their desire to kill Jesus. This is nothing new, hence not a surprising or some other item which needs explanation However, what does need explanation is the phrase "craftily" (ἐν δόλῳ). It is easy to see that 14:2 explains this point. The rulers fear defeat of their plan, and they hence want to accomplish it away from people. This is the intent of 'not in the feast,' whether it is a temporal or spatial in nature. Spatially it would refer to a 'feast crowd,' while temporally it would refer to a time when many people would be present, 'feast time.' Either way, the emphasis is on the spatial aspects, where there are many people." "Markan Sandwich Stories," 244-45.

[60] Mann correctly observes: "The Greek verb translated *were looking* (ezêtoun) [ἐζήτουν] is an imperfect tense, and implies a scheme which had been in train for some time." Mann, *Mark,* 553.

[61] Shepherd sets forth the threefold pattern of actions in the inner story for each participant: "The woman comes, breaks the flask, and anoints Jesus. The 'some' are indignant, complain, and censure her.

piling up of adjectives: an alabaster vase of ointment, pure nard, expensive (ἀλάβαστρον μύρου νάρδου πιστικῆς πολυτελοῦς). The value of her gift marks the turning point in the stories as certain, unidentified ones (τινες),[62] are reported as being inwardly aroused with disapproval (ἀγανακτοῦντες πρὸς ἑαυτούς) and asking why this ointment has been ruined (τί ἡ ἀπώλεια αὕτη τοῦ μύρου γέγονεν), since it could have been sold for nearly a year's wages (more than 300 denarii) and given to people who are poor (τοῖς πτωχοῖς). So they were reproaching, or scolding, her (ἐνεβριμῶντο αὐτῇ) (Mk. 14:4-5).

At this point in the narrative, negative questions about Jesus may be rising in the reader's mind: the religious leaders are seeking to capture and kill him; he is in the house of an unclean leper; and some woman is pouring over him very expensive oil that could have been used to help the poor.

Jesus concludes the second story and changes the direction of the narrative as he pushes back with his understanding of the woman's actions:

> Let her alone! Why do you trouble her? She has worked a good work for me. For you always have the poor with you, and whenever you wish, you are able to do good for them, but you do not always have me. What she is capable of, she did; she anticipated to anoint my body unto burial. And truly, I say to you, wherever the good news[63] is proclaimed in the whole world, what she did will be told in memory of her.[64]

Jesus then enters into a threefold speech, defense of the woman, himself contrasted with the poor, and the teaching on the woman's memorial. In each of these three parts of Jesus' speech there is a threefold pattern as well. In defending the woman he says, 'leave her alone', 'why are you troubling her?', and 'she has done a good work for me'. In comparing himself with the poor he says, 'you always have the poor with you', 'you can do good to them any time,' and 'you will not always have me.' In presenting the woman's memorial he says, 'she has done what she could', 'she has anointed my body for burial', and 'wherever the Gospel is preached throughout the world, also what she has done will be told for a memorial to her.'" "Markan Sandwich Stories," 250.

[62] In the textual witnesses of W and f^3 these nameless people are identified as the disciples (των μαθητων), as well as in D and Θ (οι δε μαθηται αυτου). This may well reflect an understanding borrowed from Matthew 26:8. More particularly, John 12:8 identifies Judas as the one who rebuked the woman, who is identified as Mary (Jn. 12:3). However, as Shepherd notes, the exclusion of Judas from the inner story and the woman from the outer story is one way in which the narrator holds the two stories apart. "The Narrative Function of Markan Intercalation," 523-24. Nevertheless, when the outer story resumes, there is a hint that Judas was with Jesus in the inner story when it states that Judas "went off" or "went away" (ἀπῆλθεν) to the chief priests (Mk. 14:10). Ibid., 527.

[63] Shepherd insightfully observes: "These gaps [concerning the death of Jesus] interconnect the stories so that there is a modification of the plot. Whereas the leaders' and Judas' story portends a tragic end to the ministry of Jesus, the inner story pulls aside the curtain and illustrates that the death of Jesus will be Good News. Even the plot to betray and kill Jesus is used in the service of the Gospel." "The Narrative Function of Markan Intercalation," 537.

[64] Jesus sets forth three prolepses: (1) "you will not always have me" (14:7); (2) "She has anointed my body beforehand for burial" (14:8), and (3) "Wherever the Gospel is preached in all the world what she has done will also be told as a memorial to her" (14:9). Shepherd comments: "Each of these prolepses is spoken by Jesus and each succeeding one has a further reach than the previous one.... All of the anachronies together have the influence of laying tremendous stress upon the significance of the woman's action. This

(Mk. 14:6-9, my translation).

Jesus' elevation of this anonymous woman exemplifies Mark's theology where the nameless are the followers of Jesus as they come out of anonymity and fade back into it. Their wealth is gladly given in devotion to God, and they do not allow conventional practices to stand in the way of their faith and love. However, the full measure of this woman is only seen against the stark relief of the outer story as it resumes in the next two verses.

Although the woman was anonymous in the inner story, the outer story begins again by specifically identifying "Judas Iscariot who was one of the Twelve" (Mk. 14:10). The juxtaposition of these two character is Mark's way of asking the reader to compare them, and accordingly, to say more through an intercalation than could have been said in either story on its own.

The gap first raised in the outer story concerning how the religious leaders are going to arrange for Jesus' secret arrest to kill him, and resumed in the inner story as Jesus is anointed for his burial, is now answered in the resumption of the outer story as we are told that Judas, one of the Twelve,[65] is going[66] to betray Jesus. In other words, it is Judas who is going to provide a way for the religious leaders to secretly[67] apprehend Jesus and then kill him (*cf.* 14:1-2):

> Then Judas Iscariot, one of the twelve, went to the chief priests in order to hand him over to them. And those hearing rejoiced and promised to give him silver. And he sought[68] how he should conveniently[69] hand him over.

---

repetitive reinterpretation of her act of devotion is what makes possible the dramatic comparison with the outer story." "Markan Sandwich Stories," 258-59.

[65] The Greek text includes the definite article, "the one of the twelve" (ὁ εἷς τῶν δώδεκα) (Mk. 14:10). Wallace identifies the article as fitting within the "well-known" category. Wallace, *Greek Grammar*, 233. Mann suggests that this use of the article emphasizes Judas among the Twelve: "Mark may be using the definite article here for emphasis: 'That one, the only one, of the Twelve' who proved treacherous." *Mark*, 560.

[66] The verb in 14:10 is the clue that this portion of the outer story is subsequent to the inner story: "It is stated that Judas 'went away' to the high priests. This implies subsequent time to the previous event where Judas was present. Although Jesus is the only character to appear in both stories, nevertheless, in 14:10 we are told that Judas 'went away,' obviously from the previous meeting place, which is Bethany. The reference in 14:10, in fact, goes out of the way to designate Judas as one of the Twelve. Hence, we can conclude that 14:10 occurs after the events of 14:3-9." Shepherd, "Markan Sandwich Stories," 242-43.

[67] Shepherd rightly states: "Thus Judas is not an agent who shifts the plan of the rulers temporally. He does not somehow lead them to carry out their plot during the feast when they did not actually plan to do so. Rather, he is the conduit through which they accomplish their goal in a secretive way." "Markan Sandwich Stories," 245 n. 1.

[68] The outer story contains an *inclusio*: Just as the religious leaders sought (ἐζήτουν) how they could seize Jesus (14:1), now Judas seeks (ἐζήτει) how he should hand him over (14:11).

[69] Shepherd observes that "In previous intercalations we have a noted return of the outer story of the inner story's point at the close of the outer story. But in the present story, the ending is about Judas the betrayer, and nothing "good" can be said of his deed. However, an ironic twist is present, for Judas seeks to

(Mk. 14:10-11).

Unlike the woman who shows her devotion to Jesus by anointing his head with expensive oil, Judas betrays his master. Unlike the woman who pours out perfume worth nearly 300 denarii, Judas receives a promise of an unspecified sum of money[70] to hand Jesus over.[71] Unlike those in Bethany who scorn the woman for the good work she has done, the chief priests rejoice over Judas' treachery. Unlike the woman who is praised by Jesus for taking what she had to perform a good work in preparation for his burial, Judas takes the knowledge he has and does a work of disloyalty.[72]

These contrasts between the nameless woman and the named member of the Twelve uniquely call out to the reader from the comparison of the two stories, leading to the inevitable conclusion that Judas is an example, *par excellence*, of a failed disciple, while the woman is an example of a true, faithful disciple.[73]

---

betray Jesus conveniently (εὐκαίρως 14:11). In the outer story alone this just adds to his perfidy, as though he enjoys or plots well how to hand over the Messiah. But the ironic twist is the way in which the εὐ-word stands in such close relation with so many "good" words in the inner story, words which convey high ideals and holy concepts in the inner story (καλός, 14:6; εὖ, 14:7, and εὐαγγέλιον, 14:9). Thus the well-laid perfidious plot against Jesus becomes forever part of the Good News. The evil is turned back to good, even though the betrayer never shares in its goodness. Thus, in a way, there is a return to the point of the inner story." "Markan Sandwich Stories," 156-57.

[70] The theme of money contributes toward dramatized irony between the two stories. "Jesus is highly valued in the inner story, but not even worthy of the specification of a betrayal price in the outer story. This irony centers on the Christological question and is closely connected with the discipleship theme. What value will the disciple place upon Jesus." Shepherd, "Markan Sandwich Stories," 263.

[71] Shepherd notes: "Whereas Judas places a low valuation upon Jesus (he is not worth even a *set sum* of money), the woman, representative of true discipleship, pours out upon her Lord the costly nard, worth more than 300 denarii. . . . The contrast between the actions of the two characters could hardly be greater. "The Narrative Function of Markan Intercalation," 537. Likewise, after discussing the concurrent responsibility to the poor and to those who are loved, Tolbert states: "But whatever the moral choices involved in using money for various loving ends, giving money to purchase betrayal and accepting money to deliver up your teacher to his enemies is clearly evil. The contrast between the generosity of the anonymous woman and the deal of Judas ('who was one of the twelve') with the chief priests to exchange Jesus for money (14:10-11) dramatizes starkly the different production of good earth and rocky ground. *Sowing the Gospel*, 274. Finally, Shepherd comments: "The plots of the two stories are interlinked. The two stories, although apparently of contrasting types, are actually similar. They are both stories of valuation. Money is mentioned in both stories and Jesus is the center of the 'money actions.' In the inner story, it is a case of giving (δίδωμι, 14:5), while in the outer story, it is a case of betrayal (παραδίδωμι, 14:10-11)." "Markan Sandwich Stories," 255.

[72] Shepherd identifies the dramatic irony in this intercalation as follows: "The nefarious plot becomes Good News. The disciple, one of the Twelve, does not value his Master aright, but a nameless woman prepares his body for burial by an expensive gift of love." Tom Shepherd, "The Narrative Function of Markan Intercalation," 540. Ironically, just as what the woman did will be remembered, so too, what Judas did will be a lasting remembrance.

[73] Similarly, Edwards states: "Is not Mark saying that in Jesus' "hour" (14:35) there can be only one of two responses to him, that of the woman or that of Judas? Mark places the woman in the middle as the ideal." James R. Edwards, "Markan Sandwiches," 209.

A summary of these two stories might be seen in the following table:

An Intercalation
Mark 14:1-11

Outer Story: *Death plot of the Leaders & Judas*	**Inner Story**: *The Anointing at Bethany*
- Leaders plot Jesus' death (gap—how?) - Judas' action is a betrayal unto death - Judas is named - Judas betrays his master	- The woman's anointing is for Jesus' burial (gap—how?) - Woman is unnamed - Woman anoints his head with expensive oil showing her devotion
- Judas receives promise of unspecified sum to betray Jesus	- Woman pours out perfume worth 300 denarii
- Priests laugh at Judas' treachery	- Some of the inner circle censure the woman
- Judas demonstrates disloyalty	- Jesus praises the woman's deed
- Judas: failed discipleship	- Woman: faithful discipleship

Once again, Mark's narrative structure brings a woman to the forefront—even over one of the Twelve.

Conclusion

Mark may never have known the meta-language of an "intercalation" to describe his combining of stories, but he skillfully used the narrative technique to aid the reader in placing the outer and inner stories against one another with the result that their sum equaled more than their parts.

Moreover, the three interactions we examined in this study uniquely highlighted the anonymous over the named whether it was "whoever does the will of God" over Jesus' mother and brothers who are seeking to apprehend him, or the faith of a woman healed from suffering over Jairus, the ruler of a synagogue who needs to trust in Jesus in the face of his own suffering, or the woman who did what she could to anoint Jesus for his burial, over against Judas, one of the Twelve, who did what he could to betray him.

While the first unit showed why a particular woman, Jesus' mother, may not have been a leader in Jesus' earthly ministry, the next two units showed not only how woman are exemplary in their faith and devotion to Jesus, but also how that faith and devotion are instructive to a male religious leader, and over against a man who was one of Jesus' inner circle.

This close reading of these three, non-controversial passages are but a few seeds from a great bushel that must be sown as a basis for a biblical theology of women against which the more difficult passages should then be read.

CHAPTER IV

THE CONTRIBUTION OF CODEX BEZAE CANTABRIGIENSIS TO AN
UNDERSTANDING OF WOMEN IN THE BOOK OF ACTS*

1. *Introduction*

This study is not another attempt to identify the 'original' text of Acts, but an examination of the passages in Acts that address women and also contain variant readings in Code Bezae Cantabrigiensis (Codex D). The goal is to identify the theological concerns, tendencies and/or motivations[1] of the variant readings in Codex D regarding women. As a side product, this study will also discuss the theological concerns of the Alexandrian text (Codex B) regarding women.

In no way will this investigation provide an exhaustive discussion of all of the passages dealing with women in Acts,[2] only those that have

*This article first appeared in Journal of Greco-Roman Christianity and Judaism 4 (2007): 158-83

1. Epp writes, '*many* variants reveal a religious viewpoint (and perhaps a religious "experience") which accounts for their origin or...which occasioned their retention in or deletion from a given text' (Eldon Jay Epp, *The Theological Tendency of Codex Bezae Cantabrigiensis in Acts* [Cambridge: Cambridge University Press, 1966], p. 17; see also pp. 10-21). Strange identifies Epp's work with 'tendency criticism' in response to 'Haenchen's description of the Western reviser as "Acts' earliest commentator" and thus as a means of obtaining insight into the period of the early second century' (W.A. Strange, *The Problem of the Text of Acts* [Cambridge: Cambridge University Press, 1992], p. 23). Strange goes on to describe common features in many Western texts, including the addition of material and alteration of style which reflect a scribal attitude toward the text, until late in the second century when the literature began to obtain respect as emerging scripture (pp. 36-37).

2. For a more exhaustive treatment of all of the passages in Acts dealing with women, see Ivoni Richter Reimer, *Women in the Acts of the Apostles: A Feminist Liberation Perspective* (trans. Linda M. Maloney; Minneapolis: Fortress Press, 1995); see also Ben Witherington, *Women in the Earliest Churches* (Cambridge: Cambridge University Press, 1988), pp. 143-57.

theologically significant variants in Codex D.³ In particular, the following passages will be examined: Acts 1.14 (the apostles with the women for prayer); Acts 16.14, 15, 40 (Lydia and her household); Acts 17.4, 12 (prominent women); Acts 17.34 (the omission of Damaris); and Acts 18.2-3, 7, 26 (Priscilla and Aquila).

The Western text, though extant in numerous sources, shows a uniformity of quality and character even though the particular witnesses to this text are not uniform.⁴ Codex D is a leading representative of the Western text and includes the four canonical Gospels and the book of Acts, dated somewhere from the fourth to the seventh century AD.⁵ Even though Codex D is bilingual containing a Latin (*d*) and Greek (D) text,⁶

---

3. Ben Witherington ventured briefly into such a selective study in his article, 'The Anti-Feminist Tendencies of the "Western" Text in Acts', *JBL* 103 (1984), pp. 82-84.

4. Epp, *Theological Tendency*, pp. 5-8; Strange rightly notes, 'Eighteenth century criticism, valuable though it was in laying the foundations of ordering of witnesses, left critics with the unhappy choice of "Western" as an adjective to describe the group of witnesses of which Codex D is the principal. This text is scarcely "Western" in a geographical sense, as has been widely recognised for some time' (*The Problem of the Text of Acts*, p. 3, cf. pp. 35-37); see also Peter Head, 'Acts and the Problem of its Texts', in Bruce W. Winter and Andrew D. Clarke (eds.), *The Book of Acts in its First Century Setting. I. The Book of Acts in its Ancient Literary Setting* (Grand Rapids: Eerdmans, 1993), pp. 415-44 (416). Nevertheless, 'Western' will be used to describe this textual tradition for the sake of common scholarly reference.

5. Epp, *Theological Tendency*, pp. 7, 10, holds to a fifth century date; Strange, *The Problem of the Text of Acts*, p. 3; Bruce M. Metzger, *The Text of the New Testament: Its Transmission, Corruption, and Restoration* (New York: Oxford University Press, 1968), p. 49, dates the text 'from the fifth or possibly sixth century'. Ernst Haenchen holds to an early sixth century date (*The Acts of the Apostles: A Commentary*. [trans. Bernard Noble and Gerald Shin; Philadelphia: Westminster Press, 1971], p. 53). Nevertheless, as Jenny Read-Heimerdinger affirms, 'Although none of these actual MSS dates from before the fourth century, it should be borne in mind that the text they transmit is of an earlier date. This much is known from readings of both the Alexandrian MSS and Codex Bezae that are found among the oldest papyri, versions and Church Fathers' (Jenny Read-Heimerdinger, *The Bezan Text of Acts: A Contribution of Discourse Analysis to Textual Criticism* [JSNTSup, 236; Sheffield: Sheffield Academic Press, 2002], p. 5).

6. Epp, *Theological Tendency*, pp. 8-10; Metzger, *Text of the New Testament*, p. 49, notes that the Greek text is on the left and the Latin text is on the right with each page in a single 'column of text, which is not written straight ahead but...

the focus of this paper will be on the textual variants in the Greek text (D).

This study is inductive,[7] examining words and phrases in view of the context of a passage, identifying variant readings in Codex D,[8] considering their cause, and their effect on a reading of the passage, and then working, where possible, toward an overall identification of the theological tendency of the variants regarding women in Acts.[9] This study will not attempt to approach the text from the presuppositions of a patriarchal or feminist perspective, but from a textual focus that permits the text to inform one's perspectives and presuppositions.[10]

Epp seems to be correct that a study limited to Acts is more helpful than a study of Luke–Acts because 'characteristic features of the "Western" text and Codex Bezae are the most prominent and abundant in Acts', and because a study of Acts avoids the possible effect of a 'harmonistic influence' of the Gospels.[11] Epp also astutely notes that it is not where texts are in agreement, but where they disagree, that the theological differences become evident.[12] The standard text against which

---

divided into κῶλα, that is, lines of varying length with the object of making the pauses in sense come at the end of lines'.

7. Epp, *Theological Tendency*, pp. 24-34, identifies a similar methodology, but he extends it to identifying the significance of variant Western readings beyond Codex D itself.

8. Read-Heimerdinger, *The Bezan Text*, pp. 5-19, argues for the benefit of focusing upon an actual manuscript, like Codex D, rather than upon 'a hypothetical text reconstructed from a range of witnesses' in the Western text, because a focused study leads to more certain results.

9. Read-Heimerdinger, *The Bezan Text*, pp. 19-25, argues forcefully for a theological purpose in Codex D even if her counterbalancing explanation of the Alexandrian text as a 'historical account' is questionable.

10. Witherington describes this interpretive tension well when, writing on the same subject, he says, 'Of course, no one comes to the text without presuppositions, but this author has tried to let the text inform and reform his presuppositions so that it is the text that has the last say about the material' (*Women in the Earliest Churches*, p. 2).

11. Epp, *Theological Tendency*, p. 26; see also Strange, *Text of Acts*, p. 1; Metzger writes, 'No known manuscript has so many and such remarkable variations from what is usually taken to be the normal New Testament text. Codex Bezae's special characteristic is the free addition (and occasional omission) of words, sentences, and even incidents' (*Text of the New Testament*, p. 50).

12. Epp, *Theological Tendency*, p. 40, says, 'Differences and only the differences reveal the distinctive driving force and direction of movement of a thinker

variants will be identified is the Alexandrian text as identified in the Nestle–Aland[27] (N–A[27]) or United Bible Societies[4] (*UBSGNT*[4]) editions.[13] However, if there is any variance in the N–A[27], I will follow Codex B Vaticanus as laid out by J.H. Ropes.[14] This study will not consider the variants which can be explained as unintentional, accidental and/or mechanical due to faulty eyesight, hearing, errors of the mind, or

closely related to a larger tradition. The objection, then, that an emphasis on textual variants overlooks the overwhelming majority of textual agreement among all New Testament texts and textual traditions is not well founded. This extensive agreement is obvious enough, but what is not so obvious is that twist or torsional strain which a specific text or textual tradition is bringing to bear upon the common textual material being transmitted. And it is precisely the textual variants which can bring to light this distinctive thrust' (see also p. 35).

13. It is understood that the Nestle–Aland critical text is not the 'original' text. Even the introduction to the N–A[27] identifies the text as 'a working text' that is 'not to be considered as definitive, but as a stimulus to further efforts toward defining and verifying the text of the New Testament' (Kurt Aland, Matthew Black, Carlo M. Martini, Bruce M. Metzger, and Allen Wilkgren, *Novum Testamentum Graece* (Stuttgart: Deutsche Bibelgesellschaft, 27th edn, 2001), p. 3. See also Epp, *Theological Tendency*, p. 36. Nevertheless, the Nestle–Aland text is an attempt to reconstruct an 'original' text from extant sources (primarily, but not exclusively, from the Alexandrian text composed of codices ℵ, A, B, C, Ψ, Papyri 45, 50, 56, 57, 58, 74, and the minuscules 33, 81, 104, 326, 1175, 1241, and 1739); see F.F. Bruce, *The Acts of the Apostles: Greek Text with Introduction and Commentary* (Grand Rapids: Eerdmans, 3rd edn, 1990), pp. 70-71; Bruce M. Metzger, *A Textual Commentary on the Greek New Testament: A Companion Volume to the United Bible Societies' Greek New Testament (Third Edition)* (Stuttgart: United Bible Societies, corr. edn, 1975), pp. 259, 271-72; Head, 'Acts and the Problem of its Texts', pp. 418-19. As such, the Nestle–Aland text is the foundation for much present New Testament study; see Haenchen, *Acts of the Apostles*, p. 50; Luke Timothy Johnson, *The Acts of the Apostles* (Sacra Pagina, 5; Collegeville, MN: Liturgical Press, 1992), pp. 2-3; Bruce, *Acts of the Apostles: Greek Text*, p. 77; Ben Witherington, III, *The Acts of the Apostles: A Socio-Rhetorical Commentary* (Grand Rapids: Eerdmans, 1998), p. 68; William J. Larkin, *Acts* (The IVP New Testament Commentary Series; Downers Grove, IL: InterVarsity Press, 1995), p. 23; I. Howard Marshall, *The Acts of the Apostles: An Introduction and Commentary* (TNTC; Grand Rapids: Eerdmans, 1980), p. 46. Consequently, the Nestle–Aland text is a viable choice as a 'base text' against which textual variants in Codex D may be identified. See Head, 'Acts and the Problem of its Texts', pp. 443-44; Metzger, *Textual Commentary*, pp. 259-72; Read-Heimerdinger, *The Bezan Text*, p. 7 n. 7.

14. J.H. Ropes, *The Text of Acts*, in F.J. Foakes Jackson and Kirsopp Lake (eds.), *The Beginnings of Christianity. Part I: The Acts of the Apostles*, III (London: Macmillan, 1926).

errors of judgment.[15] Instead, this study will consider those variants which appear to be intentional, including changes in spelling and grammar, and especially alterations made for doctrinal considerations, since these changes are in the realm of theological development.[16] The use of the term 'intentional' is not meant to be pejorative, but descriptive, as thinking scribes made good-faith emendations in an attempt to rectify apparent error in the text.[17]

2. An Examination of Selected Passages in the Book of Acts

a. Acts 1.14 (The Apostles and Women in Prayer)

1. *The Context of Acts 1.14.* The verse in question occurs within a larger logical unit, Acts 1.1–2.47, which includes the following sub-units: the prologue, (1.1-2),[18] the programmatic prelude (1.3-14),[19] and the book's

---

15. Metzger, *Text of the New Testament*, pp. 186-95.
16. Metzger, *Text of the New Testament*, pp. 195-206; Epp, *Theological Tendency*, p. 35.
17. Metzger, *Text of the New Testament*, p. 195; Metzger, *Textual Commentary*, pp. 264-65.
18. Some biblical literary critics combine Acts 1.1-2 and 1.3-14 into a single unit of 1.1-14 because of similar themes, audience (the Twelve) and the smooth transition of the prologue into vv. 3 and following. D.W. Palmer, 'The Literary Background of Acts 1.1-4', *NTS* 33 (1987), pp. 427-38 (427 n. 1) (who nevertheless recognizes the prologue as a distinct literary form); Robert C. Tannehill, *The Narrative Unity of Luke–Acts: A Literary Interpretation. II. The Acts of the Apostles* (Minneapolis: Fortress Press, 1990), p. 9. Nevertheless, the complex nature of the single Greek sentence is reminiscent of Lk. 1.1-4; therefore, it may be better to distinguish between the units of 1.1-2 and 1.3-14. See F. Blass, A. Debrunner, and Robert W. Funk, *A Greek Grammar of the New Testament and Other Early Christian Literature* (Chicago: University of Chicago Press, 1961), § 464; Joseph A. Fitzmyer, *The Gospel According to Luke (I-IX): Introduction, Translation, and Notes* (AB, 28; Garden City, NY: Doubleday, 1981), p. 288; Philip E. Satterthwaite, 'Acts against the Background of Classical Rhetoric', in Winter and Clarke (eds.), *The Book of Acts in its First Century Setting. I. The Book of Acts in its Ancient Literary Setting*, pp. 337-79 (353); Hans Conzelmann, *Acts of the Apostles* (trans. James Limburg, A. Thomas Kraabel, and Donald H. Juel; Hermeneia; Philadelphia: Fortress Press, 1987), pp. 3-4; Loveday Alexander, *The Preface of Luke's Gospel: Literary Convention and Social Context in Luke 1.1-4 and Acts 1.1* (SNTSMS, 78; Cambridge: Cambridge University Press, 1993), pp. 102-46; Charles H. Talbert, *Reading Acts: A Literary and Theological Commentary on the Acts of the Apostles* (New York: Crossroad, 1997), p. 19.

first major panel where the promise of the Father is prepared for, received, and presented (1.15–2.47).[20]

The prologue provides continuity with *Lukas*'s[21] previous work and furnishes an update on the Gospel so that the plot can develop further.[22] The prelude is unfolded through a general statement (1.3-5), which is enlarged to include more specific development (1.6-14). It is programmatic in that it foreshadows essential themes that *Lukas* will develop in Acts: the eschatological import of the coming of the Spirit,[23] baptism,[24]

---

19. William S. Kurz, *Reading Luke–Acts: Dynamics of Biblical Narrative* (Louisville: Westminster John Knox, 1993), p. 80, understands Acts 2–3 to function in the book like the first two chapters in the Gospel of Luke and the prologue in the Gospel of John. However, by delaying the programmatic chapters until ch. 2, Kurz seems to break the typical pattern of both of his examples. While it is true that themes exist in Acts 2–3 which are further developed in the book, they first arise in the prologue and programmatic prelude.

20. Satterthwaite, 'Acts against the Background of Classical Rhetoric', pp. 353-54.

21. The identity of the historical author(s)/redactor(s) of the book of Acts is beyond the scope of this study and not necessary knowledge for evaluation of textual variants. In this article, the author of the book of Acts will be referred to as *Lukas*, to distinguish the author from the name of the Gospel. This does not intend to address the question of the author's identity.

22. The formal tone of the prologue does not necessarily determine either the style or the reader's/listener's expectations for the remainder of the narrative. F. Gerald Downing, 'Theophilus's First Reading of Luke–Acts', in C.M. Tuckett (ed.), *Luke's Literary Achievement: Collected Essays* (JSNTSup, 116; Sheffield: Sheffield Academic Press, 1995), pp. 91-109 (96-98); see also Alexander, *The Preface of Luke's Gospel*, pp. 200-201, 206. Rather it provides a smooth transition from Luke's Gospel to the narrative of Acts, invokes the preface to the Gospel of Luke as controlling for both works, provides continuity between Jesus (in the Gospel) and his apostles (in Acts), continues the narrator's relationship to the reader (Theophilus), and continues the story begun in the Gospel of Luke; see Steven M. Sheeley, *Narrative Asides in Luke–Acts* (JSNTSup, 72; Sheffield: JSOT Press, 1992), pp. 134-35.

23. Acts 1.5-8; this is identified as the promise of the Father about which Jesus told the disciples. See also 2.16-21; 3.19-21; 8.17; 9.17-18; 10.44-47; 19.6. The coming of the Spirit had an Old Testament connection to and expectation of the coming of the kingdom attached to it (cf. Isa. 32.15-20; 44.3-5; Ezek. 39.28-29; Joel 2.28; Zech. 12.8-10).

24. Acts 1.5; 8.12-13, 36; 16.15, 33; 19.3-7.

being witnesses to the Jews and all peoples[25] of the death and resurrection of Jesus,[26] the return of Jesus as judge,[27] and an earlier division among the disciples[28] which was replaced by unity.[29]

In Acts 1.12-14, the narrative begins to move from its programmatic prologue into its first major panel, with the return of the apostles to Jerusalem. That the apostles are in view is emphasized through the naming of the Eleven (Acts 1.13). However, in the next verse, the group is expanded to include women, the mother of Jesus, and his brothers (Acts 1.14). Unlike the conflict and division described in the Gospel of Luke (Lk. 22.20-24, 33-34; 24.36-49), here the disciples of Jesus are unified as they pray[30] with one mind (ὁμοθυμαδόν).

2. *Textual Variant in Acts 1.14.* Against this background, Codex D offers a theologically significant textual variant regarding women in Acts 1.14:

N–A[27] (Vaticanus)	Codex D
οὗτοι πάντες ἦσαν προσκαρτεροῦντες ὁμοθυμαδὸν τῇ προσευχῇ σὺν γυναιξὶν καὶ Μαριὰμ τῇ μητρὶ τοῦ[31] Ἰησοῦ καὶ σὺν[32] τοῖς ἀδελφοῖς αὐτοῦ.	οὗτοι πάντες ἦσαν προσκαρτεροῦντες ὁμοθυμαδὸν τῇ προσευχῇ σὺν **ταῖς** γυναιξὶν **καὶ τέκνοις** καὶ Μαριὰ τῇ μητρὶ τοῦ Ἰησοῦ καὶ τοῖς ἀδελφοῖς αὐτοῦ.[33]

The inclusion of 'women' along with the apostles and the brothers of Jesus in prayer for the awaited Spirit appears to have been minimized by the addition in Codex D of 'and children'.[34] The Alexandrian text leaves

---

25. 'The ends of the earth' (Acts 1.8) is not so much a geographical reference as another way of saying 'to all peoples' (cf. Isa. 8.9; 48.20; 49.6; 62.11).
26. Acts 2–4; 7; 10; 13; 17; 22–26; 28.
27. The angels emphasize that Jesus will return as judge (1.11; cf. Luke 12.35-48; 19.11-27). See also Acts 17.
28. Lk. 22.20-24, 33-34; 24.36-49.
29. Acts 1.14-26; 2.44-46; 8; 10; 19.
30. For continuity with the Gospel see Lk. 11.9-13; 18.1-8.
31. Codex Vaticanus does not include the article τοῦ in the text.
32. N–A[27] does not include the preposition σὺν but follows the reading in ℵ, A, C* and D.
33. Here and below, significant variants in Codex D are highlighted in bold.
34. Although the critical apparatus in N–A[27] only notes the addition of καὶ τέκνοις, Metzger, *Textual Commentary*, p. 284; Josep Rius-Camps and Jenny Read-Heimerdinger, *The Message of Acts in Codex Bezae: A Comparison with the Alexandrian Tradition.* I. *Acts 1.1–5.42: Jerusalem* (JSNTSup, 257; London: T. &

the identity of these women open to include those who accompanied Jesus in his itinerate ministry from Galilee to Jerusalem (cf. Lk. 8.1-3) including those who were the first witnesses to the resurrection, and perhaps the wives of the apostles.[35] The phrase, σὺν γυναιξίν, without the article, may possibly be a reference to 'wives'.[36] However, once the article and 'children' are added to the text, the identity of the women is *limited* to the wives of the apostles.[37] Not only does this change in Codex D imply that some of the disciples were married and had children, but that the women in the upper room may not have included those who were with Jesus as he traveled. Additionally, the message is that the women in the upper room were not there as independent people alongside the men in prayer and as witnesses,[38] but as wives of the apostles tending to their children. This is a more subordinate positioning of women.[39]

In view of the contextual unity with the Gospel of Luke mentioned above in Acts 1.1-14, it appears that the ambiguity of the Alexandrian reading allows for, and, as most commentators agree, argues for the more

T. Clark International, 2004), p. 56, and Ropes, *Text of Acts,* p. 6, note that Codex D also includes the article before women, i.e. σὺν ταῖς γυναιξὶν καὶ τέκνοις. Even without the article, the phrase σὺν γυναιξὶν καὶ τέκνοις could mean 'with their wives and children' as in Acts 21.5; see the NET Bible.

35. Rius-Camps and Read-Heimerdinger, *Message of Acts,* pp. 56, 104.

36. Martin M. Culy and Mikeal C. Parsons, *Acts: A Handbook on the Greek Text* (Waco, TX: Baylor University Press, 2003), p. 13, say, 'It is unclear whether this term refers to "wives", or to "women" in general. Given the fact that the subject, "all these", refers to a list of men, a reference to "wives" is superficially the most natural way to take σὺν γυναιξίν'; Kirsopp Lake and Henry J. Cadbury, additionally note: 'It is slightly supported also by the καί before Μαριάμ, which suggests that she was not one of the γυναῖκες, and thus the γυναῖκες means "wives"' (*English Translation and Commentary,* in F.J. Foakes Jackson and Kirsopp Lake [eds.], *The Beginnings of Christianity: Part I: The Acts of the Apostles,* IV [London: Macmillan, 1933], p. 11).

37. Rius-Camps and Read-Heimerdinger, *Message of Acts,* p. 56; Metzger translates the D variant as 'with their wives and children' (*Textual Commentary,* p. 284).

38. Conzelmann writes, 'When D adds καὶ τέκνοις, "and children", it shows that it no longer understands that Luke portrays those who are present as witnesses' (*Acts of the Apostles,* p. 9).

39. As Bruce states, 'playing down the independent status of the women' (*Acts of the Apostles: Greek Text,* p. 106). See also Witherington, *Acts of the Apostles,* p. 113 n. 39; Witherington, 'Anti-Feminist Tendencies', p. 82; Culy and Parsons, *Acts,* p. 13; Haenchen, *Acts of the Apostles,* p. 154 n. 3. See also Reimer, *Women in the Acts,* p. 232.

generic sense of 'women' rather than 'wives of the apostles', including those mentioned as disciples in the Gospel of Luke (Lk. 8.1-3; 23.55; 24.1, 9, 22).[40] It also appears that this account in Acts 1.14 is one where *Lukas* has placed women in parallel with men to emphasize their mutual involvement in the gospel (cf. Ananias and Sapphira in Acts 5; Priscilla and Aquila in Acts 18; Felix and Drusilla in Acts 24; Agrippa and Bernice in Acts 25; the summary statement in Acts 5.14; Paul's persecutions in Acts 9.2; and Dionysius and Damaris in Acts 17.34).[41]

Consequently, Codex D appears to limit the meaning of the text in Acts 1.14 so as to place women in a more subordinate role in the early Church. This limiting may well imply that the scribe recognized the liberating implications of the Alexandrian text's description of women as participants equal with men in the upper room as they waited for the promise of the Spirit.

b. *Acts 16.14-15, 40 (Lydia and her Household)*

1. *The Context of Acts 16.14-15.* This is *Lukas*'s sixth panel in the book of Acts, built between two summary statements in 16.5 and 19.20. On one hand, this is a unit of continuation in that Paul's missionary journeys are continued. The fifth and sixth panels seem to have a seamless union where the mission is prepared for (Acts 16.1-5), and then commences (from Acts 16.6). On the other hand, this is a unit of distinctions in that Paul was demonstrated 'before men' to be a true apostle with the true gospel message for all peoples in the fifth panel (Acts 12.25–16.5), but in this panel Paul is demonstrated 'before God' to be a true apostle with the true gospel message for all peoples. *Lukas* emphasizes the divine direction and control of the Pauline mission in these units. The irony and sovereignty of God is seen in Paul being forbidden to preach the word in Asia (Acts 16.6), but by the end of the panel all of Asia has heard the word of God (19.10).

---

40. Witherington, *Acts of the Apostles*, pp. 113-14; Bruce, *Acts of the Apostles: Greek Text*, p. 106; Haenchen, *Acts of the Apostles,* p. 154. As Culy writes, 'Given the fact that Acts is the second of two volumes, however, and the fact that Luke spends a significant amount of time in the first chapter refreshing the memory of Theophilus, it would also be natural to "assume that Luke means the same women he has mentioned at the end of his first volume—female disciples (cf. Luke 23.55; 24.1, 9, 22)"' (*Acts*, p. 13); Reimer, *Women in the Acts*, pp. 232-33.

41. Witherington, *Women in the Earliest Churches*, pp. 143-45.

Because the remaining textual variants discussed in this study occur in this sixth panel, its macro-structure follows as a guide to context:

The Sovereign Mission at Philippi (16.6-40)
Prologue: The sovereign call to Macedonia (16.6-10)
a. The sovereign conversion of a woman (16.11-15)
b. The sovereign conversion of a man (16.16-34)
Epilogue: The sovereign vindication of God's servants (16.35-40)
The Movement of the True Gospel Mission from Thessalonica to Corinth (17.1–18.17)
Ministry toward the Jews (17.1-15)
—Negative: The mission to the Thessalonians (17.1-9)
—Positive: The mission to the Bereans (17.10-15)
Ministry toward the Gentiles (17.16–18.17)
—Negative: The mission to the Athenians (17.16-34)
—Positive: The mission to the Corinthians (18.1-17)
The Climax of the Gospel Mission in Asia at Ephesus (18.18–19.20)
Ephesus is bypassed again to leave Priscilla and Aquila there (18.18-23)
Priscilla and Aquila instruct Apollos (18.24-28)
Paul apostolically bestows the Spirit on about twelve men (19.1-7)
Paul speaks the word of God so that all of Asia hears it (19.8-10)
Paul demonstrates the uniqueness of God's power: healings, exorcism, repentance (19.11-19)

Witherington correctly identifies *Lukas*'s parallel structure in the conversion of one woman, Lydia (16.12-15, 40), and one man, the jailer (16.23-39), as a means of expressing parity in God's plan of salvation.[42]

2. *Textual Variant in Acts 16.14*. Epp argues through a phrase added at the end of Acts 18.8 (πιστεύοντες τῷ θεῷ) that Codex D is portraying a favoritism towards Gentile proselytes over Jewish proselytes, the latter of whom would have been described with κύριος following πιστεύειν.[43] However, this argument seems to break down when it comes to the variant regarding Lydia in Acts 16.14:

N–A²⁷ (Vaticanus)	Codex D*
καί τις γυνὴ ὀνόματι Λυδία, πορφυρόπωλις πόλεως Θυατείρων σεβομένη τὸν θεόν, ἤκουεν, ἧς ὁ	καί τις γυνὴ ὀνόματι Λυδία, πορφυρόπωλις τῆς πόλεως Θυατείρων σεβομένη τὸν

---

42. Witherington, *Women in the Earliest Churches*, pp. 147-48.
43. Epp, *Theological Tendency*, pp. 87-91; see also Witherington, 'Anti-Feminist Tendencies', p. 83.

κύριος διήνοιξεν τὴν καρδίαν κύριον,⁴⁵ ἤκουσεν, ἧς ὁ κύριος προσέχειν τοῖς λαλουμένοις ὑπὸ διήνοιξεν τὴν καρδίαν προσέχειν [τοῦ]⁴⁴ Παύλου. τοῖς λαλουμένοις ὑπὸ Παύλου.

Codex D's change of θεόν to κύριον in Acts 16.14 seems to be a move in exactly the opposite direction from Epp's thesis because, if he is right, Codex D is presenting Lydia as a Jewish proselyte through the use of σεβομένη τὸν κύριον rather than a Gentile one, even though in Acts 16.15 Codex D substitutes θεῷ for κυρίῳ intimating that she is a Gentile proselyte.⁴⁶

One might understand why this switch occurs in Codex D since Lydia's conversion is occurring both in a Gentile area and in a contextual setting of Paul searching for a synagogue. It appears in Acts 16.13 that Paul went outside of the city to attend a Jewish synagogue, but found none: 'on the Sabbath day we went outside the gate to a riverside, where we were supposing that there would be a place of prayer; and we sat down and began speaking to the women who had assembled'.⁴⁷ Bruce notes that this may imply that there were very few resident Jews in the city because it only took ten Jewish men to organize a synagogue.⁴⁸ Nevertheless, based upon Paul's search for a synagogue, Bruce seems to conclude that Lydia was a Jewish proselyte.⁴⁹ It seems that Codex D flips back and forth describing Lydia through the lens of the immediate context as a Jewish proselyte in 16.14 (σεβομένη τὸν κύριον) and through a broader lens as a Gentile, viewing Philippi as a place where Gentiles would live in 16.15 (εἰ κεκρίκατέ με πιστὴν τῷ θεῷ εἶναι). Witherington suggests that the term σεβομένη connotes Lydia as a

---

44. Codex B does not include the article τοῦ before Παύλου. In this sense, it comports with Codex D.

45. The term κύριον is found in D* and not in D, where θεόν is employed; see Ropes, *Text of Acts*, p. 155.

46. Epp does recognize that v. 14 is a difficulty to his view, but attempts to work his way around it when he says, 'If this difficulty is insurperable, then xvi.15 must be taken as the exception which proves the rule, or else must be considered a special, later reading of D' (*Theological Tendency*, p. 90). This argument reads as special pleading.

47. Acts 16.13 in the NASB.

48. F.F. Bruce. *The Book of Acts* (NICNT; Grand Rapids: Eerdmans, rev. edn, 1988), pp. 310-11 n. 37.

49. Bruce, *Book of Acts*, p. 359.

'Gentile who worships the biblical God', but offers no particular support based upon the terms for God as argued by Epp.[50]

Consequently, it appears that this particular textual variant does not offer any nuanced insight into Codex D's perspective on women. With either reading in 16.14 or 16.15, Lydia is viewed as a proselyte; more cannot be said.

3. *Textual Variant in Acts 16.15.* In Acts 16.15, Codex D adds to the narrative by placing the term 'all', πᾶς, before 'house' with the article, ὁ οἶκος.

N–A²⁷ (Vaticanus)	Codex D
ὡς δὲ ἐβαπτίσθη καὶ ὁ οἶκος αὐτῆς	ὡς δὲ ἐβαπτίσθη καὶ **πᾶς** ὁ οἶκος αὐτῆς

This seems to be a characteristic expansion by Codex D,[51] but the reason for the expansion is not clear. If Codex D was intending to minimize Lydia, one would not expect an expansion to identify her whole household as being baptized. The household probably included servants and children, although Witherington notes that baptism of a household may not have always included a commitment of faith by every member, since the head of a household often determined the religion of that household.[52] If that is the case, the addition by Codex D may have been an attempt to emphasize the *conversion of all* rather than the social alignment of all with the head of the house. If so, this may be a case where the expansion of Codex D compliments Lydia rather than detracts from her. It is also true that the expansion 'all' may not be an attempt by Codex D to say anything about Lydia, but to comment upon the effect of Paul's words on everyone in the household. Therefore, the theological significance of Codex D is indeterminate in this passage.

4. *Textual Variants in Acts 16.40.* The textual variants in Acts 16.40 may provide some slight insight into a concern for Codex D.

N–A²⁷ (Vaticanus)	Codex D
ἐξελθόντες δὲ ἀπὸ τῆς φυλακῆς εἰσῆλθον πρὸς τὴν Λυδίαν καὶ	ἐξελθόντες δὲ ἐκ τῆς φυλακῆς **ἦλθον** πρὸς τὴν Λυδίαν καὶ

50. Witherington, *Acts of the Apostles*, p. 493.
51. Metzger, *Textual Commentary*, p. 447.
52. Witherington, *Acts of the Apostles*, p. 493 n. 102.

ἰδόντες παρεκάλεσαν τοὺς	ἰδόντες τοὺς ἀδελφοὺς
ἀδελφοὺς καὶ ἐξῆλθαν.	διηγήσαντο ὅσα ἐποίησεν
	κύριος αὐτοῖς, παρεκαλέσαντες
	αὐτούς, καὶ ἐξῆλθαν.

Codex D first of all changes the verb in the first part of v. 40 from εἰσέρχομαι, conveying the sense of entering into the house,[53] to ἔρχομαι with the more generic sense of coming from one place to another.[54] This change may have been an attempt to protect the reputation of Paul and those with him by bringing him only up to Lydia's house, and not into her house. However, if this was a concern of Codex D, one wonders why there is not a variant reading at Acts 16.15 where Lydia urges the team to stay in her house (εἰσελθόντες εἰς τὸν οἶκόν μου μένετε), also using εἰσέρχομαι. Perhaps Codex D does not make the change in Acts 16.15 because the text emphasizes that Lydia prevailed upon them (παραβιάσατο ἡμᾶς), but in Acts 16.40, the team is coming to Lydia's house on their way out of prison and as they are departing the region, so the writer of Codex D emphasizes that they did not go into her home.

The second significant textual variant in this unit is the sentence, 'and they related the things that the Lord had done to them' (διηγήσαντο ὅσα ἐποίησεν κύριος αὐτοῖς). This expansion of Codex B's 'they encouraged the brethren' (παρεκάλεσαν τοὺς ἀδελφούς) is an attempt not only to identify the content of the team's encouragement, but to give the Lord the credit for their release from prison. Perhaps from reading 16.37-38 one might have the impression that Paul was the mastermind behind their deliverance; therefore Codex D inserts an amplification that identifies the mover behind their deliverance as the Lord, which provides encouragement to the brethren.

5. *Conclusion.* Unlike Codex D's expansion in Acts 1.14, the textual variants in Acts 16.14, 15, and 40 do not reveal a great deal about Codex

---

53. William Arndt, Frederick W. Danker, Walter Bauer, *A Greek–English Lexicon of the New Testament and Other Early Christian Literature* (Chicago: University of Chicago Press, 3rd edn, 2000) (further referred to as BDAG), *s.v.* εἰσέρχομαι p. 294; Johannes P. Louw and Eugene Albert Nida, *Greek–English Lexicon of the New Testament: Based on Semantic Domains* (New York: United Bible Societies, 2nd edn, 1996), I, p. 194.

54. BDAG, s.v. ἔρχομαι, p. 393; Louw and Nida, *Semantic Domains*, I, pp. 182, 192.

D's theological concern for women. In Acts 16.14, the writer seems to switch back and forth between κύριος and θεός so as to make the identity of Lydia as a Jewish or Gentile proselyte indeterminable. The expansion in Acts 16.15 to πᾶς ὁ οἶκος αὐτῆς may be an endorsement of Lydia, or of God's work of conversion through Paul; it is hard to know for sure. The change of the verb in Acts 16.40 from εἰσέρχομαι to ἔρχομαι may reflect an attempt to keep the team from entering Lydia's home, but if so, one wonders why the same verb was not changed in Acts 16.15. Finally, the addition to Acts 16.40 of διηγήσαντο ὅσα ἐποίησεν κύριος αὐτοῖς does seem to reflect a theological concern to give credit to the Lord for the team's deliverance, but this concern does not reflect directly on women. While the writer of Codex D appears to make expansions out of theological concerns, those discussed in this section offer little light on Codex D's view of women.

c. Acts 17.4, 12 (Prominent Women)

1. *The Context of Acts 17.4, 12.* Broadly speaking, the context of this unit was laid out in the outline above. In Acts 17.1-15, Paul followed his usual pattern of first reaching out to the Jews; then in Acts 17.16–18.7 he ministered to the Gentiles. Each broad unit includes a duality and balance. As Paul reached out to the Jews, the message was rejected by the Thessalonians (17.1-9), but accepted by the Bereans (17.10-15). Acts 17.1-9 describes the Jewish mission to the Thessalonians. Paul and Silas passed through Amphipolis and Apollonia, and came to Thessalonica where there was a Jewish synagogue, and where Paul argued for Jesus as Messiah from the Scriptures for three weeks. Acts 17.4 describes some of the positive fruit of Paul's mission as some were persuaded, including God-fearing Greeks and quite a few prominent women.

2. *Textual Variant in Acts 17.4.* The textual variant in Acts 17.4, centered upon the term γυνή, provides significant insight into the theological disposition of the writer of Codex D toward women.

N–A[27] (Vaticanus)	Codex D
καί τινες ἐξ αὐτῶν ἐπείσθησαν καὶ προσεκληρώθησαν τῷ Παύλῳ καὶ	καί τινες ἐξ αὐτῶν ἐπείσθησαν καὶ προσεκληρώθησαν τῷ Παύλῳ καὶ

[τῷ]⁵⁵ Σιλᾷ, τῶν τε σεβομένων   τῷ Σιλαίᾳ τῇ **διδαχῇ πολλοὶ**
Ἑλλήνων πλῆθος πολύ,⁵⁶ γυναικῶν   τῶν σεβομένων καὶ Ἑλλήνων
τε τῶν πρώτων οὐκ⁵⁷ ὀλίγαι.⁵⁸   πλῆθος πολύ, **καὶ γυναῖκες** τῶν
                                  πρώτων οὐκ ὀλίγαι.

The significant difference for this study between the two readings is that the Alexandrian text, γυναικῶν τε τῶν πρώτων, has the sense of 'prominent/leading women', whereas the text in Codex D, καὶ γυναῖκες τῶν πρώτων means 'wives of prominent/leading men'. Although the Alexandrian text (γυναικῶν τε τῶν πρώτων) could be translated as 'wives of the leading men' (since the genitive plural forms of πρῶτος for masculine and feminine look the same), Codex D καὶ γυναῖκες τῶν πρώτων, makes such a reading explicit by changing the case of γυνή from genitive, which agrees with πρώτων, to nominative, so that the genitive πρώτων specifically refers to men.⁵⁹ By making this change, Codex D has eliminated the possibility that the adjective πρώτων could refer to the women.⁶⁰ Although Ropes identifies Codex D as the 'better reading' because the Alexandrian text could easily have been altered for grammatical uniformity,⁶¹ Metzger prefers the reading in the Alexandrian text because of its manuscript support and because it is more likely that copyists would have replaced the connective τε with the more common καί.⁶²

Although the Alexandrian text is ambiguous, if γυναικῶν refers to 'women' rather than 'wives', the meaning would be significant. The term for 'prominent', πρῶτος, was used in the New Testament to describe people who were first, foremost, and most prominent in a social setting.⁶³ It was used to describe Peter as the 'first' among the apostles (Mt. 10.2), the 'first' one who will be 'last' in the future kingdom (Mt. 19.30), the 'leading' men among the people who were trying to destroy

---

55. Unlike Codex B, the N–A²⁷ includes the article τῷ before the proper noun Σιλᾷ.
56. The N–A²⁷ reads πολύ.
57. Codex B reads οὐχ.
58. Codex B reads ὀλίγαι.
59. See Culy and Parsons, *Acts*, p. 326.
60. Metzger, *Textual Commentary*, p. 453; Lake and Cadbury, *English Translation and Commentary*, p. 204; Witherington, 'Anti-Feminist Tendencies', p. 82.
61. Ropes, *Text of Acts*, p. 162.
62. Metzger, *Textual Commentary*, p. 453.
63. BDAG, s.v. πρῶτος, p. 893.

Jesus (Lk. 19.47), the 'leading' men of Galilee for whom Herod gave a banquet on his birthday (Mk 6.21), and the 'leading' men among the Jews who brought charges against Paul (Acts 25.2; see also Acts 28.17). Therefore, for πρῶτος to be applied to women is to identify them as those who are politically on a par with men in society—part of a social elite. Such a view also seems to comport with what was known about Macedonian women at this time.[64]

While it is possible that the scribe of Codex D was simply clarifying an ambiguous reading in Codex B, it is also possible that the change plays down the prominence of women. The motive behind this textual change may become clearer when a similar phrase appears in Acts 17.12 below.

3. *Textual Variant in Acts 17.12.* After the uproar by the Jews in Acts 17.5-9, the believers from Thessalonica sent Paul and Silas away by night to Berea, where they again went to a Jewish synagogue (Acts 17.10-11). As *Lukas* describes the identity of those who believed in Acts 17.12, a textual problem arises that is similar to the one found in Acts 17.4 above.

N–A²⁷ (Vaticanus)	Codex D
πολλοὶ μὲν οὖν ἐξ αὐτῶν ἐπίστευσαν καὶ τῶν Ἑλληνίδων γυναικῶν τῶν εὐσχημόνων καὶ ἀνδρῶν οὐκ ὀλίγοι.	τινὲς μὲν οὖν αὐτῶν ἐπίστευσαν, τινὲς δὲ ἠπίστησαν, καὶ τῶν Ἑλλήνων καὶ τῶν εὐσχημόνων ἄνδρες καὶ γυναῖκες ἱκανοὶ ἐπίστευσαν.

The difference between these readings is significant, and sheds light on what Codex D appeared to be doing in Acts 17.4. Whereas the Alexandrian text might be translated: 'Therefore many of them believed, along with a number of prominent Greek women and men',[65] the variant in Codex D can be translated: 'Some of them therefore believed, but some did not believe, and many of the Greeks, both men and women of the better class believed.'[66]

---

64. Bruce, *Book of Acts*, p. 323; Witherington, *Women in the Earliest Churches*, pp. 11-13.
65. NASB.
66. Bruce, *Book of Acts*, p. 326 n. 20. Ramsay translates Codex D more literally, but the sense is the same: 'And of the Greeks and of those of honourable estate, men and women in considerable numbers believed' (William M. Ramsay, *The Church in*

Everything is parsed 'more judiciously' in Codex D's alternative reading; Metzger identifies this as a smoothing out of the text so as to provide better Greek.[67] Instead of focusing upon *many* believing, Codex D states that *some* believed and adds that *some did not believe*.[68] But even more importantly for this study, Codex D switches the order from 'women and men' (γυναικῶν τῶν εὐσχημόνων καὶ ἀνδρῶν) to 'men and women' (τῶν εὐσχημόνων ἄνδρες καὶ γυναῖκες ἱκανοί) thereby reversing the priority given to women in the Alexandrian text.[69] This change in Acts 17.12 leads many commentators to interpret Codex D's alternative reading in Acts 17.4 to be more than a clarification of an ambiguous text; it is rather an intentional move to play down the importance of women.[70]

In both the Alexandrian text and Codex D, a strong adjective, εὐσχήμων, is used to describe these prominent women, meaning those who were 'especially worthy of public admiration, prominent, of high standing/repute, noble'[71] (see Acts 13.50). This is similar to Acts 17.4 where the adjective 'prominent' is employed (πρῶτος). Witherington suggests that εὐσχήμων probably refers to both men and women, but that placement of 'women' before the adjective (γυναικῶν τῶν εὐσχημόνων καὶ ἀνδρῶν) suggests that more women than men believed the message.[72] In any case, the order in the Alexandrian text

the Roman Empire before A.D. 170 [London: Hodder and Stoughton, 1897; repr. Grand Rapids: Baker, 1979], pp. 160-61).

67. Metzger, *Textual Commentary*, p. 454.

68. Concerning this expansion, Ramsay writes, 'Considering the mutual jealousy between Greeks of different districts which has characterized their history alike in ancient times and at the present day, we may here perhaps see that a native of Asia seizes the opportunity of emphasizing the fact that some disbelieved, whereas the received text merely says that "many of them believed"' (*The Church*, p. 160).

69. Bruce, *Book of Acts*, p. 326 n. 20; Metzger, *Textual Commentary*, p. 454.

70. Bruce, *Acts of the Apostles: Greek Text*, pp. 369, 374; Culy and Parsons, *Acts*, pp. 326, 330; Ropes describes the activity here and in Acts 18 as an '"antifeminist" tendency'. *Text of Acts*, p. ccxxxiv. Haenchen writes, 'The emphasis on noble women is here effaced' (*Acts of the Apostles,* p. 508 n. 5); Witherington, *Acts of the Apostles*, p. 509 n. 171; Conzelmann, *Acts of the Apostles*, p. 135; Ramsay writes, 'The omission [of Damaris in 17:34] may be compared with the change in the second part of xvii.12. The reason for both changes is the same: they are due to dislike to the prominence assigned to women in the accepted text' (Ramsay, *The Church*, p. 161).

71. BDAG, s.v. εὐσχήμων, p. 414.

72. Witherington, *Acts of the Apostles*, p. 509 n. 171.

does support priority of women over men. Just as a listing of the apostles emphasizes an order of importance (Mk 3.16-19), so listing women ahead of men suggests an order of importance. This theme of order and priority is one of which Codex D is aware, as will become more evident in the discussion of Priscilla and Aquila below in Acts 18.26.

4. *Conclusion*. The scribe(s) of Codex D demonstrates a much stronger theological bias against women in Acts 17.4 and Acts 17.12 than in Acts 16.14, 15, and 40. This bias seems to be more in line with the intention behind the variant in Acts 1.14. In Acts 17.4, Codex D turns what is, at most, an ambivalent text, into one where women are only the wives of leading men in the community. Even if that is the proper way of understanding the Alexandrian text, Bruce is right to emphasize that the initiative to believe was not their husbands' but theirs.[73] But the Alexandrian text allows for the women themselves to be the ones identified as prominent in society. Likewise, in Acts 17.12, the women are emphasized by being listing before the men, and before the adjective which describes them as socially prominent.[74] Codex D reduces their importance by placing them after the men with the adjective explicitly modifying both of them. On the other hand, by *Lukas*'s emphasis upon women, he contextually includes them in the group of those who 'received the word with great eagerness, examining the Scriptures daily to see whether these things were so',[75] thereby allowing them to study Scripture and emphasizing their freedom and prominence in this new gospel.[76]

These passages demonstrate a theological tendency of Codex D to flatten and deemphasize women as prominent players in *Lukas*'s story. They are present, but only in supporting roles as wives and/or alongside of, and subordinate to, men. These changes by Codex D only make the statements in favor of women by Codex B more forceful. *Lukas* sees women as prominent in society, and now in the new community being formed. They are not second-class citizens, but leaders among those following this new way of faith.

73. Bruce, *Book of Acts*, p. 323.
74. Witherington writes, 'Interestingly, in each passage it is the women, not the men, who are qualified by words indicating their importance or eminence' (*Women in the Earliest Churches*, p. 144).
75. NASB.
76. See Witherington, *Women in the Earliest Churches*, p. 144.

d. *Acts 17.34 (The Omission of Damaris)*

1. *The Context of Acts 17.34.* While Paul was in Athens waiting for Silas and Timothy, he became disturbed over the idolatry in the city. He began proclaiming the word of God in the synagogue and the market place, until at last he spoke before the Gentile philosophers at the Areopagus, where he urged a resistant people to repent from their idolatry and turn to the true God who is Creator and will one day judge the world through his vindicated Servant (Acts 17.16-31). The response to Paul's message was mixed, in that some mocked him, others wanted to hear more about his teaching some other day, and some believed (Acts 17.32-34). *Lukas* particularly identifies those who believed, included Dionysius the Areopagite, and a woman named Damaris (Acts 17.34).

2. *Textual Variant in Acts 17.34.* It is with the identification of women among those who believed in Paul's message that the textual problem in Codex D arises.

N–A²⁷ (Vaticanus)	Codex D
τινὲς δὲ ἄνδρες κολληθέντες αὐτῷ ἐπίστευσαν, ἐν οἷς καὶ Διονύσιος [ὁ]⁷⁷ Ἀρεοπαγίτης καὶ γυνὴ ὀνόματι Δάμαρις καὶ ἕτεροι σὺν αὐτοῖς.	τινὲς δὲ ἄνδρες ἐκολλήθησαν αὐτῷ, ἐπίστευσαν, ἐν οἷς καὶ Διονύσιός τις Ἀρεοπαγίτης **εὐσχήμων** καὶ ἕτεροι σὺν αὐτοῖς.

Although this textual variant may reveal Codex D's theological tendency against women, its transmission makes conclusions tentative. One might translate Codex B as: 'But some men joined him and believed, among whom also were Dionysius the Areopagite and a woman named Damaris and others with them.'⁷⁸ Metzger translates the significant changes in Codex D as 'among whom also was a *certain* Dionysius, *an* Areopagite of *high standing*, and others with them'.⁷⁹ In particular, Codex D omits 'and a woman named Damaris' (καὶ γυνὴ ὀνόματι Δάμαρις) and adds the adjective, 'prominent' or 'high standing' (εὐσχήμων).

Ramsay considers this omission to be deliberate, intentional, and another expression of the anti-feminist tendencies of Codex D,⁸⁰ while

77. N–A²⁷ includes the article, whereas it is excluded from Codex B.
78. NASB.
79. Metzger, *Textual Commentary*, p. 459.
80. Ramsay, *The Church*, p. 161; see also Witherington, 'Anti-Feminist Tendencies', p. 82; Witherington, *Acts of the Apostles*, p. 532 n. 262.

Ropes understands it as a mistaken attempt to do away with a gloss in Codex E of γυνη τιμια from *mulier honesta* in e.[81] Ropes also understands the adjective added in Codex D, εὐσχήμων, to be a survivor of the gloss,[82] while Metzger thinks a 'gallant scribe' added it after Δάμαρις, because the term is only used of women elsewhere in Acts (13.50; 17.12). He thinks the adjective was left in by a later scribe when he deleted the name Damaris.[83] Ramsay too argues that εὐσχήμων was added to the name of Damaris because of its use in Acts 13.50 and 17.12, but when the name Damaris was excised, the adjective remained in the wrong place as it now reads in Codex D.[84] Witherington argues that the textual evidence does not support so many textual emendations in D.[85] In the end, Cadbury abandons any claim to accurately reconstruct the history of εὐσχήμων in Codex D.[86]

If the deletion of καὶ γυνὴ ὀνόματι Δάμαρις in Codex D was a process of mistakes by a number of scribes, then it is not possible to impugn any theological bias to Codex D from this variant. But if the removal was intentional, there is a clear act to reduce the place of women in the text.[87] Any conclusions depend upon a reconstruction of the textual evidence. The heart of the problem in explaining Codex D as an intentional excision of the woman's name Damaris is the use of the adjective εὐσχήμων to modify Dionysius, since elsewhere in Acts the adjective is only used of women (13.40; 17.20). However, it is used of Joseph of Arimathaea, in Mk 15.43. The problem of the placement of

81. Ropes, *Text of Acts*, p. 170; see also Metzger, *Textual Commentary*, p. 459.

82. Ropes, *Text of Acts*, p. 170.

83. Metzger, *Textual Commentary*, pp. 459-60; Bruce seems to follow this reconstruction when he writes, 'The original form of the Western text perhaps described her as εὐσχήμων ("of honorable estate"), like the God-fearing Greek women of Beroea (v. 12)' (*Book of Acts*, p. 344 n. 98); see also Haenchen, *Acts of the Apostles*, p. 526 n. 5.

84. Ramsay, *The Church*, p. 161.

85. Witherington argues against Cadbury and Ramsay when he says, 'Only D omits the phrase καὶ γυνὴ ὀνόματι Δάμαρις, and only D inserts εὐσχήμων. If εὐσχήμων was original or even early and ascribed to Damaris, then there likely would be some other evidence that it was not simply D's addition' ('Anti-Feminist Tendencies', p. 82 n. 5).

86. Cadbury, in Lake and Cadbury, *English Translation and Commentary*, p. 220, says, 'It must be admitted that no more clumsy way could be found of saying that the converts included one woman, but I do not know the answer to any of these questions.'

87. Ramsay, *The Church*, p. 161.

εὐσχήμων in Codex D is that Dionysius has already been described with the prestigious title of Ἀρεοπαγίτης—as a member of the counsel or high court of the Areopagus.[88] Therefore one wonders why Codex D also calls him εὐσχήμων; this seems redundant.[89] Cadbury rings true when he says that the use of εὐσχήμων seems like a clumsy way to say that Damaris was present and has been deleted;[90] but the duplicative description of Dionysius is also problematic.

Therefore, the most one may be able to say on this problem is that it is indeterminate whether Codex D is showing a theological bias, since it is not clear whether the omission of Damaris was intentional. Witherington and Ramsay's strong assertions of D's anti-feminist bias in this passage[91] seem premature, since there is not enough evidence to satisfactorily explain the existence of the adjective εὐσχήμων in Codex D. Theories abound, but conclusions are only as strong as their underlying arguments.

On the positive side, the Alexandrian text does identify Damaris by name as one of the people[92] who joined and believed Paul. If Codex D's omission was intentional, it only highlights how *Lukas* in Codex B is emphasizing women as part of the new community that God is building through Paul. Alongside of men like Dionysius are women like Damaris, who are receiving the word about Christ and joining the Church—even in a Gentile land like Athens, where most scoff at God's wisdom.[93]

e. *Acts 18.2-3, 7, 26 (Priscilla and Aquila)*

1. *The Context of Acts 18.2-3.* In Acts 17.1-15, Paul followed his usual pattern of first reaching out to the Jews; then in Acts 17.16–18.7 he ministered to the Gentiles. We have just discussed the textual variants in the negative passage where Paul reached out to the Gentiles in Athens

88. BDAG, s.v. Ἀρεοπαγίτης, p. 129.
89. Metzger, *Textual Commentary*, p. 459.
90. Cadbury, in Lake and Cadbury, *English Translation and Commentary*, p. 220.
91. Ramsay, *The Church*, p. 161; Witherington, 'Anti-Feminist Tendencies', p. 82; Witherington, *Acts of the Apostles*, p. 532 n. 262.
92. The actual term is ἀνήρ which is usually translated as 'man' or 'husband'; but in light of the context which includes Damaris, it has more of the sense of ἄνθρωπος. BDAG offers the suggestion that, 'the term was probably chosen in anticipation of the contrasting γυνή (is Damaris the wife of one of the men?)', s.v. ἀνήρ, p. 79.
93. See Witherington's discussion of parallelism between one man and one female in this passage (*Women in the Earliest Churches*, pp. 143-44).

(17.16-34), now we move to those variants in the positive passage where Paul preached to the Corinthians (18.1-17). The first set of textual variants arises in Acts 18.1-5. The setting is after the event in Athens, when Paul went to Corinth, where he met a Jewish couple to live and work with, and proclaimed Jesus to the Jews and the Greeks.

2. *Textual Variants in Acts 18.2-3.* Although there are numerous textual variants involving Codex D in Acts 18, for the purpose of this study, I am only going to focus on those that relate to women. Acts 18.2-3 describes Paul's introduction to Aquila and Priscilla and reads as follows:

N-A²⁷ (Vaticanus)	Codex D
2 καὶ εὑρών τινα Ἰουδαῖον ὀνόματι Ἀκύλαν, Ποντικὸν τῷ γένει προσφάτως ἐληλυθότα ἀπὸ τῆς Ἰταλίας καὶ Πρίσκιλλαν γυναῖκα αὐτοῦ, διὰ τὸ διατεταχέναι <Κλαύδιον> χωρίζεσθαι πάντας τοὺς Ἰουδαίους ἀπὸ τῆς Ῥώμης, προσῆλθεν αὐτοῖς	2 καὶ εὑρών τινα Ἰουδαῖον ὀνόματι Ἀκύλαν, Ποντικὸν τῷ γένει προσφάτως ἐληλυθ<ότ>α ἀπὸ τῆς Ἰταλίας καὶ Πρίσκιλλαν γυναῖκα αὐτοῦ, διὰ το τεταχέναι Κλαύδιον χωρίζεσθαι πάντας Ἰουδαίους ἀπὸ τῆς Ῥώμης, οἳ καὶ κατῴκησαν εἰς τὴν Ἀχαίαν, προσῆλθεν αὐτῷ ὁ Παῦλος.
3 καὶ διὰ τὸ ὁμότεχνον εἶναι ἔμενεν παρ᾽ αὐτοῖς καὶ ἠργάζοντο·[94] ἦσαν γὰρ σκηνοποιοὶ τῇ τέχνῃ.	3 καὶ διὰ τὸ ὁμότεχνον ἔμενεν πρὸς αὐτούς, καὶ ἠργάζετο.

While there are numerous textual differences between the two codices, the significant variants in these verses are the following. In v. 2, Codex B reads, 'he [Paul] approached them [Aquila and Priscilla]' (προσῆλθεν αὐτοῖς), but Codex D reads, 'Paul approached him [Aquila]' (προσῆλθεν αὐτῷ ὁ Παῦλος). Although subtle, this change seems to focus upon Paul approaching the man and not the woman. This variant reflects the bias in Codex D to move women, in this case Priscilla, out of the center of the activity. Then in v. 3, Codex B reads, 'they were working' (ἠργάζοντο), using the third person plural imperfect of ἐργάζομαι, while Codex D says that only Paul worked (ἠργάζετο),

---

94. The N-A²⁷ actually follows Codex D here reading the third person singular, ἠργάζετο, unlike Codex B which reads the third person plural, ἠργάζοντο.

using the third person singular of ἐργάζομαι.⁹⁵ Codex D also deletes the phrase from Codex B 'for they were tent-makers by trade' (γὰρ σκηνοποιοὶ τῇ τέχνῃ).

These small changes all have the effect of removing Priscilla out of the reader's view. In this initial introduction, Priscilla is only identified as Aquila's wife (Πρίσκιλλαν γυναῖκα αὐτοῦ). Then in Codex D, Paul is not approaching 'them' as a couple, but only the man, Aquila. In addition, they (meaning Paul, Aquila and Priscilla) are not working their craft together, only Paul is working. And that is because they (Paul, Aquila, and Priscilla) do not even share a craft together as tentmakers. Instead of making Paul a partner with the husband-and-wife team of Aquila and Priscilla, Paul is described as working with a man, Aquila, who happens to also have a wife named Priscilla.

3. *Textual Variant in Acts 18.7.* After the introduction in Acts 18.1-3, the reader is told that Paul argued in the synagogue every Sabbath persuading Jews and Greeks (Acts 18.4). When Timothy and Silas joined Paul in Corinth, Paul spent all of his time proclaiming Jesus as the Christ to the Jews (Acts 18.5). However, when the Jews rejected Paul's teaching, he left the synagogue and went among those who believed his message. The particular identity of what it was that Paul left is the subject of the next textual variant in Acts 18.7.

N–A²⁷ (Vaticanus)	Codex D
καὶ μεταβὰς ἐκεῖθεν, ἦλθεν⁹⁶ εἰς οἰκίαν τινὸς ὀνόματι Τιτίου Ἰούστου σεβομένου τὸν θεόν, οὗ ἡ οἰκία ἦν συνομοροῦσα τῇ συναγωγῇ.	μεταβὰς [δὲ ἀπὸ Ἀκύ]λα [εἰσ]ῆλθεν εἰς τὸν [ο]ἶ[κό]ν τινος ὀνόματι Ἰούστου σεβομένου τὸν θεόν, οὗ ἡ οἰκία ἦν συνομοροῦσα τῇ συναγωγῇ.

Although there are a number of textual variants between the two codices in Acts 18.7, the one of significance for this study is the expansion in Codex D that states that Paul moved from Aquila to the house of Justus (μεταβὰς [δὲ ἀπὸ Ἀκύ]λα [εἰσ]ῆλθεν εἰς τὸν [ο]ἶ[κό]ν τινος ὀνόματι Ἰούστου). Beyond the fact that it is unlikely that the Jewish

---

95. Again, note that N–A²⁷ actually follows Codex D here reading the third person singular of the imperfect, ἠργάζετο, unlike Codex B which reads the third person plural, ἠργάζοντο.

96. Although the N–A²⁷ reads εἰσῆλθεν from εἰσέρχομαι following D*, Codex B employs the verb ἦλθεν from ἔρχομαι.

opposition would have caused Paul to change his place of residence[97] rather than his location of teaching,[98] the text in Codex D also implies that the house that Paul is going from is not Aquila and Pricilla's house, but only Aquila's. Once again, the woman, Priscilla, is removed from the scene.

3. *Textual Variant in Acts 18.26.* After Paul stood before Gallio, he stayed longer in Corinth and then left with Priscilla and Aquila for Syria (Acts 18.18a). At Cenchreae, Paul had his hair cut to end a personal vow (18.18b), arrived in Ephesus, and then left Aquila and Priscilla there as he departed for Caesarea (18.19-23).[99] The final textual variant of interest in this paper occurs in the report that Priscilla and Aquila met and instructed a gifted Alexandrian Jew named Apollos. They instructed him concerning all of the truth about Jesus, whereupon he was sent to Corinth to help the brethren in their public debates with the Jews about Jesus as Messiah. Of particular interest is the transposition of words that occurs in Acts 18.26:

N–A²⁷ (Vaticanus)	Codex D
οὑτός τε ἤρξατο παρρησιάζεσθαι ἐν τῇ συναγωγῇ. ἀκούσαντες δὲ αὐτοῦ Πρίσκιλλα καὶ Ἀκύλας προσελάβοντο αὐτὸν καὶ ἀκρειβέστερον,[100] αὐτῷ ἐξέθεντο τὴν ὁδὸν τοῦ θεοῦ.	οὑτος ἤρξατο παρ<ρ>ησιάζεσθαι ἐν συναγωγῇ. καὶ ἀκούσαντες δὲ αὐτοῦ Ἀκύλας καὶ Πρίσκιλλα προσελάβοντο αὐτὸν καὶ ἀκριβέστερον αὐτῷ ἐξέθεντο τὴν ὁδόν.

The primary textual variant in Acts 18.26 is the reversal of Priscilla and Aquila in Codex B (Πρίσκιλλα καὶ Ἀκύλας) to Aquila and Priscilla in Codex D (Ἀκύλας καὶ Πρίσκιλλα). One might argue that the meaning is the same regardless of the order of the names, since they were both involved in teaching Apollos, but the fact that Codex D changes the order of the names gives support to the idea that order is significant. Priority is often communicated by the order in which names are given in the New

---

97. See Metzger, *Textual Commentary*, p. 462; Bruce, *Acts of the Apostles: The Greek Text*, p. 393; Bruce, *Book of Acts*, p. 349 n. 19.

98. Conzelmann, *Acts of the Apostles*, p. 152.

99. It is interesting that the text in 614 (sy^p.hmg) on Acts 18.22 only describes Aquila as being left behind in Ephesus when Paul went to Caesarea: τὸν δὲ Ἀκύλαν εἴασεν ἐν Ἐφέσῳ αὐτός δὲ ἀνενέχθεις ἦλθεν εἰς Καισάρειαν.

100. The N–A²⁷ reads ἀκριβέστερον with Codex D.

Testament. For instance, in the naming of the apostles, Peter is named first and then called 'first', πρῶτος, among the apostles (see Mk 3.16-19; Mt. 10.2-4.). For Priscilla to be mentioned first implies that she was the one who was primary of the two.[101] Therefore, Codex D's inversion of the names is an intentional re-ordering of importance, placing the man first. Once again, this appears to be an intentional choice by Codex D to reduce the prominence of Priscilla.[102]

In addition, Priscilla's more prominent role is in the realm of teaching, and in particular in teaching someone who was a prominent male evangelist. Apollos is described as an eloquent speaker (ἀνὴρ λόγιος), powerful with the Scriptures (δυνατὸς ὢν ἐν ταῖς γραφαῖς), and instructed in the way of the Lord (οὗτος ἦν κατηχημένος τὴν ὁδὸν τοῦ κυρίου). Evidently, Apollos was familiar with the baptism of John, but not of the Spirit (Acts 18.25). Conzelmann suggests that the teaching by Priscilla and Aquila comprised everything from Acts 2 onward.[103] One thing is certain, Priscilla and Aquila taught him the way of God (ἐξέθεντο τὴν ὁδὸν τοῦ θεοῦ). By painting Priscilla in a prominent role as a teacher with her husband, *Lukas* was providing another model of women in leadership who stand shoulder-to-shoulder with men.[104]

5. *Conclusion.* Acts 18 provides abundant evidence that the writer of Codex D has a theological bias against women. In Acts 18.2-3, after introducing Pricilla as the wife of Aquila, he removes her from any discussion of the tent-making work that Paul did with Aquila. In Acts 18.7, Codex D inserts a phrase that not only misunderstands Paul's movement from one teaching location to another, but in the process

---

101. Haenchen describes her as 'particularly active' (*Acts of the Apostles*, p. 550 n. 11).

102. Commenting on D's interchange of names, Ropes rightly observes, 'The desire to reduce the prominence of Priscilla seems to have been at work in a number of places in this chapter. The original writer appears never to have mentioned Aquila without Priscilla, and always (except at the first introduction, vs. 2) put Priscilla's name first; the glossator departs from him in both respects. Only in vs. 18, where κειράμενος was interpreted of Aquila (cf. h) does the "Western" reviser fail to put the husband first' (*Text of Acts,* p. 178). Along this line, see Metzger, *Textual Commentary*, pp. 466-67.

103. 'Perhaps Luke understood the matter in this fashion: Apollos knew the material of the "gospel" (as far as Luke 24), but not the events from Acts 2 and on' (Conzelmann, *Acts of the Apostles*, p. 158).

104. Witherington, *Women in the Earliest Churches*, p. 567 n. 22.

makes the home only Aquila's by not even mentioning Priscilla. Finally, in Acts 18.26, Codex D inverts the order of names from Priscilla and Aquila so that the man has the appearance of taking the lead in teaching Apollos. Unlike some of the earlier examples, these textual variants strongly affirm the writer's intention to reduce any prominence given to women in the Alexandrian text.

3. Conclusion

Sometimes a light does not seem to shine very brightly until it is placed in stark relief against a dark sky. So it is that this paper has sought to highlight some of *Lukas*'s portrayals of women in Acts against alterations made in Codex D. Not every textual variant clearly demonstrates a theological perspective. The intent of some changes is not always evident, due to problems with the transmission of the text, or ambivalent readings in Codex D. But where intent is clear, so is a predisposition against women. Thus Codex D provides a window into theological thought about women in the early Church.

An additional benefit of this study is that it highlights the strong view of women contained in the Alexandrian text of Acts. *Lukas* portrays women as co-participants in the ministry of the first-century Church. They are not depicted separately from men as women blazing new trails on their own; but within the sensitivities of a first-century culture, they are portrayed as co-workers with men, placed alongside their male counterparts in the spiritual work of the ministry. They are present, in their own right, in the upper room, waiting for the promise of the Spirit along with the apostles. They are prominent in society, and prominent in the new community being formed. They are not second-class citizens, but leaders among those following this new way of faith. They are teachers of teachers, who are having an impact on the Christian movement from the very top.

This study demonstrates the value of textual criticism beyond the task of identifying the most probable reading of a text. By examining textual variants, the reader gains insight into theological tensions in the earliest Church. In addition, by examining the theologically motivated variants regarding women in Codex D, positive pictures of women are highlighted in Codex B.

CHAPTER V

NARRATIVE LOGIC AND THE "SIGN-SERMON" PATTERN IN ACTS

Introduction

Although not as developed as Robert Alter's "type scenes,"[1] the author of Acts uses a convention of typological symbolism which this writer identifies as a sign-sermon pattern to unify smaller units and develop narrative logic. Its source may well reach back into Hebrew, emblematic parallelism where the author uses images to convey the poetic meaning. While one line conveys the main point in a direct fashion, the second line illuminates it by an image. There is a movement from point to picture or picture to point (*see* Ps. 23:1, 2, 4; 103:13; 113:5, 6; 57:1).[2]

This poetic device was artfully applied to miracles that were joined with other narratives in the Hebrew and Greek Scriptures.[3] As Raymond Brown observes, "miracles are important external signs of revelation."[4] Revelation seems to be precisely the function of miracles, but not in terms of expressing new content as in affirming, in almost an existential sense, the truth expressed in the sermon (whether it precedes or follows the sign). Raymond Brown touches upon this when he says that the sign had a prophetic, symbolic action in that, "[t]he sign performed by the prophet (e.g., Is. 20,3) was important only in what it graphically portrayed, e.g., God's coming judgment, or God's intervention."[5] This correlation of sign to sermon can be seen in a brief examination of several passages.

Genesis 9

After the floodwaters had receded and Noah scarified a thank offering (Gen 8), God blessed Noah and covenanted never to destroy the earth again by flood (Gen 9:8-11).

---

[1] Robert Alter, *The Art of Biblical Narrative* (New York: Basic Books, Inc., Publishers, 1981), 47-62.

[2] *See* Allen P. Ross, *Commentary on the Psalms* (vol. 1, 3 vols.; Grand Rapids, MI: Kregel Publications, 2011), 88.

[3] Kurz affirms that "inserting speeches to explain the meaning of the events they accompany" is a common pattern in both Greco-Roman and biblical narratives. William S. Kurz, *Reading Luke-Acts: Dynamics of Biblical Narrative* (1st ed.; Louisville, KY: Westminster/John Knox Press, 1993), 78.

[4] Raymond Edward Brown, "Gospel Miracles," in *Bible in Current Catholic Thought* (New York: Herder & Herder, 1962), 185.

[5] *Ibid.*, 199.

He then gave a sign of the covenant in his "bow" which was to be seen in the cloud (Gen 9:12-17). This sign graphically portrayed the message (covenant) in that it was called a קֶשֶׁת which referred to a hunter's bow as in Genesis 27:3; 48:22.[6] As a picture of God's promise never to destroy the earth again by water, he hung his weapon in the sky.

Jeremiah 13 and 19

Though neither of these events are "miracles," they are signs to support the prophet's messages of judgment to Judah.

In Jeremiah 13 the form is "sign-sermon." Jeremiah was told by the Lord to purchase a new waistband, wear it and place it among the rocks along the Euphrates. Then Jeremiah was told to dig it up. It was naturally ruined and totally worthless (Jer. 13:1-7). The Lord compared Judah to the waistband in that they were to cling to God as a waistband clings to a waist; but since they did not, God would destroy them because they went after other gods (symbolized by placing the band along the Euphrates) and became totally worthless (Jer. 13:8-11).[7] Although the sign was given first, its significance was not ascertained until the sermon was spoken. It was the sermon that contained the revelation; the sign provided an emotional illustration.

In Jeremiah 19, the form is "sermon-sign-sermon." Verses 1-9 proclaimed the destruction of the nation. Jeremiah was then told to break a jar in verse 10. He consequently proclaimed that the destruction of Judah would be a shattering which could not be repaired (11-13).[8] Once again the supportive nature of the sign is seen in terms of its emotional confirmation of the message.

---

[6]Francis A. Brown, S. R. Driver, and Charles A. Briggs, *A Hebrew and English Lexicon of the Old Testament* (BDB), 1959 reprint ed., s.v. "קֶשֶׁת", 905-906; see also Allen P. Ross, *Creation and Blessing: A Guide to the Study and Exposition of the Book of Genesis* (Grand Rapids, MI: Baker Book House, 1988), 206; Bruce K. Waltke and Cathi J. Fredricks, *Genesis: A Commentary* (First Edition; Grand Rapids, MI: Zondervan, 2001), 146; Gerhard Von Rad, *Genesis* (Revised edition.; Philadelphia: Westminster John Knox Press, n.d.), 134; Nahum M. Sarna, *JPS Torah Commentary: Genesis* (1st edition.; Philadelphia: The Jewish Publication Society, 2001), 63.

[7] Robert B. Chisholm, *Handbook on the Prophets: Isaiah, Jeremiah, Lamentations, Ezekiel, Daniel, Minor Prophets* (Grand Rapids, MI: Baker Academic, 2002), 171; J. A. Thompson, *The Book of Jeremiah* (The New international commentary on the Old Testament; Grand Rapids, MI: Eerdmans, 1980), 365.

[8] See Chisholm, *Handbook on the Prophets*, 177–178; Thompson, *The Book of Jeremiah*, 445, 452.

Hosea

It is common knowledge that the first half of Hosea is built around the "sign-sermon" motif. From the start Yahweh tells Hosea that his wife is a symbol of the relationship that the northern kingdom has with Yahweh (Hos. 1:1–2:1).[9] Then using the figure of a faithless wife, Yahweh indicts the northern kingdom for its faithlessness against Him (Hos. 2:2-23). Finally, Hosea's redemption of Gomer is symbolic of Yahweh's redemption of Israel (Hos. 3:1-5). This interweaving of the sign with the sermon provides an emotional charge to the revelation of the prophet and is central to revealing the heart of God's work for the nation.

The Gospels

Although contained in a single pericope, Jesus' healing of the paralytic in Luke 5:17-26 (= Mk. 2:1-12 = Matt. 9:1-8) provides a concise, gospel example of a miracle designed to picture the words of Jesus. At first Jesus does not heal the lame man, but proclaims that his sins are forgiven (a sermon, Lk. 5:20). But when the scribes and Pharisees reason that Jesus is blaspheming because only God can forgive sins (Lk. 5:21), Jesus heals the man as a sign in the physical realm that confirms his words in the spiritual realm, when he says, "Which is easier, to say, 'Your sins have been forgiven you,' or to say, 'Rise and walk'? But in order that you may know that the Son of Man has authority on earth to forgive sins,' –He said to the paralytic- 'I say to you, rise, and take up your stretcher and go home.'" (Lk. 5:22-24, NASB). Throughout Acts, and most of the New Testament, the lame function as a physical metaphor for the spiritual condition of a contextual people (cf. John 5:1-9; Acts 9:32-34). The dead will also play a similar role in Acts (9:36-42; 20:6-12).[10]

This particular study will examine the use of the sign-sermon pattern as a literary technique Luke employs to unify smaller units and develop narrative logic in four passages: (1) Acts 3:1-26; (2) Acts 9:32—10:48; (3) Acts 13:4-14:20; and (4) Acts 20:1-38.[11]

---

[9] See Chisholm, *Handbook on the Prophets*, 336; Hans Walter Wolff, *Hosea: A Commentary on the Book of the Prophet Hosea* (Philadelphia, PA: Fortress Press, 1973), 16, 23.

[10] This paper has utilized an example from the Gospel of Luke because of the literary connection between Luke and Acts. However, in the Gospel of John, all miracles are specifically identified as "signs" (σημεῖον) (*see* Jn. 2:11, 23; 3:2; 4:54; 6:2, 14, 26; 7:31; 9:16; 11:47; 12:18, 37; 20:30).

[11] These are not the only passages in Acts where the sign-sermon technique is employed (see also Acts 2:1-36 for example). Nevertheless, these passages have been chosen because they provide either concise, clear examples of the literary technique, or because a recognition of the technique brings clarity to the narrative as in Acts 20:1-38.

The Healing of the Lame Man in Acts 3:1-26

The book of Acts begins with a prologue (Acts 1:1-2),[12] a programmatic prelude (Acts 1:3-14),[13] and the book's first major panel where the promise of the Father is prepared for, received, and presented as forming a people distinct from Israel through whom God is applying and offering the salvific benefits of Jesus' Messiahship to all people—especially Israel (1:15—2:47).[14] Now the Twelve (represented here by Peter and John)[15] begin to

---

[12] Some biblical literary critics combine Acts 1:1-2 and 1:3-14 into a single unit of 1:1-14 (or 1:1-11) because of similar themes, audience (the Twelve) and the smooth transition of the prologue into verses 3 and following. C. K. Barrett, *The Acts of the Apostles: Vol. 1: Preliminary Introduction and Commentary on Acts I-XIV.* (New York: T & T Clark, Ltd.) 57, 71-90. D. W. Palmer, "The Literary Background of Acts 1:1-4," *New Testament Studies* 33 (1987): 427, n. 1 (who nevertheless recognizes the prologue as a distinct literary form); Robert C Tannehill, *The Narrative Unity of Luke-Acts: A Literary Interpretation: Volume 2: The Acts of the Apostles* (Minneapolis: Fortress Press, 1990), 9-25; Joseph Rius-Camps and Jenny Read-Heimerdinger, *The Message of Acts in Codex Bezae: A Comparison with the Alexandrian Tradition.* Vol. 1: Acts 1.1—5.42: Jerusalem (New York: T&T Clark International, 2004), 45-47; Darrell L. Bock, *Acts,* Baker Exegetical Commentary on the New Testament (Grand Rapids: Baker Academic, 2007), 46, 49-71; Craig S. Keener, *Acts: An Exegetical Commentary: Volume 1: Introduction and 1:1-247* (vol. 1, Har/Com edition.; Baker Academic, 2012), 646.

Nevertheless, the complex nature of the single, Greek sentence in Acts 1:1-2 is reminiscent of Luke 1:1-4; therefore, it may be better to distinguish between the units of 1:1-2 and 1:3-14 (or 3-11). *See* F. Blass, A. Debrunner, and Robert W. Funk, *A Greek Grammar of the New Testament and Other Early Christian Literature: A Translation and Revision of the ninth-tenth German edition incorporating supplementary notes of A. Debrunner* (Chicago: The University of Chicago Press, 1961), § 464; Joseph A. Fitzmyer, *The Gospel According to Luke (I-IX): Introduction, Translation, and Notes,* The Anchor Bible, Volume 28 (Garden City, NY, Doubleday & Company, Inc., 1981), 288; Philip E. Satterthwaite, "Acts against the Background of Classical Rhetoric," in *The Book of Acts in Its First Century Setting,* vol. 1, *The Book of Acts in Its Ancient Literary Setting,* ed. Bruce W. Winter and Andrew D. Clarke (Grand Rapids: William B. Eerdmans Publishing Company, 1993), 353; Hans Conzelmann, *Acts of the Apostles,* trans. James Limburg, A. Thomas Kraabel, and Donald H. Juel, Hermeneia (Philadelphia: Fortress Press, 1987), 3-4; Loveday Alexander, *The Preface of Luke's Gospel: Literary Convention and Social Context in Luke 1.1-4 and Acts 1.1.* SNTS Monographs 78 (Cambridge: Cambridge University Press, 1993), 102-146; Charles H. Talbert, *Reading Acts: A Literary and Theological Commentary on the Acts of the Apostles* (New York: Crossroad Publishing Company, 1997), 19; Robert W. Wall, "The Acts of the Apostles: Introduction, Commentary, and Reflections," in *The New Interpreter's Bible: A Commentary in Twelve Volumes,* vol. 10 (Nashville: Abingdon Press, 2002), 35, 37 n.51: Craig S. Keener, *Acts An Exegetical Commentary,* vol. 1, *Introduction and 1:1—2:47* (Grand Rapids: Baker Academic 2012), 579, 649.

[13] Kurz understands Acts 2–3 to function in the book like the first two chapters in the Gospel of Luke and the prologue in the Gospel of John. Kurz, *Reading Luke-Acts,* 80. However, by delaying the programmatic chapters until chapter 2, Kurz seems to break the typical pattern of both of his examples. Therefore, while it is true that themes exist in Acts 2–3 which are further developed in the book, they first arise in the prologue and programmatic prelude.

[14] *See* Satterthwaite, "Acts against the Background of Classical Rhetoric," in *The Book of Acts in Its First Century Setting,* 1:353-54; Keener, *Acts An Exegetical Commentary,* 577.

[15] Peter may be the focal point of the action but John is always nearby as a second witness who authenticates the testimony of Peter (cf. Acts 4:19-20; Luke 21:12-13) and represents the Twelve. Leo O'Reilly, *Word and Sign in the Acts of the Apostles: A Study in Lucan Theology.* (Roma: Editrice Pontifica

bare effective testimony of Jesus to Israel. This is accomplished through the literary technique of a sign-sermon.[16] The sign consists of healing a lame man at the Beautiful Gate[17] (3:1-11) and the related sermon to Israel is in 3:11-26. Together they comprise the message of the unit as Leo O'Reilly states:

The miracles are not just incidental to the message of salvation; they form a constitutive part of that message itself. Simply by taking place they announce the arrival of the messianic age, the near approach of the Kingdom of God. Then the power of Satan and sin, symbolized by disease and demonic possession, will be broken and the ruptured relations between God and man will begin to be restored. The new community of the saved begins to take shape.[18]

The Sign (3:1-11)

This unit provides a seamless union with the summary statement that precedes it. As Mikeal Parsons writes, "The opening verses (3:1-2) particularize the general description of the community of believers found in the preceding narrative summary."[19]

Universita Gregoriiana 1987), 124; Ernst Haenchen, *The Acts of the Apostles: A Commentary* (Philadelphia: Translated by Bernard Noble and Gerald Shin from the 14th German edition [1965]. The Westminster Press, 1971), 201-202. In addition Jesus had recommended that his messengers go out in pairs (Luke 10:1); this pattern is thus repeated throughout Acts here with Peter and John and later with Barnabas and Paul, and Paul and Silas. Kurz, *Reading Luke-Acts*, 79; see also Bock, *Acts,* 159 n. 2.

Interestingly, Talbert argues for a double witness in the literary structure of the unit: "the 'sign + speech' pattern provides the testimony of the two witnesses necessary under Jewish law to guarantee truthfulness (Deut 19:15; John 8:17): apostles and Holy Spirit (5:32)." Talbert, *Reading Acts*, 52, 53.

[16]Talbert affirms that the healing of the lame man is the first example of the "signs and wonders" alluded to in the summary of Acts 2:43 (cf. 4:30; 5:12). *Ibid.,* 50. Actually, the miracle in Acts 3:1-11 is called a "sign" (σημεῖον) by the council in Acts 4:16 and the narrator in Acts 4:22. Concerning the placement of these terms, O'Reilly observes: "This designation clearly refers to the miracle as it has been interpreted throughout the whole section rather than simply to the healing as an extraordinary phenomenon. Once again ... Luke allows us to experience the reality of the 'sign' in all its dimensions in his narrative before formally designating it as such. It is only when he has already in various ways pointed out the miracle's *sign*ificance that he can encapsulate this verbally in the word *sêmion*. O'Reilly, *Word and Sign,* 158.

[17] This may have been the eastern gate or the Nicanor Gate. See discussion by Keener, *Acts* II, 1048-49.

[18] O'Reilly, *Word and Sign,* 147, see also 194-97. Not all seem to view such a close connection between the miracle and the message. Bock identifies some broad correlation between the miracle and the sermon but focuses upon each pericope in a more distinct way as he divides the discussions into separate chapters in his commentary. Bock, *Acts,*158-83. Nevertheless, he does affirm the connection through the word play of σῴζω in Acts 4:9 and 4:12. *Acts,* 192; see also Barrett, *The Acts,* I:175.

[19] Mikeal C. Parsons, "Christian Origins and Narrative Openings: The Sense of a Beginning in Acts 1–5," *Review and Expositor* 87 (1990): 411. Similarly, Wall correlates this unit with the broader Pentecost narrative: "The first story of the Jerusalem mission begins abruptly. The literary pattern and

The two units hold several concepts in common: (1) signs, (2) community property (thus Peter and John have no silver or gold), and (3) attendance at the temple. Luke has linked this next unit with the preceding description of the new covenant community.

The linear structure of this unit might well be: a statement of the problem (a lame man) 3:1-2, a description of the cure (the miracle) 3:4-8, and the reactions of the people in 3:9-11.[20] However, the broader argument is visible by discussing the literary function of the unit. Throughout Acts and much of the Gospels the lame function as a physical metaphor for the spiritual condition of a contextual people (cf. John 5:1-9; Luke 5:17-26; Acts 9:32-34). The dead also play a similar role in Acts (9:36-42; 20:6-12). This sign pictures, in the physical realm, the spiritual salvation experience that Peter will proclaim for Israel in chapter 3.[21] It was natural for First Century readers to look at remarkable events as omens from the gods (cf. Luke 23:44-47).[22] The miracle offers symbolic elements which transfer to the sermon which follows.[23]

---

images recall the earlier story of Pentecost, suggesting that the two should be read together reflexively, the one expanding the meaning of the other." Wall, "The Acts of the Apostles," 76; see also Craig S. Keener, "This account thus becomes a dramatic example of the summary that precedes it. . . . Peter's lack of silver (3:6) illustrates the sacrificial lives of those serving the Lord in 2:44-45. . . . Most clearly, this event illustrates the continuing apostolic signs (2:43) and is a particularly dramatic case of continuing conversations (2:47; 4:4)." *Acts: An Exegetical Commentary 3:1—14:28*. Vol. 2 (Grand Rapids: Baker Academic, 2013), 1042.

[20] Talbert, *Reading Acts*, 52.

[21] As Wall observes: "Healing miracles are 'enacted parables' of the manner or experience of God's saving grace. For this reason, Luke sometimes uses the verb "to save" for 'to heal" (see Luke 7:50; 8:36, 48, 50; Acts 4:9; 14:9)." Wall, "The Acts of the Apostles," 85. The explicit connection is actually found later in the first confrontation narrative of Acts 4:9-12. Haenchen writes that the miracle "paves the way not only for the following speech by Peter, linked to the healing, but also for the consequent arrest and inquisition. For at the trial Peter, by referring to the healed cripple, will be able to declare impressively that only in the name of Jesus is σωτηρία given to men (4.12)." Haenchen, *The Acts*, 202. Likewise, O'Reilly writes that this is a sign of messianic salvation. "It is a partial and individual realization of the salvation of which Peter speaks in 4,12, and this is a salvation which embraces the whole man in his physical and spiritual dimensions and which is offered to all men. The miracle is a striking proclamation of the message of salvation in concrete terms, it is a sign which points forcefully to the reality of salvation which is the content of the apostolic preaching." O'Reilly, *Word and Sign*, 159.

[22] Haenchen, *The Acts*, 202.

[23] O'Reilly writes, "We shall see that the healing is a sign of salvation and that it bears witness to the power of the word to effect the salvation which it proclaims." O'Reilly, *Word and Sign*, 88. Bock writes: "the miracle is a visual act that points to a deeper reality." *Acts*, 158. M. Dennis Hamm asserts, "Indeed, not only is the healing the *occasion* of the speeches, but the healed man's physical presence is a dramatic part of the narrative and becomes, as it were, part of the dialogue (3,11; 4,10.14)." "Acts 3, 1-10: The Healing of the Temple Beggar as Lucan Theology," *Biblica Roma* 67:3 (1986): 305.

Note the parallels between the healing of the lame man in Acts 3 and the lame man in John 5:[24]

John 5	Acts 3
Jesus	Peter
Sick (paralytic)	Lame from birth
Certain man	Certain man
Man looks for help	Man looks for help (money)
Healed by command	Healed by command
Immediately well	Immediately well
Man goes into the temple	Man goes into the temple
The man separates himself from Jesus	The man clings to John and Peter
The leaders respond negatively	The people respond positively
Jesus speaks pointing to himself	Peter speaks pointing to Jesus
Jesus is persecuted	Peter and John are arrested
(Response – not given)	Many people believe

Much like a type-scene,[25] the healing of a lame man causes the reader to look for the related spiritual significance in another contextual group. In John 5 the contextual group was unbelieving Jews. In Acts 3 the contextual group is believing Jews in the temple. In John 5 the man that was healed became the transition to unbelieving Jews as he separated from Jesus and betrayed him to the Jews (John 5:10-15). In Acts 3 the man that was healed became the transition to believing Jews as he clung to John and Peter,[26] and the people responded well (Acts 3:9-11). The differences that arise in the two scenes are the clues to the meaning of the miracle. In John 5 the Jews were like the lame man–they had no faith

---

[24] This correlation of Acts 3 with John 5 demonstrates that New Testament writers were familiar with using the metaphor of a physical healing of the lame to picture the spiritual condition or opportunity of another people in the narrative. O'Reilly provides a similar discussion comparing the miracle in Acts 3 to the account in Luke 5:17-26 and Acts 14:8-11. A repeated pattern by Jesus, Peter, and Paul emphasizes continuity for the reader in Peter and Paul's teaching with the message of Jesus. O'Reilly, *Word and Sign*, 129-34.

[25] Alter, *Art of Biblical Narrative*, 47-62.

[26] Ben Witherington, III, overlooks this significance when he writes, "The man who was healed clung to Peter and John as they moved to Solomon's portico, and it may be that we are meant to see this move as an attempt to avoid too much attention being focused on the miracle." *The Acts of the Apostles: A Socio-Rhetorical Commentary* (Grand Rapids: William B. Eerdmans Publishing Company, 1998), 179.

and rejected the work of Jesus. In Acts 3 the people were like the lame man–they accepted God's work and had faith (4:4). The miracles are meant to be tied to the sermons (discourses) that follow them.[27]

Comparisons between the man and the people are significant. The man is lame. In the Hebrew Scriptures, "walking" symbolizes a moral lifestyle (Psalm 1:1),[28] and the setting of Acts 3 is very Jewish. The beggar's condition appears to represent the nation's inability to walk with God. Israel is lame.[29] The man in Acts 3 is a beggar in need of physical grace,[30] so too the nation is in need of spiritual grace.[31] The beggar is outside of the temple suggesting that the nation, though injured and impoverished sits at the threshold of the kingdom of God.[32] After being healed, the beggar enters the temple leaping (ἐξαλλόμενος) and praising God. (*See* the LXX of Isaiah 35:6, "Then shall the lame one leap (ἄλλομαι) as a deer.")[33] This suggests the arrival of the Messianic salvation which Peter is about to offer

---

[27] Kurz also sees the interdependence of miracles and accompanied explanatory speeches. *Reading Luke-Acts*, 78-79.

[28] Commenting on the verb "walks" in Psalm 1:1, Allen P. Ross states: "The first [verb] is 'walks' (הָלַךְ, an implied comparison that becomes an idiom), which signifies how one lives, whether morally and ethically or not; here it would refer to living according to the advice of the ungodly." Ross, *Commentary on the Psalms*. 1:187.

[29] The correlation of the salvation of the lame man with the salvation of Israel is more explicitly made in Acts 4:9-12 where the lame man's salvation is offered to the leaders of Israel. See also Bede the Venerable who identified Israel with the lame man in his *Commentary on the Acts of the Apostles* 3.2A, in *Acts,* Ancient Christian Commentary, vol. V, ed. Francis Martin (Downers Grove: Intervarsity Press, 2006), 39; Mikael C. Parsons also notices the symbolic nature of this miracle when he writes: "Just as the blind man who sees in John 9 is the ideal disciple in the Fourth Gospel where believing is symbolized as a kind of seeing, so the lame man who walks of Acts 3 is the symbol of salvation in a story where journey narratives occupy much narrative space, and where the Christian movement is referred to simply as the 'Way' (see 9:2; 19:9, 23; 22:4; 24:14, 22)." Parsons, "Christian Origins and Narrative Openings: The Sense of a Beginning in Acts 1—5," *Review and Expositor* 87 (1990): 414; see also Hamm, "Acts 3,1-10," 305.

[30] The expression of faith is not explicitly recounted as part of the miracle. Peter states that the man was healed by faith in Acts 3:16. However, the owner of that faith is not clear; Talbert suggests that Peter is describing the faith of the apostles rather than the lame man. Talbert, *Reading Acts*, 54; see also Wall, "The Acts of the Apostles," 81 n. 162. However, the lame man's response of "praising God" and "clinging to Peter and John" reflects his faith and is certainly different from that of the healed man in John 5 who gives Jesus up to those who wish to harm him.

[31] These concepts are interrelated. Talbert argues that, "in Luke-Acts salvation encompasses the whole person. . . . The physical healings of the bodies of the afflicted are foretastes of the resurrection of the dead, just as one's conversion is a foretaste of the ultimate redemption from all sin. There is in Luke-Acts no reduction of salvation to a purely spiritual transaction any more than there is a reduction of it to a purely physical or political reality. The whole person is affected." *Reading Acts*, 54.

[32] Hamm, "Acts 3,1-10," 309-311, 312.

[33] τότε ἁλεῖται ὡς ἔλαφος ὁ χωλός,

the nation.³⁴ The miracle is a demonstration of the power of Christ's name (Acts 3:16) to meet the nation's salvation, even for each individual since the nation's need includes individual needs (see Acts 3:26, "every one of you," "ἕκαστον").

Parallels exist between the miracles of Jesus and Peter (and later Paul);³⁵ this is a literary device employed by Luke to provide continuity in the larger double-work of Luke and Acts. As O'Reilly affirms, "The apostles and disciples in Acts can work miracles like those of Jesus because they have become sharers in his prophetic mission to restore sight to the blind and hearing to the deaf, to liberate captives, to make the lame walk, and to preach the good news."³⁶ This was Jesus' mission (Luke 4:18-19; 7:22 cf. Isaiah 35:5-6; 61:1) and Luke makes a similar allusion in Peter's healing of the lame man who "walks" and "leaps" (Acts 3:8 cf. Isaiah 35:5-6; 61:1).³⁷ Luke is showing the reader that Peter stands in line with Jesus; there is unity and continuity in their messages.³⁸

The Sermon (3:12-26)

The sermon explains and applies the miracle of healing to the Jews in the temple. It has a simple structural divider at the beginning of 3:17 (Καὶ νῦν, ἀδελφοί,). The first section argues that what has happened was not of Peter and John, but of God (3:12-16); the second section tells what the hearers should do in response to the miracle (3:17-26).³⁹

---

³⁴ O'Reilly confirms: "The allusion to Is 35 implies that Luke sees in Peter's first miracle a fulfillment of this scriptural prophecy. It is a concrete realization of the messianic salvation promised for the last times. O'Reilly, *Word and Sign*, 129, cf. 127. See also Talbert, *Reading Acts*, 53; M. Dennis Hamm, "Acts 3:12-26: Peter's Speech and the Healing of the Man Born Lame." *Perspectives in Religious Studies* 11:3 (Fall 1985): 201.

³⁵ O'Reilly notes well that discontinuities also exist between the miracle workings of Jesus and the apostles, especially with respect to authority. Jesus needs no higher authority to perform his miracles, whereas the apostles are given authority by Jesus (Luke 9:1) and often invoke his name as their authority (Acts 3:6). O'Reilly, *Word and Sign*, 153.

³⁶ *Ibid.* See also Parsons, "Christian Origins," 412.

³⁷ Parsons writes, "As in Isaiah, the lame man in Acts symbolizes the potential restoration of Israel (see Acts 1:6) as part of the establishment of God's cosmic reign, inaugurated by Jesus and continued through the ministry of the apostles and Paul. In this light, it is difficult to resist giving symbolic value to the more than forty years of the lame man's illness in terms of the exiled and restored Israel." Mikeal C. Parsons, "The Character of the Lame Man in Acts 3—4." *Journal of Biblical Literature* 124:2 (2006): 309.

³⁸ Again O'Reilly states, "The apostles and missionaries continue Jesus' ministry, that of a prophet, mighty in deed and word. As prophets their role is to speak the word of God and, just as in Jesus' case that proclamation was expressed in preaching and in mighty works, in word and in sign, so too their prophetic ministry consists of preaching and of working miracles." O'Reilly, *Word and Sign*, 159.

³⁹ Talbert holds to a similar structure of (1) "how the healing happened" in vv. 12-16, and (2) "what the healing demands and why" in vv. 17-26. Talbert, *Reading Acts*, 52. See also Parsons, "Christian Origins," 413; Bock, *Acts*, 165.

In this sermon Peter offers spiritual, kingdom blessings to his audience just as the lame man received physical, kingdom blessings. The physical healing of the lame man pictured and foreshadowed the spiritual healing available for the Jews upon their reception of Peter's word about Jesus.[40] The correlation between the physical and spiritual kingdom blessings is implied in Acts 3:16ff, and later made textually explicit before the religious leaders through the terms σέσωται and σωτηρία.[41]

Peter's talk is heavily colored by Jewish references demonstrating that it is a message for the nation of Israel to repent and receive the blessings which are found in Jesus. The local is Solomon's portico, on the east side of the court of the Gentiles (3:11),[42] alluding to the Solomonic age, the highest point in Israel's history never to be repeated until Messiah comes with the kingdom. In addition, "all the people" (πᾶς ὁ λαὸς) come connoting as William Kurz affirms that, "Peter is addressing God's chosen people as Moses and Jesus had done."[43] The audience is called, "Men of Israel" in 3:12. God is called the "God of Abraham, Isaac, and Jacob," and the "God of our fathers" representing the Abrahamic covenant (3:13; cf. Ex. 3:6, 15-16; 4:5; 6:3). Many primitive and archaic Christological titles are employed including, "servant" (παῖς) 3:13, 26 (cf. Isa. 52:13 LXX), "holy" (ἅγιος) and "righteous one" (δίκαιος) 3:14 (cf. Isa. 53:11 LXX), and "the ruler/author of life" (τὸν δὲ ἀρχηγὸν τῆς ζωῆς) 3:15. Just as the man was raised (ἐγείρω) in Christ's name (3:7), so is it that Jesus, the ruler of life, was raised (ἐγείρω) by God in 3:15. As Dennis Hamm states, "The sense is this: God, who vindicated Jesus by raising him up . . . has further vindicated him by raising up this lame man in the Risen One's name. The healing is a sign of the resurrection."[44] In addition, the healing demonstrates Jesus to be the ruler of life in that he gives new life to the lame man.[45] Peter stresses the fulfillment of prophecy for Israel (3:18,

---

[40] O'Reilly writes, "What Luke is now proclaiming, through the lips of Peter, is not only that this particular realization of salvation (the miracle at the temple) has taken place by means of the name of Jesus, but that all salvation takes place by this means." O'Reilly, *Word and Sign,* 151.

[41] See Acts 4:9, 12; O'Reilly, *Word and Sign,* 143-52; Robert C. Tannehill, "The Functions of Peter's Mission Speeches in the Narrative of Acts," *New Testament Studies* 37 (1991): 407.

[42] Keener notes: "Because the eastern colonnade's masonry was pre-Herodian, people assumed that it derived from the time of Solomon (*War* 5.184-85; *Ant.* 15.397-400; 20.221). The putative connection with Solomon, builder of the original temple (Acts 7:47), may have helped play into an eschatology emphasizing the temple's restoration even if the believers chose the site for its utility." *Acts* II, 1074-75.

[43] Kurz, *Reading Luke-Acts,* 79.

[44] Hamm, "Acts 3:12-26," 203. In the fourth century A.D. John Chrysostom stated, "This act [the healing of the lame man] made manifest the resurrection, for it was an image of the resurrection." *Homilies on the Acts of the Apostles.* 8.24 in Martin, ed. *Acts,* Ancient Christian Commentary, 41.

[45] Haenchen, *The Acts,* 206 n5. Hamm notes that, "the healing is a demonstration of just how concretely Jesus leads into fullness of life. The phrase calls to mind the words of Ps 16 (originally the prayer of a sick person) applied to the resurrection of Jesus in Acts 2:28: 'Thou has made known to me the ways

22, 24, 25); he affirms that his listeners are "the sons of the prophets" (3:25), so it is important for their sins to be forgiven so that Messianic, kingdom blessings may come upon them[46] as they have to this lame man (3:20-24).[47] These Jewish hearers are the natural heirs to the promises to Abraham (3:25-26).

The implied correlation of the lame man's physical healing with the nation's spiritual healing is first *shown* through the narrative logic of the sign-sermon motif. It is then explicitly affirmed through the use of a leadword in Acts 4:9 and 4:12. In Acts 4:9 Peter says, "If we are on trial today for a benefit done to a sick man, as to how this man has been made well (σῴζω)" only to affirm three verses later in 4:12 that, "And there is salvation (σωτηρία) in no one else; for there is no other name under heaven by which we must be saved (σῴζω)." Since not everyone to whom Peter was speaking was physically lame at the time, Luke has Peter explicitly identifying the physical salvation which the man received with the spiritual salvation being offered to the nation through Jesus.[48] In other words, Luke has used the sign-sermon pattern to communicate his narrative logic regarding salvation in Acts 3.

Two Miracles By Peter And Cornelius' Conversion
In Acts 9:32—10:48

The fourth of Luke's panels in Acts unfolds between the two summary statements in 9:31 and 12:24. One strand which unifies this segment with those that preceded it is the reappearance of Peter. After chapter 12, though, Peter is never again the central figure in any of Luke's narratives. This is at first a surprise to the reader. But this

---

of life.' All of this gives added reason for naming God as the God of Abraham, Isaac, and Jacob, for it is precisely under this title that God was proclaimed by Jesus in his earthly ministry as 'the God not of the dead but of the living' (Luke 20:37-39)." Hamm, "Acts 3:12-26," 203.

[46] Bock, *Acts*, 175-78; Witherington, *Acts*, 186-87. Hamm argues well that the term ἀποκατάστασις refers to the end-time restoration of Israel to their Lord and their land. With respect to the restoration of the lame man he writes that: "it provides the ideal verbal link between the healing of the man born lame and what that healing signifies." Hamm, "Acts 3:12-26," 209-10, 216.

[47] Hamm understands the blessings not to be future, as in the *parousia*, but present with "times of refreshing" referring to the effects of conversion in apocalyptic language as in 4 Ezra 11:46a and Isa. 32:15 in the LXX version of Symmachus. "Acts 3:12-26," 207-208, see also 212-14, 216.

[48] As Bock affirms, "With the repetition of the term in its broader sense in verse 12, a wordplay is set up here. The man was saved (i.e., delivered) by Jesus physically (v. 10), but this symbolized the fact that Jesus saves (v. 12). *Acts*, 192. Likewise Barrett affirms, "*Salvation* . . . is in part a spiritual equivalent to the healing of a lame man. Man, who is spiritually lame and unable to act as it was intended that he should, is so restored as to be able to move and act freely." *The Acts*, I:228. Mikeal C. Parsons arguing for physiognomy in the miracle states, "The outer physical healing thus provides empirical proof of the inner moral and spiritual transformation, a point underscored by the double sense of σῴζω in 4:9 as both 'heal' in a physical sense and 'save' in a moral/spiritual sense, a double entendre that conforms nicely to physiognomic expectations." "The Character of the Lame Man," 307; see also Hamm, "Acts 3:12-26," 200.

unit plays out Peter's role as he makes official transition to the larger inclusion of Gentiles into the new community by: (1) preparing the way for the Gentile mission, and (2) preparing the way for Saul/Paul.

The overall structure of the panel revolves around two lengthy narratives with Peter as the central figure: (1) The conversion of Cornelius; and (2) The Imprisonment of Peter. Both narratives are preceded with preparatory materials: (1) The two miracles of Acts 9; and (2) The brief narrative about the church in Antioch. In addition, both narratives are followed by sequels: (1) The report to the church in Jerusalem; and (2) The death of Herod.[49] One might chart this unit as follows:

Preparatory Material	Two Miracles
Narrative One	**The Conversion of Cornelius**
Sequel	The Report to the Church in Jerusalem

Preparatory Material	The Church at Antioch
Narrative Two	**The Imprisonment of Peter**
Sequel	The Death of Herod

The two, large segments within this panel relate to one another as complementary opposites which demonstrate the panel's overall message that, "The Lord lays the groundwork for the Gentile mission while rebellious Israel slips on toward divine judgment."[50]

The central unit on the conversion of Cornelius is the climax of expansion in the larger story of Acts. Luke focuses upon God's sovereign work through Peter to enlarge the new community with Gentiles. Since this people of expansion is so all-inclusive, the narrative requires repeated preparation before the conversion of Cornelius, and repeated explanation after his conversion to convince the reader that God's hand was behind the events.

---

[49] Zane C. Hodges, class notes of student in 219 The Book of Acts (Dallas Theological Seminary, Fall 1984).

[50] *Ibid.*

Luke employs the preparatory units to move Peter toward the Gentiles as he ministers in a path through Samaria to Caesarea–a city where both Philip and Saul, those who foreshadowed the Gentile mission in the previous panel, have recently been (Acts 8:40; 9:30), and where Cornelius dwells (10:1).[51] After Cornelius' conversion, the story of God's work will have to be repeated to those in Jerusalem so that they may walk through the experience that God used in Peter's life to accept the inclusion of Gentiles into the new community.

The Signs: Two Miracle Stories (Acts 9:32-42)[52]

In addition to the structure of "Preparatory Material," "Narrative," and "Sequel," one may suggest a larger construct of "sign-sermon" for these units. The two miracles which precede Cornelius' conversion speak, in the physical realm, of the spiritual healing about to be bestowed on Cornelius.[53] The first "sermon" would be the Cornelius event itself, and the second would be Peter's defense of the Cornelius event in Jerusalem. Perhaps Luke is emphasizing a double witness to this significant event.

Geographically these miracles move Peter in the direction of Caesarea. This is the city where the narrator left Philip (Acts 8:40) after his involvement with one who might have been a Gentile (the Ethiopian Eunuch).[54] It is also the city from which Saul, the future apostle to the Gentiles, was sent to Tarsus (9:30).[55] Luke uses this common city[56] to bring

---

[51] Luke Timothy Johnson writes, "These two miracle stories therefore serve as something of a narrative transition. Geographically, they draw Peter from Jerusalem to the coastal city of Joppa, and therefore closer in the reader's imagination to the wider world of the Gentiles, which boundary will be crossed in the story of Cornelius' conversion." Luke Timothy Johnson, *The Acts of the Apostles*. Sacra Pagina, vol. 5, ed. Daniel J. Harrington, (Collegeville, Minnesota: The Liturgical Press, 1994), 179; see also Talbert, *Reading Acts*, 104; Haenchen does not find much use for these miracles beyond this geographical progress and affirming Peter's ministry. Haenchen, *The Acts,* 340-41.

[52] For a more in-depth discussion of this section see David E. Malick, "The Significance of Three Narrative Parallels of Men and Women in Luke 1, John 3-4, and Acts 9," *Priscilla Pap.* 28.3 (2014): 15–25 (included as Chapter I in this book).

[53] Johnson writes, "Notice that Peter tells both Aeneas and Tabitha to 'rise up' (ἀνίστημι), using the word associated so frequently with the resurrection of Jesus. The reader is given an early signal that the conversion of the Gentiles that Luke will now relate is to be understood similarly as coming from the 'Holy Spirit,' that is the power of the resurrected one, and also as itself an extension of the 'resurrection/rebuilding' of Israel (Acts 15:16-17)." *Acts*, 180.

[54] "But Philip found himself at Azotus, and as he passed through he kept preaching the gospel to all the cities until he came to Caesarea." (NASB).

[55] "But when the brethren learned *of it*, they brought him down to Caesarea and sent him away to Tarsus." (NASB).

[56] Leland Ryken identifies this literary device as the functional use of geography to communicate a message in the Gospel of Mark: "Sometimes the geography is used for structural purposes. The Gospel of

into fruition the earlier adumbrates of Gentile inclusion.[57] Ironically, Caesarea will also be the place where the antagonist to Peter and the gospel, Herod, will be sovereignly slain (Acts 12:19-23). God will vindicate Peter, and the expansion of the movement, through the events which are played out around Caesarea.

Thematically, the miracle stories demonstrate the continuing power of Peter's ministry as a representative of the resurrected Lord. Peter is vindicated as he does the works of Jesus.[58] The raising of Tabitha (Dorcas)[59] ties into the Elijah/Elisha miracles (1 Kgs. 17; 2 Kgs. 4:8-37) affirming that Peter also functions with the authority of an Old Testament prophet.[60]

Mark, for example, is structured on a grand contrast between Galilee, place of acceptance, and Jerusalem, which symbolizes rejection of Jesus." Leland Ryken, *Words of Life: A Literary Introduction to the New Testament* (Grand Rapids: Baker Book House, 1987), 33.

[57] Witherington also argues for a movement toward the Gentile mission due to the Greek nature of these cities and peoples in these transitional narratives when he states, "Peter was traveling in increasingly more Hellenized territory, and so we should not be surprised that it was in this sort of locale that the question of Gentiles and the Christian faith seems to first have arisen in a significant way." Witherington *Acts*, 330. F. F. Bruce writes, "Since much of this territory was semi-Gentile in population, a further widening of the range of the saving message is implied." F. F. Bruce, *The Book of Acts*, rev. ed. The New International Commentary on the New Testament (Grand Rapids: William B. Eerdmans Publishing Company, 1988), 198, see also 201. In other words, the ethnic nature of the people in these two miracles also foreshadows a movement to the Gentiles in the Cornelius narrative.

[58] See Jesus with the paralytic (Luke 5:17-26), with the son of the widow of Nain (Luke 7:11-17), and with the daughter of Jairus, the official of the synagogue (Luke 8:40-56). See also Johnson, *Acts*, 179-80; Tannehill, *The Acts*, II:126-27; Talbert, *Reading Acts*, 103.

[59] Josep Rius-Camps and Jenny Read-Heimerdinger correlate the two names given for this woman (Tabitha/Dorcas) as symbolizing the Hebrew-Greek nature of this community when they write, "The fact that her name is given in Aramaic indicates that she was not of Hellenistic origin but the translation of her name and the use of it a second time (cf. 9.39) would imply that the community of believers included Greek as well as Aramaic speakers." Continuing they write, "'The reference to the gazelle in this context occurs three times in the course of the reformed laws in the book of Deuteronomy, and could be a way of indicating here that Tabitha represented a community of both Hebrews (clean) and Hellenists (unclean); the use of her name in Greek suggests as much." *The Message of Acts in Codex Bezae: A Comparison with the Alexandrian Tradition. Volume 2: Acts 6.1—12.25: From Judaea and Samaria to the Church in Antioch.* Library of New Testament Studies 302. Ed. Mark Goodarcre. (New York: T&T Clark, 2006), 212. This is another way in which Peter is being moved toward the Gentiles, namely, Cornelius.

[60] This theme is especially clear in Jesus' healing of the son of the widow of Nain. The New Testament town was just on the other side of the hill from where Elisha healed the son of the widow of Shunem (2 Kgs. 4:8-37). The connection between Christ and Elisha is implicit in the response of the people from Nain who said, "And fear gripped them all, and they *began* glorifying God, saying, 'A great prophet has arisen among us!' and, 'God has visited His people!'" (NASB). Tannehill identifies explicit textual parallels between the two events in *The Acts*, II:126-27; *see also* Talbert, *Reading Acts*, 103; Witherington, *Acts*, 327; Bock, *Acts*, 375, 378-79; Keener, *Acts* II: 1711.

In addition, the miracles themselves suggest the spiritual benefits which are about to be bestowed upon the Gentiles.[61]

The parallels between those physically healed[62] and Cornelius are striking:

Two Miracles by Peter & the Cornelius' Conversion			
Persons	Aeneas (9:32-36)	Tabitha (9:37-42)	Cornelius (9:43–10:48)
Opening	"Now it came about ..." (9:32)	"And it came about ..." (9:37)	"And it came about ..." (9:43)
The City	Lydda (9:32)	Joppa (9:36)	Caesarea (10:1)
Identification	"A certain man–Aeneas" [a Man] (9:33)	"A certain disciple–Tabitha" [a Woman] (9:36)	"A certain man–Cornelius [a Man] (10:1)
Condition	Bedridden & Paralyzed (9:33)	Sick & Died (9:40)	(*Like Aeneas he goes nowhere; like Tabitha he needs new life*)
Peter's Words	"Arise" (9:34)	"Arise" (9:40)	"Arise" (10:26)
Response	"He arose" (9:34)	"She sat up" (9:40)	"The Holy Spirit fell upon those who were listening" (10:44)
The Result	Many "turned to the Lord" (9:35)	"many believed in the Lord" (9:42)	"They were hearing them speaking with tongues and exalting God" (10:46)

The explicit textual parallels between the three units invite the reader to compare them—especially in terms of the opening for each unit, the identity of each main character,[63] the

---

[61] Hodges, class notes of student. This spiritual focus is also hinted in the fact that the miracles had an evangelistic effect (*cf.* Acts 9:35, 42); *see* Witherington, *Acts*, 330. But even more foundational is Jesus' healing of the paralytic in Mark 2:1-12 (= Matt. 9:1-8 = Luke 5:17-26), where a man is physically healed to demonstrate that Jesus has authority to forgive sins. See Bruce, *Acts*, 216.

[62] Barrett sees many of the parallels between Aeneas and Tabitha, but he does not continue the correlations to Cornelius. *The Acts*, I: 477.

[63] As Rius-Camps and Read-Heimerdinger state, "Aeneas is a representative character ('a certain', τινά) . . ., and man (ἄνθρωπος), which establishes him as a universal character (as opposed to ἀνήρ, one with a specific function)." They also identify this sense with the use of τίς with the introduction of Tabitha (9:36), Simon the Tanner (9:43), and Cornelius (10:1). *The Message of Acts*, 2:209, 212, 216, 244.

naming of each city, the condition of each main character, and Peter's repeated exhortation for each to arise.[64]

As in the sign-sermon of Acts 3, the lame man pictures the spiritual condition of another,[65] who in this case is Cornelius–a man whose sins are un-forgiven and is thus unable to walk with God.[66] This theme is further pictured in that Cornelius goes nowhere in chapter 10; rather, he sends emissaries (Acts 10:5-8). The resurrection of Tabitha pictures the spiritual life which Cornelius is about to receive through the ministry of Peter (*cf.* Acts 11:18).[67] She was physically dead but abounded in *charity* (ἐλεημοσύνη; Acts 9:36); likewise Cornelius was spiritually dead but gave many *alms* (ἐλεημοσύνη) to the Jewish

---

Regarding the use of characters as types in narratives, Robert Scholes and Robert Kellogg affirm: "In every case, whenever we consider a character as a type, we are moving away from considering him as an individual character and moving toward considering him as part of some larger framework. This framework may be moral, theological, referable to some essentially extra-literary scheme; or it may be referable to a part of the narrative situation itself. When we consider characters . . . we are thinking of them not as characters in themselves but as elements which contribute to the whole, as part of the plot or meaning of a work." *The Nature of Narrative*. Fortieth Anniversary Edition, Revised and Expanded. (Oxford University Press, 2006), 204.

[64] The term used in each case is an imperative form of ἀνίστημι, namely ἀνάστηθι (cf. 9:34, 40; 10:26). Although Witherington does note the use of the term, "to rise," in the two miracles, he does not connect it to the Cornelius account. *Acts*, 328.

[65] Bede connected Aeneas with "the ailing human race." *Commentary on the Acts of the Apostles*, 9.33 in Martin, ed. *Acts*, Ancient Christian Commentary, 115. Rius-Camps and Read-Heimerdinger also identify the physical paralysis as symbolic of a "spiritual rigidity" and correctly identify echoes in the terms to describe Aeneas with those in the Gospel's account of the healing of the paralytic: "κατακείμενον, cf. Lk. 5.25 B03; ἦν παραλελυμένος" 5.18, 24 B03 (παραλυτικός " D05, cf. 5.19 D05), ἐπὶ κραβάττου is found in the Bezan text of Luke's Gospel (Lk. 5.19 D05, 24 D05) and in Mark's parallel account (Mk. 2.4, 9, 11, 12) whereas Luke according to B03 uses κλινιδίον (Lk. 5.19.24)," but wrongly connect it with the state of the church in Lydda rather than with Cornelius. *The Message of Acts*, 2:210 n. 124. Barrett sees little, Lucan function in the healing of Aeneas: "It is hard to see any motive that Luke could have had in telling the story beyond the following: (1) It provided a further example (cf. 5.15, 16) of the power of Jesus working through Peter; (2) it was connected in tradition with Lydda and thus served to bring Peter on the way to Caesarea (ch. 10)." *The Acts*, I:477.

[66] Luke employed the image of "walking" (πορεύομαι) in 9:31 to describe the conduct of the church in Judea, Galilee, and Samaria. As Rius-Camps and Read-Heimerdinger state, "The verb πορεύομαι, 'walk', expresses the typically Lucan concept of walking in the paths of the Lord (cf. Lk. 8.14; 9.57; 10.38; 13.33 *et al*; Acts 8.36, 39) as distinct from the way of Judaism (21.21, cf. v. 24 D05) or the Gentiles (14.16)." *The Message of Acts*, 2:209 n. 120. In addition, to "walk" is wisdom imagery from the Hebrew Scriptures depicting close fellowship (cf. Gen 5:24; Ps 1:1); see Allen P. Ross, *A Commentary on The Psalms*. Vol. 1 (1-41) (Grand Rapids, Kregel Academic & Professional, 2011), 187.

[67] Barrett does not understand the raising of Tabitha to have much usefulness in the narrative: "The latter story, as a resurrection, is even more striking and is told more fully, but it seems to acquire no additional motivation and to have been intended to teach no further truth." *The Acts*, I: 477-78.

people (Acts 10:2).⁶⁸ Together they picture Cornelius as one who does good things but is spiritually dead, unable to walk with God, and in need of God's miraculous deliverance.

Aeneas and Tabitha function as stepping stones to confirm, prepare and bring Peter to Cornelius. Peter will be explicitly shown to be reluctant to move in God's direction toward the Gentiles in the next section (Acts 10:14-16).⁶⁹ Through the two miracles in chapter 9, Peter is confirmed to be "God's man" as he does miracles similar to Christ. Why would things change with the advent of Cornelius? Peter is prepared in the physical realm for the spiritual need of Cornelius (a Gentile), and sovereignly brought to Cornelius through the need of several people.⁷⁰ God is going to bring Cornelius to spiritual life, just as He brought Tabitha to physical life,⁷¹ and He is going to enable Cornelius to walk with Him spiritually, just as He enabled Aeneas to physically walk.

---

⁶⁸ Both individuals are described by the same Greek term, ἐλεημοσύνη, describing alms, or charitable giving. William Arndt, Frederick W. Danker, Walter Bauer, *A Greek-English Lexicon of the New Testament and Other Early Christian Literature* (3rd ed. Chicago: University of Chicago Press, 2000), s.v. "ἐλεημοσύνη," 315. Interestingly, this same term is also used to describe the lame man in Acts 3:2. Even though Bock identifies the use of the term with Tabitha and Cornelius, he does not connect the two figures any further. *Acts* 386; see also Rius-Camps and Read-Heimerdinger, *The Message of Acts*, 2:212.

⁶⁹ Rius-Camps and Read-Heimerdinger write: "Taking into account the symbolical significance of Tabitha's death as the death of Jewish attitudes to Gentiles (9.37a above), Peter's uncertainty can be linked to the situation he finds himself confronted with concerning the Jewish Law – as he sees the old mentality being challenged, he struggles to explore new territory, feeling his way step by step. *The Message of Acts*, 2:215.

⁷⁰Peter was traveling through the region and found Aeneas in Lydda (9:32-33); then he was called by the people of Joppa to quickly come for Tabitha (9:37-38). Then Cornelius (at God's command) called Peter to Caesarea (10:3-8). Peter appears to be an actor on the stage, but he is in fact just a pawn in God's hand. Alter describes this dual aspect well in his discussion of Hebrew Scriptures' narrative when he states that, "The Hebrew Bible is animated by an untiring, shrewdly perceptive fascination with the theater of human behavior in the textual foreground, seen against a background of forces that can be neither grasped nor controlled by humankind." Robert Alter, *The World of Biblical Literature* (New York: BasicBooks, 1992), 22.

⁷¹ Another link between the Tabitha/Cornelius stories may be found with the "upper room" as Rius-Camps and Read-Heimerdinger affirm: "The location of the upper room will set up a further parallel with the next episode as it is told in the text of Codex Bezae (Acts 10.9 d05, *in cenaculum*) for it is again in an 'upper room' that Peter receives his vision of the ritually unclean animals (cf. 'rooftop', AT)." *The Message of Acts*, 2:213. Likewise, the transitional nature of these narratives extends to Peter staying with a certain Simon the Tanner: "Peter has clearly learnt something from the practical experience of Tabitha's death, and yet has still to discover the full extent of the teaching that the distinction clean/unclean no longer has any force. This will follow while he is staying with Simon the Tanner, with whom Peter's affinity is indicated by the shared name." *Ibid.* 2:216.

The Sermons: The Conversion of Cornelius and Its Defense (Acts 9:43–11:18)

What was foreshadowed through the miracles is now realized through the conversion of Cornelius. The inclusion of the Gentiles into the new community is such an enormous shift in thinking that the rhetoric of repetition weaves its way throughout the Cornelius narrative and its defense. The repetition has the function of making the reader certain that God was involved in this expansion.[72]

Cornelius' vision was given in Acts 10:3-6, and then alluded to, or repeated, four more times to emphasize that God had taken the initiative with Cornelius in this meeting (Acts 10:8, 22, 30-32; 11:13-14). Likewise, Peter's vision was given in Acts 10:9-16, and then alluded to, or repeated, four more times (Acts 10:17, 19, 18; 11:5-10) to emphasize that God had taken the initiative with Peter in this meeting. It was God who was bringing this Gentile and Jew together. Finally, the bestowal of the Spirit upon Cornelius is discussed twice in the narrative and alluded to as a repetition of the work of God in Jerusalem on the Day of Pentecost (Acts 10:44-46; 11:15-17; *cf.* Acts 1:4-5; 2:1-13). Just as God identified a new remnant within Israel in Acts 2, and included the Samaritans in this new community in Acts 8, He was now including the Gentiles.

Therefore, through the literary techniques of sign/sermon, repetition and leadwords, Luke brings his readers to the conclusion that Gentiles should be included in this new community because God has willed it.

The First Missionary Journey in Acts 13:4—14:20

This fifth panel of the Book of Acts falls between the summary statements of 12:24 and 16:5 containing narrative (12:25–14:28) and then the Jerusalem Council (15:1–16:5). This panel is built upon the narrative logic of the "sign-sermon" motif. The "sign," or picture, is Paul's first missionary journey. That sign is then vindicated through the "sermon," or discourse, of the Jerusalem Council. By relating these larger units to one another, Luke desires to authenticate Paul. His overall message to the panel is: "Even though most Jews continually reject the gospel message, Paul, as a genuine apostle, is

---

[72] Allen P. Ross identifies the significance of repetition in Genesis's Joseph narratives when he writes, "The fact that there are repeated elements in the narratives does not prove that the material was handed down in two different traditions. Repetition is the hallmark of Hebrew style; it serves to heighten the message by a double emphasis." Allen P. Ross, "The Exegetical Exposition of the Pentateuch: Genesis," unpublished class notes in 117 Exegesis in the Pentateuch: Genesis (Dallas Theological Seminary, Fall 1982), 113. Continuing he writes, "The nature of the Joseph stories is akin to wisdom literature itself; its distinct emphasis must be kept in mind–if not declared–in the exegetical exposition of the passages. The features that characterize this section are: . . . the parallel cycles stressing the providential dealings of God in life, i.e., if something is done once, it may be a coincidence, but if it is done twice, it is of God." *Ibid.*, 114. Witherington states, "Luke has used the device of repetition to emphasize the importance of the issues involved, as he does in the telling of Paul's conversion." *Acts*, 345; *see also* Bock, *Acts*, 394.

demonstrated to spread the true gospel of God's grace to all peoples–both Jews and Gentiles."[73] The panel might be charted as follows:

Paul's Ministry to Both Jews and Gentiles in Acts 12:25–16:5	
Sign: First Mission (12:25–14:28)	Sermon: Mission Vindicated (15:1–16:5)
• *Prelude* (12:25–13:3) • Sign: A Microcosm of mission (13:4-12) • Sermon: To the Jews (13:13–14:7) • Sermon: To the Gentiles (14:24-28) • *Postlude* (14:24-28)	• *Prelude* (15:1-5) • Sermon: Vindication (15:6-21) • Sign: Council Letters (15:22-35) • *Postlude*–Return to the Field (15:36–16:5)

The macro structure of this unit is logically built upon cause and effect. Paul's first missionary journey (the cause) raises questions about the inclusion of Gentiles, as Gentiles, into the church bringing about the Jerusalem Council (the effect).

The Sign: Paul's First Missionary Journey (12:25–14:28)

Even though the narrative of this unit has many subunits, they function as a whole to vindicate Paul's first missionary journey. Paul will also be authenticated through the many parallels between Peter and Paul.[74]

Prelude to the First Missionary Journey (12:25–13:3). After the strong rejection of Stephen and then Peter in Jerusalem, Luke intimates a new center for the church in Antioch through the initial scene of this panel (13:1-3) which bares resemblance to the earlier prelude to Pentecost in Acts 1–2.

---

[73] Zane C. Hodges, class notes of student in 219 The Book of Acts (Dallas Theological Seminary, Fall 1984).

[74] Charles H. Talbert, *Literary Patterns, Theological Themes, and the Genre of Luke-Acts* (Missoula: Scholars Press, 1974), 23-25. Susan Praeder emphasizes the continuity between Jews and Gentiles in the parallels of healing the lame: "Luke's portrayal of lame men in the two miracle stories invites a comparison of the Jewish and Gentile missions (Acts 3:1-10; 14:8-18). Peter heals a Jewish man 'Lame from birth' in Jerusalem, and Paul heals a Gentile man 'lame from birth' in Lystra. Both lame men 'leap' in their new health. The language of the two portrayals suggests that God's promises are fulfilled in the Christian mission and are the common inheritance of Jews and Gentiles (Isa. 35:6: 'Then the lame man will leap like the hart'). Paul's mission to the Gentiles continues and complements Peter's mission to the Jews." Susan M. Praeder, "From Jerusalem to Rome," *The Bible Today* 24 (1986): 80-81; see also Craig S. Keener, *Acts: An Exegetical Commentary 3:1—14:28*. Vol. 2 (Grand Rapids: Baker Academic, 2013), 1043.

Sign: A Microcosm of the Mission (13:4-12). The movement of the larger narrative will be foreshadowed through the characters and events in this unit.[75] The cyclical themes of Jewish rejection and Gentile acceptance will be lived out through the two characters who meet the missionary team in Paphos on the west side of the island of Cyprus.[76]

Luke is careful to identify this missionary journey as being under the command of God, implying divine approval.[77] Although many events may have transpired on the island of Cyprus, Luke only brings one to the reader's attention–the encounter of the missionary team with a Jewish man and a Gentile man (13:5-7). These two characters foreshadow others in the narrative by the descriptions given to them: The first man, perhaps representing the first ones that the missionary team will go to, is described as a "certain magician, a Jewish false prophet whose name was Bar-Jesus" (13:6).[78] The second man, perhaps representing the latter ones whom the team will go to, is described as, "the proconsul, Sergius Paulus, a man of intelligence" (13:7). These descriptions point to their later actions.

The names themselves may express an ironic twist in the narrative which is also the irony of the book of Acts. The Jewish man bears the name of Jesus, (Βαριησοῦ) but shows himself to hardly be a "son of Jesus" as he resists the message. He is actually so far

---

[75] Praeder also sees the unit as introducing a "theme of acceptance and rejection." Praeder, "From Jerusalem to Rome," 81.

[76] Rius-Camps and Read-Heimerdinger emphasize the symbolic nature of the journey to Cyprus: "it [Cyprus] has a symbolic value signifying exodus from the constraints of Judaism. The sea in Luke's work is a recurrent theme with this meaning; in the Gospel Jesus himself never crossed the sea (except the inner sea of Galilee) to go to the non-Jewish country for he himself never had direct dealings with the Gentiles and his own 'exodus' was undertaken from Jerusalem (Lk. 9.31). It was the community of his disciples who would be the first to have contact with a Gentile country, which Peter having the very first taste of it when he stayed with Simon the Tanner 'whose house was beside the sea' (Acts 10.5-6) before going to the town of Caesarea." *The Message of Acts in Codex Bezae: A Comparison with the Alexandrian Tradition. Volume 3: Acts 13.1—18.23: The Ends of the Earth First and Second Phases of the Mission to the Gentiles.* Library of New Testament Studies 365. Ed. Mark Goodarcre. (New York: T&T Clark, 2007), 3:34.

[77] "So, being sent out by the Holy Spirit, they went down to Seleucia and from there they sailed to Cyprus" (13:4).

[78] Rius-Camps and Read-Heimerdinger argue that with the use of the indefinite pronoun, τινὰ, "this person stands as a representative of a type, not just as an individual in his own right." However, they believe that he represents Jewish believers, rather than the Jews overall who reject the message. *The Message of Acts,* 3:37.

from Jesus' message that Paul describes him as trying to undo the work of John the Baptizer by making, "crooked the straight ways of the Lord?"[79]

On the other hand the Gentile official is named, "Sergius Paulus" (Σεργίῳ Παύλῳ, 13:7) in the same subunit where the reader learns that Saul also went by the Roman name of Paul (Παῦλος, 13:9).[80] Through a play on words, i.e., names, this Jewish believer who has been called to also proclaim God's message to the Gentiles is linked with a Gentile who will believe his message. [81]

Probably the highest level of irony occurs when the Jewish false prophet receives a similar consequence as Saul did in his rebellion, namely, blindness.[82] Of the two, the Gentile is the one who summons Barnabas and Saul so that he might hear the word of God; but the Jewish man sought to turn the proconsul away from the faith (13:7-8). The result is

---

[79] "διαστρέφων τὰς ὁδοὺς [τοῦ] κυρίου τὰς εὐθείας." 13:10; cf. Lk 3:4 reads, "ἑτοιμάσατε τὴν ὁδὸν κυρίου". Witherington astutely observes: "Paul, full of the Holy Spirit, cast a withering stare . . . and then offers us a play on words – he calls him Bar-Satan (or in Greek "υἱὲ διαβόλου") instead of Bar-Jesus." *Acts*, 402, *see also* n. 171. Keener sets forth a chart laying out numerous parallels/contrasts between Elymas and Saul. Keener, *Acts* II: 2009.

[80] Keener observes: "the primary reason for Luke's transition at this point is that Paul's ministry to Gentiles begins here, inviting Paul as well as Luke to shift to emphasis on his Roman name." Keener, *Acts II*, 2021.

[81] In the late fourth and early fifth century, Jerome believed that Saul took his new name from Sergius Paulus "because he had subdued him to faith in Christ." *On Illustrious Men*, 5.4, in Martin, ed. *Acts*, Ancient Christian Commentary, 160.

[82] "'And now, behold, the hand of the Lord is upon you, and you will be blind and not see the sun for a time.' And immediately a mist and a darkness fell upon him, and he went about seeking those who would *lead him by the hand*." 13:11, *cf.* 9:8, "And Saul got up from the ground, and though his eyes were open, he could see nothing; and *leading him by the hand*, they brought him into Damascus." (Emphasis added). Chrysostom wrote, "It was the sign by which [Paul] was himself converted, and by this he wished to convert this man. And these words, 'for a season' were spoken by one who seeks not to punish but to convert. For if he had wanted to punish, he would have made him blind forever. This is not what happens here, but only 'for a season,' so that he may gain the proconsul. For the man was prepossessed by sorcery, and he had to teach him a lesson by this punishment, just as the magicians [in Egypt] were taught by the boils." *Homilies on the Acts of the Apostles*, 28.7 in Martin, ed. *Acts*, Ancient Christian Commentary, 161. Bock affirms that: "The prophet has a punishment much like what Saul faced. In a sense, Paul judges his former self here. . . . As the magician is led away, one can imagine Paul recalling that he himself was led away after seeing the Lord and being rendered temporarily blind." *Acts*, 446. Witherington writes, "The parallels with the experience of Saul himself are striking: (1) both strongly opposed God's word, (2) both were struck blind for a time, (3) both were said to need being led by the hand thereafter." *Acts*, 402. Rius-Camps and Read-Heimerdinger affirm that: "Saul/Paul's experience of being blind is now mirrored in what happens with Bar-Iesoua as he intervenes to stop the magician from hindering the proconsul from believing the message about Jesus; in response to his perverting the 'ways of the Lord, those that are straight', he loses his sight as a divine chastisement." Continuing they write, "he [Bar-Iesoua] will be blind, a physical manifestation of his spiritual blindness to the truth of Jesus which Paul himself had experienced when he first encountered Jesus on the road to Damascus. *The Message of Acts*, 3:44, 45.

that a curse falls upon the Jewish man (13:9-11), and the Gentile believes the message (13:12).

This theme of Jewish rejection and Gentile inclusion is the essence of the cyclic-story of Acts and runs itself throughout the remainder of this panel. Luke has crafted this "sign" as a microcosm of things to come—a foreshadow of the nature of the following mission in the Galatian region.

Sermon: The Message to the Jews is Clarified (13:13—14:7). The cyclic-story will now be amplified as the theme of Jewish rejection is unfolded through the proclamation of the gospel message to the Jews in two distinct speeches.[83]

The plot revolves around two speeches to the Jews. In the mission at Pisidian Antioch Paul clarifies the message to the Jews leading primarily to rejection and a statement of expansion to the Gentiles (13:13-52); and in the mission at Iconium Paul's Jewish message is again followed by rejection (14:1-7). In accordance with Jewish law, these two subunits may form a double witness against the Jews.[84]

Sermon: The Message to the Gentiles is Clarified (14:8-23). Although this unit has been structurally titled as a "sermon," it is introduced by a "sign" that is similar in its function to Peter's healing of the lame man (Acts 3:1-11).[85] The very terms which Luke employs echo the earlier healing.

---

[83] Bock writes, "The act-preaching sequence recalls Luke 4:16-44 and Acts 2, but as in Acts 2 we have the act first and then the preaching." *Acts* 447.

[84] *See* Deuteronomy 19:15; cf. also Matt 18:16; and the literary picture of a double witness in the *two* blind men (Matt 20:29-34), and *two* proclamations of innocence in Jesus' trials by Pilate (Lk 23:4, 14, 22) and Herod (23:15).

[85] Charles H. Talbert, *Literary Patterns, Theological Themes, and the Genre of Luke-Acts* (Missoula: Scholars Press, 1974), 23-25. Susan Praeder emphasizes the continuity between Jews and Gentiles in the parallels of healing the lame: "Luke's portrayal of lame men in the two miracle stories invites a comparison of the Jewish and Gentile missions (Acts 3:1-10; 14:8-18). Peter heals a Jewish man 'Lame from birth' in Jerusalem, and Paul heals a Gentile man 'lame from birth' in Lystra. Both lame men 'leap' in their new health. The language of the two portrayals suggests that God's promises are fulfilled in the Christian mission and are the common inheritance of Jews and Gentiles (Isa. 35:6: 'Then the lame man will leap like the hart'). Paul's mission to the Gentiles continues and complements Peter's mission to the Jews." Susan M. Praeder, "From Jerusalem to Rome," *The Bible Today* 24 (1986): 80-81.

Keener charts the parallels as follows:[86]

Acts 3:1-6	Acts 14:8-10
Man disabled "from birth" (3:2)	Man disabled "from birth" (14:8)
Peter and John "gaze intently" (3:5)	Paul "gazes intently" (14:9)
Leaping and walking (3:2)	Leaping and walking (14:10)
Near temple gates (3:2)	Near temple gates (14:9)
Human "adulation" rejected (3:11-16, esp. 3:12)	Human "adulation" rejected (14:11-18, esp. 14:15)

In both cases the man is described as "lame from his mother's womb."[87] In Acts 3:4 Peter, along with John, "fixed his gaze upon him."[88] In Acts 14:9 Paul "fixed his gaze upon him.[89]" In Acts 3:6-7 Peter and John command the man to "walk" raising him up, and in Acts 14:8 Paul commands the man to stand up straight on his feet whereupon in both cases the lame man is said to "leap" and "walk."[90] The "leaping" is an allusion to Isaiah 35:6–signs of the coming kingdom. This continuity argues for unity as it places Paul in line with Peter,[91] but its discontinuity argues for expansion as the miracle once done with a Jewish man, before a Jewish speech in Jerusalem, is now done with a Gentile man, before a Gentile speech in Lystra. In true narrative form the author *shows* divine approval of the movement toward the Gentiles instead of explicitly stating it. Parallels offer visual confirmation for the reader. The "Gentile" emphasis becomes obvious as the people observe the miracle and begin to identify Barnabas and Paul as Greek gods (Zeus and Hermes, 14:11-13).

In response to this "Gentile" understanding of the healing of the lame man, Barnabas and Paul offer a speech which is less Jewish than those above and more sensitive to their Gentile audience which is seeking to worship the missionary team (14:15-18). [92]

---

[86] Craig S. Keener, *Acts: An Exegetical Commentary 3:1—14:28.* Vol. 2 (Grand Rapids: Baker Academic, 2013), 1043; he sets forth a second chart with some permutations at 2130.

[87] χωλὸς ἐκ κοιλίας μητρὸς αὐτοῦ.

[88] ἀτενίσας δὲ Πέτρος εἰς αὐτὸν σὺν τῷ Ἰωάννῃ

[89] ὃς ἀτενίσας αὐτῷ.

[90] Acts 3:8, "καὶ ἐξαλλόμενος ἔστη καὶ περιεπάτει," Acts 14:10, "καὶ ἥλατο καὶ περιεπάτε."

[91] Talbert, *Literary Patterns,* 23; Keener likewise asserts: "The parallels among Jesus, Peter, and Paul here are characteristic of Luke-Acts, suggesting the continuity of divine activity in salvation history." *Acts: An Exegetical Commentary 3:1—14:28.* Vol. 2 (Grand Rapids: Baker Academic, 2013), 1043.

[92] Actually, there are no distinctly Jewish elements to this speech: no Hebrew Scripture quotations, no arguments from typological patterns, no references to a Davidic messiah. While the theme of

Many of the themes are similar to Peter's speech to Cornelius (Acts 15)[93] and a future speech of Paul to those in Athens (Acts 17).[94] Nevertheless, this speech barely dissuades the crowd from sacrificing to them (14:18)—another affirmation that these listeners are pure "Gentiles."

Therefore, through the narrative logic of the sign-sermon pattern, Luke has not only unified the whole of this panel (12:25—16:5), but provided foreshadows of the cyclic story that is worked out in Paul's first missionary journey where the Jews reject the proclamation of the message of Jesus (as with Bar-Jesus) and the Gentiles receive the message (as with Sergius Paulus). In addition, the healing of a lame man in Lystra not only provided a sign before the message proclaimed in that city, but pictured the continuity and expansion of the work begun by Peter, before the Jews, as God's vindicated messenger, Paul, reaches the Gentiles.

Troas, Eutychus, and Paul's Farewell Address in Acts 20:1-38

The seventh, and last, of Luke's panels in the Book of Acts falls between the summary statements in 19:20 and 28:30-31. This panel marks the climax of the logical development of Acts. Here Luke once again proclaims that the gospel message is not anti-Jewish. Paul, the one accused most strongly of being anti-Jewish, is actually demonstrated to be for all peoples through events, and a series of defense speeches. Once again the movement to the Gentiles is emphasized to have occurred through rejecting Jews and receptive Gentiles.

God as creator and sustainer of life may be found in the Hebrew Scriptures, it is not nuanced in Old Testament terms. None of the speech's concepts require the listener to have a Jewish pre-understanding to comprehend them. This speech is crafted for a distinctly Gentile audience.

[93]In both speeches the listeners seek to worship the speakers (10:25; 14:12, 13, 18), the speakers identify themselves as mere men (10:26; 14:15), and God is described being over all people (10:28, 34-36, 42; 14:15-17) with an invitation to turn to him (10:43; 14:15). The speech in Acts 10 does include Jewish themes which are absent in Acts 14 (*cf.* 10:36-43). Perhaps this is because Cornelius was geographically closer to Jerusalem and had thus already heard of the events surrounding the life of Jesus (*see* the refrain, "You know" in 10:37, 38). Here Paul speaks to a Gentile audience which appears not to "know" about Jesus. Therefore, his arguments will be more "generic" and less Jewish.

[94]The parallels are striking: both speeches are given to peoples of multiple gods (14:12; 17:16, 23); both speeches refer to God as the one who provides for all people (14:17, 17:28), who has ordained all life (14:15; 17:24-28), who has allowed the nations to wander in ignorance (14:16; 17:30), and who has provided a witness to himself through creation (14:15, 17; 17:24). Both speeches have an exhortation for the listeners to repent (14:15; 17:30).

The macro structure of the unit is as follows:

As Paul Goes to Jerusalem, he demonstrates that his message is for all peoples — even those who reject him of the Gentiles and the Jews (19:21—26:32)

• **Demonstrated through parallel temple/speech scenes to the Gentiles and the Jews (19:21–22:29)**
 	
—The *Gentiles* (19:21–20:38)
  –Ephesian Temple Riot (19:21-41)
  –Speech to Ephesian Elders (20:1-38)
—The *Jews* (21:1–22:29)
  –Jerusalem Temple Riot (21:1-37)
  –Speech to Unbelieving Jews (21:37–22:29)
• **Demonstrated through apologies before the Jews (22:30–26:32)**
  —First apology before the Sanhedrin (22:30–23:11)
  —Second apology before Felix (23:12–24:27)
  —Third apology before Festus and Agrippa (25:1–26:32)

Paul goes as God's vindicated messenger to Rome among receptive Gentiles, then presents his message in Rome to Jews who reject it, whereupon he proclaims his message to be for all peoples (27:1–28:31)
• **The Gentiles:** Paul is shown to be God's vindicated messenger to receptive Gentiles (27:1–28:6) • **The Jews**: Paul presents his gospel message to the Jews, even though many reject it (28:7-29) • **Summary Statement**: Paul continues to declare his gospel message to all peoples (28:30-31)

The message of this panel would be that: "The Church's mission through the apostle Paul is demonstrated to not be anti-Gentile or anti-Jewish despite their rejection, but a proclamation of the gospel to all peoples—including the Jews."

The Sign-Sermon: Eutychus in Troas and Paul's Farewell Address

As Paul moves toward Rome in obedience to the Holy Spirit, he begins to prepare the Gentile churches to be faithful to their calling by trusting in God's provision for them during difficulty. Paul's meeting with the church at Troas (20:6-12) is part of a sign-sermon literary structure. After the riot in Ephesus (19:22-41), Paul departed for Macedonia as he had planned in 19:21. In 20:1-2 Luke simply states that Paul exhorted (παρακαλέω) those in Ephesus and Macedonia without any mention as to how, or unto what end. It seems that 20:1-2 states in a narrative, declarative statement that which is illustrated in Paul's visit to the church at Troas in 20:7-12, and is then explained, or developed, in Paul's speech to the Ephesian elders in Miletus in 20:17-38. In other words, Acts 20:2 states the fact of Paul's exhortations; Acts 20:7-12 pictures these exhortations and their results, and Acts 20:17-38 provides the content of Paul's exhortations.

Acts 20:7-12 forms a concentric structure which is inverted[95] at its conclusion for emphasis:

    A Paul speaks before the meal (20:7)

      B Luke comments about the room (20:8)

        C Eutychus dies (20:9)

        C' Eutychus lives (20:10)

    A' Paul speaks after the meal (20:11)

      B' Luke comments about the people (20:12)

This structure emphasizes the death and resuscitation of Eutychus as central to the story. Also it emphasizes the response of the people through the inversion of A' and B' in verses 11-12. It is the people's response to the death and resuscitation of Eutychus, in light of Paul's instruction, which is the thrust of this passage.[96]

Verse 7 gives the setting for the events which occur in Troas. The Church as gathered together seven days after Paul arrives (20:6) to partake of a meal[97] However, the act of fellowship is interrupted by Paul who begins to speak (διαλέγομαι). This term is always used by Luke to describe Paul's reasoning, or persuading of people who are not in agreement with him whether they be Jews (Acts 17:2; 18:19; 19:8; 24:12) or Gentiles (Acts

---

[95] Talbert notes well that perfect symmetry was not always valued in Greek and ancient Near Eastern cultures. *Literary Patterns*, 78-79.

[96] C. K. Barrett does not view the story as having much significance in the narrative logic of Acts: "It is a straightforward miracle story, the intention of which is to show the supernatural (cf. e.g. Peter in 9:36-42). Attempts to find an allegorical intention in the story (even Weiser's, 564) are unconvincing." *The Acts*, II: 950.

[97] Could this meal be communion? It is described as "breaking bread" (κλάσαι ἄρτον); see Acts 2:42, 46; so Augustine, *Letters*, 36.12.28 in Martin, ed. *Acts*, Ancient Christian Commentary, 247; against this, see Barrett, *The Acts*, II: 950.

17:17; 18:4).[98] If this passage pictures the authentication of what is explained in Paul's speech in 20:17-38 and even 21:4, 12, then Paul is persuading the church at Troas that it is God's will that he go to Jerusalem, and ultimately Rome, and never see them again. Therefore they need to be faithful to God as he has been faithful to them. The phrase, "intending to depart the next day" supports the idea that the discussion may have been about his leaving (Acts 20:7).[99]

In verse 8 the narrator leaves Paul to focus on the setting for the death of Eutychus which occurred while Paul was continuing to persuade (διαλέγομαι) the church (cf. v. 9). This tragic interruption had the potential of erasing all which Paul had said because in verse 10 the people are already engaged in mourning (θορυβέω; cf. Matt 9:23; Lk. 5:39). However, Paul turns the event into a divine affirmation of his words.

The act of Paul falling upon the child and embracing him is meant to remind the reader of Elijah (1 Kgs. 17:21ff) and Elisha (2 Kgs. 4:34)—prophets of God who, like Paul, demonstrated the power of God by raising children from the dead. There is also continuity in this activity with Jesus and the raising of the widow's son (Lk. 7:11-15), Jairus' daughter (Luke 8:49-56), Lazarus (Jn. 11:38-44), with Peter and the raising of Tabitha (Acts 9:36-43), and now with Paul as he raises Eutychus. This display of God's power through Paul authenticated his words as being from God and ended Paul's dialogue with the people.[100]

As the narrative story returns in verse 11, Paul does not resume his arguing as in verses 8 and 11 through the use of the term διαλέγομαι. Rather, bread is broken, and they engaged in more casual conversation (ὁμιλέω; cf. Lk. 24:14, 15; Acts 24:16). The event in Troas closes as it was about to begin in verse 7 with acts of fellowship and Paul leaving. But the emphasis in the unit is on the next verse with the people's response.

---

[98] Concerning this term, Witherington writes: "As is the case throughout the account of Paul's third missionary venture, we find again in vv. 7 and 9 the emphasis on Paul's using persuasion or rhetoric to convince his (mainly?) Gentile audiences." *Acts,* 607 n. 197; against this see Barrett, *The Acts,* II: 951.

[99] Chrysostom writes, "But why did he speak at night? Because [Paul] was about to depart and never see them again. This he does not tell them, since they are too weak, but he did tell the others." *Homilies on the Acts of the Apostles,* 4.3 *see also* Augustine, *Letter,* 26.12.28 in Martin, ed. *Acts,* Ancient Christian Commentary, 245, 247.

[100] Bock argues regarding Acts 20:10 that: "μὴ θορυβεῖσθε . . . does not mean 'stop being troubled' merely because it is a present imperative. The exact meaning must be determined from the context (Curly and Parsons 2003: 387)." *Acts,* 620. However the context of this command includes the long dialogue (διαλέγομαι) which Paul was having with the people in Troas where he was telling them of things that were difficult to hear (cf. 20:25). Therefore, this prohibition may well have the sense that the people should stop fearing—fearing what Paul is telling them is going to occur, and fearing what has just occurred with Eutychus. H. E. Dana and Julius R. Mantey, *A Manual Grammar of the Greek New Testament* (New York: The MacMillan Company, 1955), 302; Daniel B. Wallace, *Greek Grammar: Beyond the Basics* (Grand Rapids: Zondervan, 1996), 724-25.

The key term, or *leitwort*, is encouragement (παρακαλέω). In the active voice it refers to someone being exhorted unto action (cf. Acts 2:40). In the passive voice this term carries the same nuance but with the emphasis on the result of the exhortation, being encouraged (Acts 11:23; 14:22). The scene in Troas closes with the people having been greatly encouraged (παρεκλήθησαν οὐ μετρίως). They have the child with them as a reminder of God's enabling power in the midst of difficulty—even death—and as an authentication of Paul's message. Therefore, they are encouraged, even with the loss of Paul, to continue to be faithful.[101] However, the projected content of their encouragement would only be speculation were it not for the sermon that follows in 20:17-38 as a compliment to this sign.

The Sermon: Farewell Address to the Ephesian Elders

In the first segment of this unit (20:1-2), the narrator directly stated that Paul was *exhorting* the churches in Macedonia. In the second segment (20:7-12) it was demonstrated how it was that Paul *exhorted* or *encouraged* the church in Troas. Although the term for exhort (παρακαλέω) is not present in the third segment (20:17-38) there is a specific section of exhortation in Paul's meeting with the Ephesian elders (20:18-35) followed by a brief time of fellowship (20:36-38) which parallels the first and second segments of Acts 20:7-12. Therefore, by the juxtaposition of these narratives it appears that Acts 20 is logically developed through a statement, a sign, and then a sermon. This is a movement from general to specific wherein Luke at first tells the reader what Paul is doing generally (20:2), gives a specific illustration in Troas (20:7-12), and then gives the explicit content of the message in Miletus (20:17-38). Each situation was undoubtedly distinct; but Paul's basic thrust was the same, i.e., to encourage the Gentile church, during difficulties, to be faithful to its calling as Paul has been, and now must be, faithful to his calling.[102]

Within the flow of the book of Acts, this segment can more specifically be seen as Paul's leaving the Gentile churches which he had established in order to go to the center of the Gentile domain—Rome—via Jerusalem. However, Paul does not just leave his churches; he first encourages them to also be faithful in the face of difficulties as he himself is faithful.

---

[101] Chrysostom affirms: "At the same time, the miracle that took place made them remember that evening forever. Great was the pleasure experienced by his audience; though interrupted, it was further extended. So the fall took place to the benefit of the teacher." *Homilies on the Acts of the Apostles*, 4.3 in Martin, ed. *Acts*, Ancient Christian Commentary, 245.

[102] Even though Bock does not explicitly correlate this speech with the material in Acts 20:1-12, he does see the speech as relevant in its application: "Paul likewise is preparing the churches for his absence. What he says to the community of Ephesus could be said to any of the communities to which he has a ministry. Indeed, this is how the passage functions in Acts. It tells churches how to carry on now that they will minister without figures such as Paul present." *Acts*, 623.

Conclusion

The sign-sermon pattern is one of many literary devices Luke employs to communicate narrative logic in the Book of Acts. Using typological symbolism, the sign-sermon pattern unifies smaller units and logically develops argumentation within the larger work. The narrative signs not only introduce narrative discourses that follow them, but are central to the messages contained in those discourses. The healing of the lame man in Acts 3 pictures, in the physical realm, the spiritual deliverance that Peter is offering to the people in his speech that follows. The healing of Aeneas and Tabitha in Acts 9 foreshadow, in the physical realm, the immaterial healing of Cornelius who cannot walk with God and is spiritually dead. Bar-Jesus' rejection of the message, and Sergius Paulus' acceptance in Acts 13 are a microcosm of the First Pauline mission where the Jews overall reject the message in Pisidian Antioch and Iconium, while the Gentiles receive it in Lystra. The healing of the lame man in Lystra also correlates Paul's ministry with that of Jesus and Peter, and thus authenticates the work to the Gentiles in Acts 14. Finally, the encouragement that comes from Paul's raising Eutychus from the dead adumbrates the encouragement that Paul is giving to all the Gentile churches in the face of his difficult announcement that they will no longer see his face.

Recognition of the sign-sermon pattern in Acts enables the reader to identify Luke's narrative logic with the result that individual pericopies are connected into a more-synthetic whole. In addition, an awareness of this pattern deepens the reader's visceral and theological understanding of the message in Acts.

CHAPTER VI

THE CYCLICAL STORY AS A UNIFYING, LITERARY DEVICE IN ACTS

Introduction

The Single Story

Leland Ryken identifies the single story, or monomyth, as an archetypal plot motif, explaining that:
> [t]his composite story is made up of all the individual stories we will ever read and is shaped like a circle with four separate phases. As such, it corresponds to some familiar cycles of the sequence summer-fall-winter-spring."[1]

In literary terms, the movement from summer to winter is a movement from romance to anti-romance, or tragedy. Works like Shakespeare's *Macbeth*, and Dostoevsky's *The Idiot* end in the winter of tragedy. However, the movement from anti-romance to romance is comedy. Almost every Walt Disney story ends in the summer of romance. Dostoevsky's *Crime and Punishment* leans toward summer as it pushes into spring from the winter of a Siberian prison.

In theological terms, the movement from summer to winter is a movement from blessing to cursing that is brought about through sin, and the movement from the winter of cursing to the summer of blessing is a redemption that occurs through repentance. The cycles of Israel in the book of Judges continually emphasize this story as the people live in rest, sin, are brought into servitude, but pray to the Lord, who restores them to a position of rest.

It seems that this singular story has its ultimate roots in the redemptive story of the Scriptures. Humankind was created in the summer and rest of Genesis 1—2. However, God permitted evil in mankind, and this led to judgment of the evil one and oracles against the man and the woman in a winter, east of Eden. However, with the coming of Christ there was a deliverance of mankind from the evil one that will ultimately culminate in a new creative order.

---

[1] Leland Ryken, *Words of Delight: A Literary Introduction to the Bible*. (Grand Rapids: Baker Book House Company, 1987), 48.

The Cyclical Story as a Unifying Literary Device in Acts

A permutation of the single story becomes the overall plot of the book of Acts as the story is repeated throughout the work.[2] Over and over again the main characters present the message, whereupon some accept it, but others reject it leading to an inevitable expansion of those who will hear the message. Michael Goulder touches on the pattern well:

> The first thing that strikes a reader who stands back from the Acts enough to view it as a whole is that it is a *cyclical book*. Mighty works of God are expounded by the Church in preaching which achieves both the conversion of the open-minded and the alienation of the hard-hearted. While the converted flood into the Church, and enrich it with their charity and devotion, the alienated raise persecution against her leaders. The faithfulness of those leaders in tribulation is answered by divine intervention triumphing over the powers of darkness; and so to more mighty works, and fresh preaching to expound them, and round the cycle again. The movement of the book is like a spiral, always moving on and out into new territory, into deeper trials, into new communities, like a series of waves breaking higher and higher on the sea-shore.[3]

These repeated cycles are one way the author unites the various episodes into a larger story.

This cyclical story is one of *Luke's* literary devices which offers unity to the many episodes in Acts. It encompasses the macro plot of Acts with: (1) the inauguration of the kingdom of God through the promised bestowal of the Holy Spirit by Israel's Messiah—Jesus, (2) the middle of the story with the conflict of Jewish (and Gentile) rejection of Jesus, and (3) conflict resolution in the conclusion of the story when many Gentiles are seen to share in Israel's kingdom blessings as they join the few Jews who also trust in Jesus.

The cyclical story also contributes to unify the numerous pericopes within each subunit as it is repeated, with appropriate permutations, to match the progression of the overall message of the book.

---

[2] Norman Petersen touches on this observation as he discusses parallel relations between Luke and Acts and especially what he identifies as the Stephen cycle. *Literary Criticism for New Testament Critics*, Guides to Biblical Scholarship (Philadelphia: Fortress Press, 1978), 84-91.

[3] Michael D. Goulder goes on to identify a growth of this cycle in the Book of Acts over a series of nine repetitions: three brief cycles in Jerusalem, one fuller cycle with Stephen's death, and then four under Paul; however, he does not specifically relate the cycles to the panels of material marked off by summary statements. *Type and History in Acts* (London: SPCK, 1964), 16, 32-33, 46-47.

The Structure of Acts

Acts is generally unfolded around one of four structures: (1) the geographical progression in the book referred to in Acts 1:8, (2) the parallels between Peter and Paul, (3) the speeches in Acts, or (4) the progress reports provided through the summary statements in the book. While valid observations have given rise to each of these textual, literary clues, the progress reports seem to best identify Luke's organization of Acts. The following seven panels provide the macro structure of Acts for the purposes of this study: (1) 1:1–2:47, (2) 3:1–6:7, (3) 6:8–9:31, (4) 9:32–12:24, (5) 12:25–16:5, (6) 16:6–19:20, (7) 19:21–28:31. This study is not arguing that the cyclical story in Acts provides explicit support for the division of the book into seven panels. Instead, it will show that the cyclical story is another literary technique that Luke employs, like geography, duality and balance, parallelisms, and the work of the Spirit, to unify the many diverse pericopies in the book.

The Cyclical Story Throughout the Book of Acts

Acts 1:1–14

The cyclical story does not appear in the prologue to the book of Acts. The book begins with a prologue and a programmatic prelude. The Prologue, in Acts 1:1-2, provides continuity with Luke's previous work and furnishes an update on the Gospel so that the plot can further develop. The programmatic prelude foreshadows themes to be developed in Acts. After the prologue and programmatic prelude, we are introduced to the first major panel in the book where the cyclical story appears in seed form.

Acts 1:15—2:47

In Acts 1:15—2:47 the promise is prepared for, received, and presented, followed by a summary statement in 2:41-47.

As the first panel of material unfolds, the cyclical story of Acts is delayed because there is a necessity for the community to prepare itself for the initial message.

Acts 2:1-13 describes the reception of the promise on Pentecost. The sound of the wind symbolizes the sound of speech which the Spirit will give. As the house was filled, so will the people be filled, and tongues of fire is an image of many languages.

As part of a sign-sermon motif, the miracle is not only an occasion for the message that follows, but part of the message itself. Therefore, there is a response by the multitude in 2:5-13. The table of nations shows the wide range of languages which the Spirit gave. This is a taste of the extent of the message—to all peoples (1:8). The table of nations is not exhaustive but representative of all nations. Already some are open (Acts 2:12), but some mock (2:13) as it says, "others were mocking and saying, 'They are full of sweet wine.'" This divided house is the story of the gospel and of Israel, and where the first elements of the singular story are briefly shown as the message is proclaimed but with some conflict.

Peter then fully presents the coming of the Spirit as the fulfillment of promise in Acts 2:14-36. Completing the first of the cyclical stories, resolution is realized as about three thousand people received the word and were baptized.

Acts 3:1–6:7

The second of Luke's panels in the Book of Acts begins after the summary statement in 2:47 and continues until the next summary statement in 6:7. This larger unit is introduced through the literary convention of a sign-sermon in chapter 3 and is then developed through the technique of interchange as the new community, formed on the day of Pentecost, is attacked from: without (4:1-31), within (4:32–5:16), without (5:17-42), and within (6:1-7).

This panel unfolds around the cyclical story with an emphasis upon the element of rejection. The message will be presented to the Jews in the sign/sermon (3:1-26), accepted by many (4:4), rejected by the religious leaders (4:1-3, 5-22; 5:17-42), and threatened within the community (4:32—5:11; 6:1-6); but the rejection leads to an expansion of those who will hear and receive the message in the next panel.

The Sign–Sermon (3:1-26). Now that the promise of the Holy Spirit has been prepared for, received and presented on the day of Pentecost resulting in the formation of a new community (1:15–2:47), the Twelve (represented here by Peter and John)[4] begin to bare effective testimony of Jesus to Israel. This is accomplished through the literary technique of a sign sermon.[5] The sign consists of healing a lame man at the Beautiful gate

---

[4] Peter may be the focal point of the action but John is always near by as a second witness who authenticates the testimony of Peter (cf. Acts 4:19-20; Luke 21:12-13) and represents the Twelve. Leo O'Reilly, *Word and Sign in the Acts of the Apostles: A Study in Lucan Theology*. (Roma: Editrice Pontifica Universita Gregoriiana 1987), 124, Ernst Haenchen, *The Acts of the Apostles: A Commentary* (Philadelphia: Translated by Bernard Noble and Gerald Shin from the 14th German edition [1965]. The Westminster Press, 1971), 201-202. In addition, Jesus had recommended that his messengers go out in pairs (Luke 10:1); this pattern is thus repeated throughout Acts here with Peter and John and later with Barnabas and Paul, and Paul and Silas. William S. Kurz, *Reading Luke-Acts: Dynamics of Biblical Narrative* (Louisville: Westminster/John Knox Press, 1993), 79.

Interestingly, Charles H. Talbert argues for a double witness in the literary structure of the unit: "the 'sign + speech' pattern provides the testimony of the two witnesses necessary under Jewish law to guarantee truthfulness (Deut 19:15; John 8:17): apostles and Holy Spirit (5:32). *Reading Acts: A Literary and Theological Commentary on the Acts of the Apostles* (New York: Crossroad Publishing Company, 1997), 52, 53.

[5] See additional discussion in Chapter V of this book. In addition, the healing of the lame man is the first example of the "signs and wonders" alluded to in the summary of Acts 2:43 (cf. 4:30; 5:12). Charles H. Talbert, *Reading Acts*, 50. Actually, the miracle in Acts 3:1-11 is called a "sign" (σημεῖον) by the council in Acts 4:16 and the narrator in Acts 4:22. Concerning the placement of these terms, O'Reilly

(3:1-11) and the related sermon to Israel is in 3:11-26. Together they comprise the message of the unit.

The sermon explains and applies the miracle of healing to the Jews in the temple. In this sermon Peter offers spiritual kingdom blessings to his audience just as the lame man received physical, kingdom blessings. The physical healing of the lame man pictured and foreshadowed the spiritual healing available for the Jews upon their reception of Peter's word about Jesus.[6] The correlation between the physical and spiritual kingdom blessings is implied in Acts 3:16ff, and later made textually explicit before the religious leaders through the terms σέσωται and σωτηρία in Acts 4:9 and 4:12.[7]

Now that Peter has interpreted the miracle around kingdom blessing which are available through Jesus for those of Israel who will repent (3:19-20), the cyclical story progresses in the next half of the panel through the insurgence of pressure from without and within the new community. While the first portion of the panel is marked by an event that leads to proclamation, the second portion is marked by both internal and external struggles. Nevertheless, the church will emerge with a spiritual power that enables it to be even more effective with its testimony.

The Church Triumphant in Conflict (4:1–6:7). This large unit connects immediately with chapter three in a cause and effect manner: effective testimony of Jesus in Jerusalem leads to the persecution of the new community. But the persecution of the community will expand to include affronts from without and within its borders.

---

observes: "This designation clearly refers to the miracle as it has been interpreted throughout the whole section rather than simply to the healing as an extraordinary phenomenon. Once again . . . Luke allows us to experience the reality of the 'sign' in all its dimensions in his narrative before formally designating it as such. It is only when he has already in various ways pointed out the miracle's *sign*ificance that he can encapsulate this verbally in the word *sêmion*." *Word and Sign*, 158.

[6] O'Reilly writes, "What Luke is now proclaiming, through the lips of Peter, is not only that this particular realization of salvation (the miracle at the temple) has taken place by means of the name of Jesus, but that all salvation takes place by this means." Ibid., 151.

[7] See Acts 4:9, 12; Leo O'Reilly, *Word and Sign*, 143-52; Robert C. Tannehill, "The Functions of Peter's Mission Speeches in the Narrative of Acts," *New Testament Studies* 37 (1991): 407.

Literarily, the structure of this overall unit is built upon the technique of interchange:[8]

The Assaults Alternate	Without (4:1-31)	Within (4:32–5:16)	Without (5:17-42)	Within (6:1-7)
Physical and Spiritual Assaults	Peter & John Arrested	Ananias & Sapphira	The Twelve Arrested	Grecian Murmuring
Spiritual Results in the New Community	A Fresh Filling of the Church	The Fear of God on All	Joy and Continued Witness	Submission of the Many to the Few

In accordance with the cyclical story, these conflicts appear to threaten the community and its message, but each one turns out to result in an expansion of the community's influence as many believed (4:4), multitudes of men and women were added to the Lord (5:14), the great teacher of Israel, Gamaliel, came to the defense of the apostles (5:38-39), and the number of disciples, including priests, increased and were obedient to the faith (6:7).

Now that the gospel message has been presented in sign and sermon to Israel by the leaders (Peter and John) of the new community, and the community has shown itself to be triumphant through four conflict scenes, the cyclical story will begin once again in the next unit as Stephen speaks to those from outside of Jerusalem (Hellenists) and provides the turning point in the Book of Acts for the message to move beyond the borders of Jerusalem.

Acts 6:8–9:31

This third panel of Acts is neatly crafted between two more summary statements: one in 6:7 and one in 9:31. The prominent characters are three men who are, for the most part, new to the reader: Stephen, Philip, and Saul.[9] This panel might be charted as follows:

---

[8] Mikeal C. Parsons does not develop this pattern as extensively as this writer, but he does identify interchange with the two inner sub-units with a focus upon an inside (4:32–5:11) and an outside (5:12–42) look. "Christian Origins and Narrative Openings: The Sense of a Beginning in Acts 1–5," *Review and Expositor* 87 (1990): 415-19.

[9] Stephen and Philip were introduced (previewed) in the list of those "seven men of good reputation, full of the Spirit and of wisdom" in Acts 6:7.

The Book of the Three Preachers

Acts 1:8 Revisited	Jerusalem	Judea & Samaria	Uttermost Part of the Earth?	
	Stephen	Philip	Saul	
		Simon Magnus 8:9-24	Ethiopian Eunuch 8:26-40	To Tarsus
	6:8–7:60	8:1-40	9:1-31	
The Persecution	Stephen Martyred	Philip driven to Samaria	Saul driven to God	Rest 9:31

All three men are connected to each other in some way. (1) Stephen and Philip were of the "seven" in Acts 6:5, (2) Saul was at Stephen's execution in Acts 7:58, (3) Philip demonstrates the effect of Stephen's persecution and foreshadows the future ministry of Saul to the Gentiles. Although Simon Magnus and the Ethiopian eunuch are both related directly to Philip, these two minor characters have a thematic relationship to the major characters around them. Simon Magnus exemplifies those to whom Stephen says God shows Himself (e.g., those outside of the immediate scope of the temple). The Ethiopian Eunuch exemplifies those whom Paul will eventually reach—the Gentiles. With these two minor characters Luke provides an implicit foreshadow of those whom God will reach. Peter plays a minor role in the section. He will re-emerge in chapters 10–11 as the explicitly strong link to the Gentile mission.

The unit revolves around the first complete development of the repeated, cyclical story line of Acts: the conflict arises with Jewish rejection of the message; the conflict is resolved through an expansion of the peoples included in the new community. When the Jews reject Stephen and his message, they propel believers out of Jerusalem leading to the work of God among believing Samaritans (north of Jerusalem) and a possible foreshadow of His work among the Gentiles (south of Jerusalem). The Christian church faces its first general persecution and its first martyr in this unit. But this enables the gospel message to break beyond the boundaries of Judaism.[10]

---

[10]This does remind the reader of Jesus' words in Acts 1:8.

Stephen rapidly rises from the role of servant to witness before the Sanhedrin (Acts 6:15; cf. Luke 16:10). His testimony before the Sanhedrin and his death are the turning-point in Acts. It is Hellenists (Greek, freed, Jews)[11] who argue with Stephen in 6:9. Saul/Paul will later come back to argue with them forming a literary *enclusio* through the image of "Stephen revived" (9:29).

Stephen is accused of two things as he speaks about Jesus: (1) speaking against the temple, and (2) speaking against the Law (Acts 6:11, 13-14). If these could be authenticated, the Sanhedrin would have the "right" to stone Stephen.[12] In response Stephen produces a theological *apologia* which emphasizes two motifs throughout: (1) God is transcendent of the temple, speaking outside of the land, and (2) the Sanhedrin fulfills the evil of their fathers by rejecting God's deliverance (6:15–7:53).[13] Although Stephen is accused, he becomes the accuser.

Luke once again tells the reader that the listeners are cut deeply by God's word, but unlike Acts 2:37, these listeners retaliate (7:54); the rejection of Israel is moving toward a climax. Stephen is then stoned for blasphemy while Saul is present (7:57-59). The narrator's reference to Saul is more than an initial, incidental introduction of a character who will arise later in his account to be the main character. It is strategic theologically. Saul, like Zecharias in Luke 1–2, is a Jew who hears God's word (through Stephen) but initially rejects it. He will only turn in his understanding through personal difficulty (Acts 9).[14] But the grace for God's pursuit of Saul is found in this unit just as the grace for God's continued pursuit of Israel was found in Christ's crucifixion in Luke's Gospel. Stephen's death is a willing one (Acts 7:59) with words of forgiveness (7:60), just as Jesus' death was (cf. Luke 23:34). In Acts 3–6 the nation of Israel had more opportunities to repent as an answer to Christ's prayer. Now Stephen, this later Christ figure, prays the same prayer as Christ providing for another opportunity of repentance. Stephen's prayer will be realized in Saul's conversion (Acts 9).

Therefore, the remainder of this panel is set in motion through the speech and stoning of Stephen. God's work beyond the confines of Jerusalem and the temple is proclaimed through Stephen's speech. Now God will work outside of Jerusalem. Saul's

---

[11]This may well have been what the Apostle Paul also was (Acts 23:34).

[12]B. Talmud, *Sanhedrin*, 49b.

[13]See Rex A. Koivisto, "Stephen's Speech: A Theology of Errors?" *Grace Theological Journal* 8 (1987): 105-110.

[14]See David E. Malick, "A Literary Approach to the Birth Narratives in Luke 1–2," in *Integrity of Heart, Skillfulness of Hands: Biblical and Leadership Studies in Honor of Donald K. Campbell*, ed. Charles H. Dyer and Roy B. Zuck (Grand Rapids: Baker Books, 1994), 96-100; see also Chapter I in this book.

conversion (Acts 9) is foreshadowed in Stephen's prayer of forgiveness. And a great persecution of the church is sparked under Saul which drives Philip to Samaria where he will minister (8:4-5).[15] This unit forms a nexus where all three "preachers" touch.

To the Samaritans (8:4-25). In the wake of the first persecution of the church many went out preaching the word (8:4). Philip is a case in point (8:5-13). His story was probably one of many that could have been told from that time. Luke chooses these accounts because they serve his overall story well. With Israel's rejection of the message, an expansion begins among those closest, yet distinct from the Jews–the Samaritans–and even those further away–the Ethiopian eunuch.

The repeated story of Jewish rejection leading to a larger inclusion is seen as the bestowal of the Holy Spirit expands along the geographical lines of Jerusalem, Samaria, and the uttermost parts of the earth (Ceasarea and Ephesus, cf. Acts 1:8). Peter is present in the first three accounts to confirm God's work of including the Samaritans and the Gentiles in this new community begun at Pentecost (cf. Acts 11:17).

To the Ethiopian Eunuch (8:26-40). The expansion realized in Samaria is then further developed as Philip touches the Gentile world in 8:26-40. The reader does not know for sure if the eunuch was a Gentile. Luke gives the reader the impression that he might be,[16] but he does not explicitly state it. This taste causes the reader to ask, "Is God going to save the Gentiles too?" Philip baptizes the eunuch (8:36, 38), but the reader is not told that the eunuch received the Holy Spirit. This will be reserved for Cornelius in Acts 10 when once again continuity will be stressed through the presence of the Apostle Peter.

The Conversion of Saul (9:1-30). This closing unit of the panel develops the hint which Luke foreshadowed in the previous unit that the people of God are going to be expanded to include the Gentiles. If the gospel in the last unit appeared to be moving toward the Gentiles, it is only appropriate to now discuss the conversion of the one who will someday proclaim it to many Gentiles. After the rejection by the Jews of Stephen, God called a Satanic magician (Simon), and a man on a road (the eunuch). Now Saul who was present at the stoning of Stephen appears as an instrument of Satan on a road away from

---

[15]Kurz affirms that, "The ironic theme in Acts, which plays a major role in its plot structuring, is that persecuting attempts to suppress God's word lead to the spread of that word. This theme is a major instance of the Lukan motif of reversal–God reverses or overrules human attempts to control history and is a natural occasion for irony. One of the strongest such ironies in Acts is that the persecution associated with Saul occasions the spread of Christianity, eventually to Antioch, where the converted Paul is summoned (coming full circle) to minister to Christians." *Reading Luke-Acts*, 144.

[16]The man in the chariot is described as: (1) a eunuch, (2) a court official of Candace, queen of the Ethiopians, (3) someone who had come to Jerusalem to worship. It is not possible for him to have been a Jew since he was a eunuch (Dt 23:1). Nevertheless, he may have been a God-fearer. The point is, however, that the narrative is unclear. This serves Luke's purpose well.

Jerusalem. He is an appropriate climax to the cyclical story since he holds all of the elements of the story in his person.

Saul's conversion experience has no connection with Jerusalem, but with an unknown convert named Ananias. Ananias's objections give an occasion for God to reveal His sovereign purposes for Saul in 9:15-16. These purposes more explicitly announce the extent of expansion which will result from Jewish rejection—to Gentiles and kings.

Luke provides a gap in Saul's chronology from his conversion to an event in Damascus.[17] He picks up on Saul's life at this point because it immediately shows the truth of the oracle from Ananias, and because the Jerusalem account nicely rounds off the panel begun in Jerusalem with Stephen.

In Damascus Saul has an astounding impact. People are amazed that he is saved (9:21) and he shows himself to be a great teacher (9:22). However, in fulfillment of the prediction, he also provokes opposition and suffers.[18] These same events occur in Jerusalem where the Christians cannot believe that he is saved, and Barnabas must bring Saul into the presence of the Apostles (9:26-27). However, the unit in Jerusalem ends with Saul looking very much like a "Stephen" revived. Saul returns to Jerusalem (cf. 8:1-4 with 9:26) and closes the scene by arguing with the Hellenists (9:29); the Jews who began the disruption with Stephen in Acts 6:9 were also Hellenists.[19] The story has now come full-circle.

Acts 9:32–12:24

The fourth of *Luke's* panels in Acts unfolds between the two summary statements in 9:31 and 12:24. It ties in a seamless way with the cyclical story begun at the end of the last panel where Saul returned to Jerusalem as "Stephen revived" to argue with the Hellenistic Jews only to be rejected and have to flee to Caesarea and Tarsus.[20] This panel picks up on and develops the cyclical story with the theme of expansion after Jewish rebellion. Nevertheless, Jewish rebellion will resurface as a theme at the end of the panel

---

[17]If Paul provides a more chronological order of his post-conversion life in Galatians 1:15-18, then time in the wilderness of Arabia elapsed between his conversion and this event in Damascus. See F. F. Bruce, *Paul: Apostle of the Heart Set Free* (Grand Rapids: William B. Eerdmans Publishing Company, 1977), 80-82.

[18]Paul develops this suffering in 2 Corinthians 11:32—12:10.

[19]It seems that these Jews were either free or descendants from free men under Roman law. They were from the places of Cyren, Alexandria, Cilicia and Asia and probably had a synagogue in Jerusalem.

[20]"Rejected" may be a bit euphemistic; more literally "they were seeking to kill him" just as they did Stephen (9:29; cf. 7:54-60). Once again, the "Jews" have rejected the message from God's messenger and the messenger(s) will spread the message outside of Jerusalem. See Kurz, *Reading Luke-Acts*, 144-46.

to provide a contrastive context to the expansion, and foreshadow the judgment which will come upon those who continue in their rejection of Messiah.

The overall structure of the panel revolves around two lengthy narratives with Peter as the central figure: (1) The conversion of Cornelius, and (2) The Imprisonment of Peter. Both narratives are preceded with preparatory materials: (1) The two miracles of Acts 9, and (2) the brief narrative about Antioch. In addition, both narratives are followed by sequels: (1) The report to the church at Jerusalem, and (2) The death of Herod. One might chart this unit as follows:

Preparatory Material	Two Miracles
Narrative One	***The Conversion of Cornelius***
Sequel	The Report to the Church in Jerusalem

Preparatory Material	The Church at Antioch
Narrative Two	***The Imprisonment of Peter***
Sequel	The Death of Herod

The two large segments within this panel relate to one another as complementary opposites which demonstrate the panel's overall message that, "The Lord lays the groundwork for the Gentile mission while rebellious Israel slips on toward divine judgment."

Peter's Ministry toward the Household of Cornelius (9:32–11:18). The central unit on the conversion of Cornelius is the climax of expansion in the larger story of Acts. Therefore, the cyclical story in this unit is inverted from its normal starting point of Jewish rejection.[21] Rather, Luke focuses upon God's sovereign work through Peter to enlarge the new community with Gentiles. Since this people of expansion is so all inclusive, the narrative requires repeated preparation before the conversion of Cornelius and repeated explanation after his conversion to convince the reader that God's hand is behind the events.

---

[21]As in all literary (and artistic) patterns, variation becomes a means of emphasis See Robert Alter's discussion of variation in the type scene in *The Art of Biblical Narrative* (New York: Basic Books, Inc., Publishers, 1981), 47-62. By beginning the panel with inclusion Luke emphasizes the importance of this expansion. There could be no greater inclusion with the remnant of Israel than the incorporation of Gentiles.

Luke employs the preparatory units to move Peter towards the Gentiles as he ministers in a path through Samaria to Caesarea–a city where both Philip and Saul, those who foreshadowed the Gentile mission in the previous panel, have recently been (8:40; 9:30) and where Cornelius dwells (10:1). Luke uses this common city to bring into fruition the earlier foreshadows of Gentile inclusion.[22] After Cornelius' conversion, the story of God's work will have to be repeated to those in Jerusalem so that they may walk through the experience that God used in Peter's life to accept the inclusion of Gentiles into the new community.

The Continuing Hostility of Jerusalem (11:19–12:24). This panel ends on a tragic note as Jerusalem continues in its persecution of those who proclaim the Gospel; therefore, it develops the cyclical theme of Jewish rejection in the repeated story of Acts. Again, this theme falls at the bottom of this panel rather than at the top because the overall emphasis of the unit is one of inclusion rather than rejection. Nevertheless, the rejection theme will resurface at this point with a vengeance to demonstrate the reason why Gentiles are being included in the new community. Israel continues to slip toward judgment as she rejects God's message.

The Peter/Herod Narrative (12:1-25). This narrative is a New Testament version of David and Goliath. Although Herod, the evil king,[23] is great with power, he dies, and Peter walks away through supernatural deliverance. As a counterpart to the narrative on Cornelius' conversion, this narrative brings the cyclic-story back to the theme of rejection by the Jews.[24] However, Herod's rejection will result in judgment in the sequel before the cycle moves on to further inclusion.

The narrative holds two climaxes: (1) the release of Peter, and (2) the death of Herod. The two men stand out as adversaries in this story. Herod is the opponent of the gospel, and dies. Peter is the proponent of the gospel and lives. But there is a deeper opposition which these two men represent. Herod represents Jerusalem and the Jews who

---

[22]Ryken identifies this the functional use of geography to communicate a message in the Gospel of Mark: "Sometimes the geography is used for structural purposes. The Gospel of Mark, for example, is structured on a grand contrast between Galilee, place of acceptance, and Jerusalem, which symbolizes rejection of Jesus." *Words of Life: A Literary Introduction to the New Testament* (Grand Rapids: Baker Book House, 1987), 33.

[23]Ryken writes, "To heighten the danger, the story locates the threat in a villain, the archetypal evil king with absolute power to annihilate people whom he dislikes." And continuing he affirms that "Herod is suddenly the most dangerous type of villainous king–the one who hopes to win favor with his constituency by killing leaders of a religious minority." Ibid., 82-83.

[24]Concerning Herod's murder of James, Ryken observes that "[v]erse 3 enlarges on this hostility against the Christians by indicating the Jews' approval of Herod's crime. All the Jewish hostility delineated in the Gospels and the Book of Acts here becomes aimed against Peter, the leader of the Christian church in Jerusalem." Ibid.

are against Peter, the proclaimer of God's word. What Herod tried to do, the Jews will also attempt (cf. 12:3), but they, like he, will be foiled.

The death of Herod is the second climax to this narrative functioning as God's evaluation of "Israel's" rejection of his messenger, Peter. Herod will slay those "responsible" for Peter's escape (12:18-19), but will be slain by the One "responsible" for Peter's escape (12:7, 23).[25]

Once again, the reader has been transported to the city of Caesarea (12:19). It is appropriate that Herod meets his end in Caesarea (12:19) where the Word of God grows. Philip's gospel message took him to Caesarea after he moved the inclusive message from the Samaritans to one who might have been a Gentile (8:40). Paul, the future missionary to the Gentiles was brought to Caesarea. Then Peter was brought to Cornelius in Caesarea to clearly expand the community to include Gentiles. Now in Caesarea, Herod dies as the one who has resisted the Gospel message. Through irony Luke has demonstrated that the resistance to God's good news only expands it; and those who resist will be resisted by God.[26]

The two major Petrine narratives and their surrounding materials have emphasized both cyclical story themes of expanded inclusion and Jewish rejection. The order has been inverted from its usual logical progression of "cause and effect" to emphasize the expansion of the community to include Gentiles.

Now that the pattern of the cyclical story has been concretely established to include Samaritans and Gentiles through the main character of Peter, it will be developed in the following panels through Paul. God's work had to first be seen through Jesus[27] and then Peter before it could be recognized as God's work through Paul. Now as Paul follows in the steps of his Lord and Peter, the reader will recognize that he has not begun something

---

[25]In both cases "an angle of the Lord" (ἄγγελος κυρίου) performs God's work.

[26]Kurz, *Reading Luke-Acts,* 136-37, 144.

[27]Although this study has not established the pattern of the cyclical story in Jesus' life due to its emphasize upon Acts, it is most keenly seen in the rejection of Jesus in Nazareth (Lk 4:16-30)–a unit which many scholars believe has been moved forward (chronologically) in Luke for emphasis; see I. Howard Marshall, *The Gospel of Luke* (Grand Rapids: Eerdmans, 1978), 177-178; Walter L. Liefeld, "Luke," in *The Expositor's Bible Commentary* 8:866-67; Joseph A. Fitzmyer, *The Gospel According to Luke I-IX: Introduction, Translation, and Notes,* 1st edition. (Garden City, N.Y: Doubleday & Co., 1982), 1:529; Darrell L. Bock, *Luke 1:1--9:50.* Baker Exegetical Commentary on the New Testament, edited by Moisés Silva (Grand Rapids: Baker Books, 1994), 394, 396-97.

After Jesus' own people turn away from him (Lk 4:22*b*), he then speaks of his going to the Gentiles as Elijah and Elisha did (Lk 4:25-27). Once again, Jewish rejection leads to an expansion of those who will receive the gospel message–even Gentiles like the widow of Zarephath (1 Ki 17:8-16) and Naaman the Syrian (2 Ki 5:14).

with the church radically different than those who preceded him; rather, he has followed in the pattern of the cyclical story of Jewish rejection leading to necessary expansion. Nevertheless, just as this panel added the theme of judgment for Jewish rejection, so will future panels expand the basic story to include related themes and subthemes.

Acts 12:25–16:5

This fifth panel of the Book of Acts falls between the summary statements of 12:24 and 16:5. Through narrative (12:25–14:28) and then the Jerusalem Council (15:1–16:5) the entire cyclical story plays and replays itself. The Jewish rejection which Jesus and Peter experienced will be repeated, over-and-over-again (with a hint of Gentile rejection), only to be followed by an expansion of the movement to the Gentiles on Paul's first missionary journey.[28] Then the question of Gentile expansion will once again be developed through the Jerusalem Council (15:1–16:5). In this way Peter, who reappears as a minor character, and Paul will be brought together so that Luke can again emphasize his theme that God is pleased with the Gentile expansion and thus the Pauline mission. As in the previous panel, "expansion" is the cyclical story theme that is emphasized through the proportion of discussion given to it in this panel. Luke wants his readers to be certain that they see his favorable connections between Paul's ministry and God's work in the church.

The panel might be charted as follows:

Paul's Ministry to Both Jews and Gentiles in Acts 12:25–16:5	
Sign: First Mission (12:25–14:28)	**Sermon:** Mission Vindicated (15:1–16:5)
• Prelude (12:25–13:3)	• Prelude (15:1-5)
• **Sign:** A Microcosm of mission (13:4-12)	• **Sermon:** Vindication (15:6-21)
• **Sermon:** To the Jews (13:13–14:7)	• **Sign:** Council Letters (15:22-35)
• **Sermon:** To the Gentiles (14:24-28)	• Postlude–Return to the Field (15:36–16:5)
• Postlude (14:24-28)	

---

[28] Even though Susan M. Praeder does not identify a "cyclic story" in this unit, she notes well many of the essential elements of the cycle under her category of "progressive itinerary." "The *progressive itinerary* traces the trend 'first to the Jews, then to the Gentiles.' Although the progressive and repetitive itineraries are one in literary sequence, they are not united in logical sequence. The *repetitive itinerary* features the same historical and theological themes *before and after* the turnings to the Gentiles: preaching in synagogues, conversions of Jews and Gentiles, and opposition from Jews and Gentiles." "From Jerusalem to Rome," *The Bible Today* 24 (1986): 81.

The macro structure of this unit is logically built upon cause and effect. Paul's first missionary journey (the cause) raises questions about the inclusion of Gentiles, as Gentiles, into the church bringing about the Jerusalem Council (the effect).

Sign: A Microcosm of the Mission (13:4-12). The movement of the larger narrative will be foreshadowed through the characters and events in this unit.[29] The cyclical-story themes of Jewish rejection and Gentile acceptance will be lived out through the two characters who meet the missionary team in Paphos on the west side of the island of Cyprus.

Although many events may have transpired on the island of Cyprus, Luke only brings one to the reader's attention—the encounter of the missionary team with a Jewish man and a Gentile man (13:5-7). These two characters foreshadow their roles in the narrative by the descriptions given to them: The first man, perhaps representing the first ones that the missionary team will go to, is described as a "certain magician, a Jewish false prophet whose name was Bar-Jesus" (13:6). The second man, perhaps representing the latter ones whom the team will go to, is described as, "the proconsul, Sergius Paulus, a man of intelligence" (13:7).[30]

Of the two, the Gentile is the one who summons Barnabas and Saul so that he might hear the word of God; but the Jewish man sought to turn the proconsul away from the faith (13:7-8). The result is that a curse falls upon the Jewish man (13:9-11), and the Gentile believes the message (13:12).

---

[29] Praeder also sees the unit as introducing a "theme of acceptance and rejection." "From Jerusalem to Rome," 81.

[30] The names themselves may express an ironic twist in the narrative which is also the irony of the book of Acts. The Jewish man bears the name of Jesus, (Βαριησοῦ) but shows himself to hardly be a "son of Jesus" as he resists the message. He is so far from Jesus' message that Paul describes him as trying to undo the work of John the Baptizer by making, "crooked the straight ways of the Lord?" "διαστρέφων τὰς ὁδοὺς [τοῦ] κυρίου τὰς εὐθείας." 13:10; cf. Lk 3:4 reads, "ἑτοιμάσατε τὴν ὁδὸν κυρίου."

On the other hand, the Gentile official is named, "Sergius Paulus" (Σεργίῳ Παύλῳ, 13:7) in the same subunit where the reader learns that Saul also went by the Roman name of Paul (Παῦλος, 13:9). Through a play on words, i.e., names, this Jewish believer who has been called to also proclaim God's message to the Gentiles is linked with a Gentile who will believe his message.

Probably the highest level of irony occurs when the Jewish false prophet receives a similar judgment as Saul in his rebellion, namely, blindness ("'And now, behold, the hand of the Lord is upon you, and you will be blind and not see the sun for a time.' And immediately a mist and a darkness fell upon him, and he went about seeking those who would *lead him by the hand*." 13:11, cf. 9:8, "And Saul got up from the ground, and though his eyes were open, he could see nothing; and *leading him by the hand*, they brought him into Damascus." [Italics added]). However, unlike the narrative in Acts 9, this man does not receive his sight back. Instead, the blindness remains as a kind of judgment upon the man reminiscent of the judgment upon the Jews expressed in Herod's death at the end of the previous unit (12:20-23), and pronounced by Paul in Acts 28:26-27 using Isaiah 6:9-10. From Luke's point of view, judgment can be that which either awakens a Jew from rebellion, as with Zacharias and Saul, or remains upon a Jew in his rebellion, as in Herod (King of the Jews) and now Bar-Jesus.

This theme of Jewish rejection and Gentile inclusion is the essence of the cyclical story of Acts and runs itself throughout the remainder of this panel. Luke has crafted this "sign" as a microcosm of things to come–a foreshadow of the nature of the following mission in the Galatian region.

Sermon: The Message to the Jews is Clarified (13:13–14:7). The cyclical story will now be amplified as the theme of Jewish rejection is unfolded through the proclamation of the gospel message to the Jews in two distinct speeches.

In the mission at Pisidian Antioch, Paul clarifies the message to the Jews leading primarily to rejection and a statement of expansion to the Gentiles (13:13-52); and in the mission at Iconium Paul's Jewish message is again followed by rejection (14:1-7). In accordance with Jewish law these two subunits may form a double witness against the Jews.[31]

Sermon: The Message to the Gentiles is Clarified (14:8-23). Although this unit has been structurally titled as a "sermon," it is introduced by a "sign" that is similar in its function to Peter's healing of the lame man (Acts 3:1-11).[32] This continuity argues for unity as it places Paul in line with Peter,[33] but its discontinuity argues for expansion as the miracle once done with a Jewish man, before a Jewish speech in Jerusalem, is now done with a Gentile man, before a Gentile speech in Lystra.[34] The "Gentile" emphasis becomes obvious as the people observe the miracle and begin to identify Barnabas and Paul as Greek gods (Zeus and Hermes, 14:11-13).

In response to this "Gentile" understanding of the healing of the lame man, Barnabas and Paul offer a speech which is less Jewish than those above and more sensitive

---

[31]See Deuteronomy 19:15; cf. also Matt 18:16; and the literary picture of a double witness in the *two* blind men (Matt 20:29-34), and *two* proclamations of innocence in Jesus' trials by Pilate (Lk 23:4, 14, 22) and Herod (23:15).

[32]The very terms which Luke employs are echoes of the earlier healing. In both cases the man is described as "lame from his mother's womb" (χωλὸς ἐκ κοιλίας μητρὸς αὐτοῦ). In Acts 3:4 Peter, along with John, "fixed his gaze upon him" (ἀτενίσας δὲ Πέτρος εἰς αὐτὸν σὺν τῷ Ἰωάννῃ). In Acts 8:8 Paul "fixed his gaze upon him" (ὃς ἀτενίσας αὐτῷ). In Acts 3:6-7 Peter and John command the man to "walk" raising him up, and in Acts 14:8 Paul commands the man to stand up straight on his feet whereupon in both cases the lame man is said to "leap" and "walk" (Acts 3:8, "καὶ ἐξαλλόμενος ἔστη καὶ περιεπάτει," Acts 14:10, "καὶ ἥλατο καὶ περιεπάτε"). The "leaping" is an allusion to Isaiah 35:6–signs of the coming kingdom.

[33]Charles H. Talbert, *Literary Patterns, Theological Themes, and the Genre of Luke-Acts* (Missoula: Scholars Press, 1974), 23.

[34]In true narrative form, the author shows divine approval of the movement toward the Gentiles instead of explicitly stating his approval all the time. Parallels offer visual confirmation for the reader.

to their Gentile audience which is seeking to worship the missionary team (14:15-18).[35] Nevertheless, this speech barely dissuades the crowd from sacrificing to them (14:18)—another affirmation that these listeners are pure "Gentiles." The message has now expanded to the Gentiles.

The Jews reappear to emphasize their rejection of the message by stoning Paul, but Paul rises and moves on to Derbe. After returning to encourage the churches, Paul returns to Antioch to report the expansion of the mission reporting how God opened a door of faith to the Gentiles (14:27).

The Jerusalem Counsel (15:1—16:5). The theme of this unit is the confirmation and vindication of the Pauline mission. In Acts 13—14 Paul has been shown to be an Apostle with a true gospel. In Acts 15, Paul's mission is vindicated. The controversy over the law challenges Paul's and Barnabas's work (cf. 14:27; 15:1, 3, 5). However, the counsel's deliberations confirm the expansion seen in the cyclical story with prohibitions given as an exhortation to the new Gentile converts to not offend the Jews but win them to Christ. Even though in the cyclical story the Jews, overall, are rejecting Christ, the church is not rejecting the Jews.

Paul's Triumphant Return to the Field (15:36—16:5). This epilogue to the Jerusalem Counsel narrative shows Paul as a source of comfort to the Jews after he is vindicated by how he deals with Timothy. After Barnabas leaves with John Mark, Paul shows his concern for the Jewish community by circumcising Timothy. The departure of John Mark in Acts 13:13 may well have symbolized Jewish rejection. Mark's ties were with Jerusalem; he is a Jerusalem background figure. Jerusalem was reluctant about the Pauline mission. The reluctance ended with the Jerusalem Counsel. There is no place for this reluctance in the Gentile fields. Therefore, just as in the cyclical story the rejection of the message leads to an expansion of the mission, so is it that a rejection of a messenger leads to the expansion of the mission team as a new team arises. Silas is a prophet connected with the Jerusalem decree; he is a good Jew from Jerusalem. Timothy is a physical representative of the message—a physical half-way house (16:1). Luke is recording a changing of the guard which roughly corresponds to the major transition in Acts. Paul is senior, supported by a prophet and accompanied by Timothy who shows the counsel's decision in his flesh. Barnabas and the former chain of command are gone. Gone is the man reluctant to go all

---

[35]There are no distinctly Jewish elements to this speech: no Old Testament quotations, no arguments from typological patterns, no references to a Davidic messiah. While the theme of God as creator and sustainer of life may be found in the Old Testament, it is not nuanced in Old Testament terms. None of the speech's concepts require the listener to have a Jewish pre-understanding to comprehend them. This speech is crafted for a distinctly Gentile audience.

the way with Paul; gone is the reluctance of the earlier church to go all the way with Paul. The cyclical story is now poised to continue.

Acts 16:6–19:20

This is Luke's sixth panel in the Book of Acts built between the two summary statements of 16:5 and 19:20. On one hand, this is a unit of continuation in that Paul's missionary journeys are continued. On the other hand, this is a unit of distinctions in that Paul was demonstrated "before men" to be a true apostle with the true gospel message for all peoples in the previous panel (12:25–16:5), but in this panel, Paul is demonstrated "before God" to be a true apostle with the true gospel message for all peoples. Luke emphasizes the divine direction and control of the Pauline mission in these units.

The panel's macro structure is as follows:

The Sovereign Mission at Philippi (16:6-40)

• Prologue: The sovereign call to Macedonia (16:6-10)
    • The sovereign conversion of a woman (16:11-15)
    • The sovereign conversion of a man (16:16-34)
• Epilogue: The sovereign vindication of God's servants (16:35-40)

The Movement of the True Gospel Mission from Thessalonica to Corinth (17:1–18:17)

• Ministry toward the **Jews** (17:1-15)
    —*Negative*: The mission to the Thessalonians (17:1-9)
    —*Positive*: The mission to the Bereans (17:10-15)
• Ministry toward the **Gentiles** (17:16–18:17)
    —*Negative*: The mission to the Athenians (17:16-34)
    —*Positive*: The mission to the Corinthians (18:1-17)

The Climax of the Gospel Mission in Asia at Ephesus (18:18–19:20)
• Ephesus is bypassed again to leave Priscilla and Aquila there (18:18-23) • Priscilla and Aquila instruct Apollos (18:24-28) • Paul apostolically bestows the Spirit on about twelve men (19:1-7) • Paul speaks the word of God so that all of Asia hear it (19:8-10) • Paul demonstrates the uniqueness of God's power: healings, exorcism, repentance (19:11-19)

Once again, the cyclic story unifies the panel with its emphasis upon an offer of the Gospel message to the Jews, some acceptance, Jewish rejection, an expansion of the message to the Gentiles, and Gentile rejection.[36]

The Sovereign Mission at Philippi. The cyclical story begins in this unit with the sovereign expansion of the message. The story revolves around the conversions of Lydia and the Philippian Jailer.

God overrules the missionaries' efforts to go to Asia (south) or to Bythinia (north) (16:6-7). God's direction is given through the vision of a man—an individual man of Macedonia. This fits with the individual accounts in Philippi of Lydia and the Jailer. God is looking for individuals.

The Movement of the True Gospel Mission from Thessalonica to Corinth. Whereas in the first unit, the mission is being expressed as the sovereign work of God, in this unit the mission is being shown to still be the presentation of the true gospel to all people: Jews and Gentiles.

Acts 17:1-15 emphases ministry toward the Jews. The mission to the Thessalonians is a negative, compressed narrative. The cyclical story begins as a presentation in a synagogue and leads to oppression (17:5ff). This typical situation sets the reader up for a contrast in other cities. God allows the hostility of people (Jews) to further the missionary enterprise from Thessalonica to Berea, to Athens (the Greeks).

The Bereans are more noble than those at Thessalonica. This is a testimony to what might have been if the Jews had not been rebellious (17:11-12). However, opposition from the Thessalonian Jews overthrows Berea and brings an end to prosperity. Now the cyclical story expands to the Greeks.

Ministry toward the Gentiles (17:16—18:17). Not only does God allow Jewish activity to drive His gospel forward, but He has a place for it to go—to the Gentiles. As there is rejection of Paul's message in Athens, with some acceptance, Paul moves on to Corinth. This is parallel with the rejection in Thessalonica that led Paul to Bereoa. The Greek rejection is in the cultural form of suspended judgment rather than persecution, but it, nevertheless thrusts Paul onto the positive field of Corinth.

God has sovereignly prepared for the Pauline mission before Paul arrives by using Claudias' decree from Rome to move Priscilla and Aquila to Corinth. God then frees up Paul to minister full time with the arrival of Silas and Timothy. The cyclical story

---

[36] Again, Praeder sees these cyclic elements under her category of "progressive itinerary" "From Jerusalem to Rome," 82-83.

reappears as Paul testifies to the Jews that Jesus is Messiah, and the Jews reject Paul's message providing an echo of what occurred in Thessalonica.

This Jewish rejection causes Paul to then turn to the Gentiles, as has been the cyclical pattern throughout Acts, however this scene is unique because Paul does not flee, as before, but is encouraged by the Lord to remain in Corinth (18:9).

No revolt follows by the Jews, and God works in 18:12-17 to fulfill His word from 18:9-10 to Paul. The Jews brought Paul before the Judgment seat trying to argue that The Way is not part of Judaism, and thus not a legal religion. As Paul is about to defend himself, Gallio, the proconsul of Achaia (Greece), answers (as Pilate did for Jesus in Luke 23) judging this to be an internal, religious dispute that the Jews must solve. No doubt, this is Luke's view as well.

When Paul arrives in Ephesus, he immediately begins the cyclical story by presenting the message to the Jews (18:19). This Jewish emphasis is prolonged as Paul leaves to go to the church in Jerusalem and as a Jew named Apollos is more fully instructed by Priscilla and Aquila. Then Paul returns to Ephesus during the sustained Jewish cycle of the story and bestows the Spirit on about twelve men (19:1-7). There is ambiguity about the identity of these disciples. Because they were baptized in the baptism of John, they may have been Jewish. When Paul laid his hands upon these men, they received the Holy Spirit and began speaking in tongues (19:6) creating a new "Pentecost" with about twelve disciples (as with the Twelve Apostles). Thus, Ephesus becomes a microcosm of the larger history of the church with: (a) John the Baptizer being parallel to Apollos, (b) Christ bestowing the Holy Spirit on the Twelve (and 120, i.e. 12 x 10) being parallel to Paul with the twelve, and (c) the word going to Jerusalem and then the ends of the earth, being parallel with the Jews and all of Asia hearing the word (19:10).

Then after the prolonged Jewish phase of the story, the cyclical story moves forward as Paul continues to speak to the Jews for three months (19:8), the Jews rebel, Paul withdraws and reasons daily outside of the synagogue in the school of Tyrannus, and after two years, all of Asia hears the word of God—both Jews and Greeks.

Acts 19:21–28:31

The seventh, and last, of Luke's panels in the Book of Acts falls between the summary statements in 19:20 and 28:30-31. This panel marks the climax of the logical development of Acts. Here *Luke* once again proclaims that the gospel message is not anti-Jewish. Paul, the one accused most strongly of being anti-Jewish, is demonstrated to be for all peoples through narratives, and a series of defense speeches. Once again, the movement to the Gentiles is emphasized in the cyclical story to have occurred through rejecting Jews and receptive Gentiles. However, this unity also includes an emphasis upon Gentiles who reject the message.

The macro structure of the unit is as follows:

As Paul goes to Jerusalem he demonstrates that his message is for all peoples– even those who reject him of the Gentiles and the Jews (19:21–26:32)

• **Demonstrated through parallel temple/speech scenes to the Gentiles and the Jews (19:21–20:38)**
—The *Gentiles* (19:21–20:38)
  –Ephesian Temple Riot (19:21-41)
  –Speech to Ephesian Elders (20:1-28)
—The *Jews* (21:1–22:29)
  –Jerusalem Temple Riot (21:1-37)
  –Speech to Unbelieving Jews (21:37–22:29)
• **Demonstrated through apologies before the Jews and Gentiles (22:30–26:32)**
  —First apology before the Sanhedrin (22:30–23:11)
  —Second apology before Felix (23:12–24:27)
  —Third apology before Festus and Agrippa (25:1–26:32)

Paul goes as God's vindicated messenger to Rome among receptive Gentiles, then presents his message in Rome to Jews who reject it, whereupon he proclaims his message to be for all peoples (27:1–28:31)
• **The Gentiles:** Paul is shown to be God's vindicated messenger to receptive Gentiles (27:1–28:6) • **The Jews**: Paul presents his gospel message to the Jews, even though many reject it (28:7-29) • **Summary Statement**: Paul continues to declare his gospel message to all peoples (28:30-31)

Paul's Message Is Demonstrated to Be for All People through Parallel Temple/Speech Scenes (19:21–22:29). The units of 19:21–22:29 are connected through the literary techniques of duality and balance.[37] Both express a threat on religion; both relate to a "temple;" both are initiated by a limited group and then spread to a larger group, and both include an accusation and then a call to action.

The cyclical story takes a different turn in the final panel of Acts. Instead of rejection of the message leading to an expansion of those who will receive the message, the emphasis in the last panel seems to be upon <u>confirming</u> the message to the Gentiles and Jews as Paul moves toward his final days with the communities.

---

[37]Robert C. Tannehill, *The Narrative Unity of Luke-Acts: A Literary Interpretation: Volume 2: the Acts of the Apostles* (Minneapolis: Fortress Press, 1990), 242.

Rejection by the Gentiles: Temple Riot (19:21-41). The Gentile temple riot scene in Ephesus follows an emphasis in Acts of Paul having just completed the climax of his ministry among the Gentiles in Ephesus. The temple riot scene demonstrates the effect of Paul's mission upon the religion of the Gentiles—they do not like it, because the message of The Way threatens the future of the temple Artemis. Like Jesus, Paul is vindicated by the Secretary. However, the effect of this rejection by the Gentiles is for Paul to return to the Gentile churches from Ephesus, through Macedonia and Greece, and back up to Macedonia, due to Jewish hostility, to Troas so that he can encourage (παρακαλέω) the churches.

The event in Troas pictures the tension between the churches and Paul as they debate late into the night what we later come to know as his decision to go to Jerusalem, be bound, and sent to Rome. The complementary sermon that follows the sign in Troas is Paul's farewell speech to the Ephesian elders in Miletus. Part of that speech emphasizes Paul's gospel of grace for all peoples (20:21). This meeting reminds the reader of the Ephesian mission because the elders represent the Pauline churches from the high point of his ministry among those in Asia. Therefore, in this cyclical story, the rejection of the message of Paul in Ephesus leads to an expansion in the sense of encouraging the Gentile churches where Paul has ministered to continue in the message and pattern of Paul in the face of resistance, infiltration, and Paul's absence.

Rejection by the Jews: Temple Riot (21:1-27). When Paul arrives in Jerusalem, the issue starts off as one between Paul and Jewish Christians (21:17-25), but it turns into an issue between Paul (Christianity) and the Jews, who in this case are Asian Jews. In both cases, Paul, and implicitly his message, is being accused of being against Jewish people. The riot comes as Paul is trying to demonstrate that he is not anti-Jewish (21:23-24, 26). Paul is accused of the same things as Jesus and Stephen (that he is against the Law and the temple) and has the crowds against him as Jesus did (21:36).

This is another temple riot like in Ephesus. Paul is delivered by the Romans, and the cyclical story unfolds through irony. Paul goes to the temple as a loyal Jew, but is arrested as a renegade. However, the arrest enables Paul to continue his mission before kings (cf. Acts 9:15).

The rejection of the Jews in the Jewish temple riot immediately allows Paul to give testimony to unbelieving Jews in a speech that has its parallel to that in Acts 20 before the Gentiles following the temple riot in Ephesus. However, Paul is not only shown as a Jew in this unit (22:2-3), but when he reveals his Roman citizenship he proclaims himself to be a member of both worlds to whom he was sent (22:25-29).

Paul Declares His Message to Be for All Peoples—Especially the Jews (22:30—26:32). In this extended defense section, which arose out of the Jewish rejection in the temple riot, Paul overtly argues that his message is not anti-Jewish, but for all peoples—especially the Jews.

In Paul's first apology before the Sanhedrin, he does not try to argue for the Jewishness of Christianity, but to bridge the gap between his mission and Judaism through the doctrine of the "hope of Israel"—the resurrection. Paul's mention of the resurrection was not just a tactical move (23:6), but a central issue which he redefines in order to turn the trial into a testimony—ultimately before King Agrippa (Acts 26).

God now acts in a new way in this final panel of Acts. Previously, he delivered his witnesses. Now God enables his witnesses to persevere in their witness of him (23:11). Paul is a witness for Jesus and not just for himself in these speeches.

In Paul's second apology before Felix (23:12—24:7), two accusations are brought against him: (a) that he is a danger to society (24:5), and (b) that he tried to defile the temple (24:6). There is a movement toward Paul being a societal danger as an enemy of the Jews as there was with Jesus. Since there are no witnesses to the first charge, Paul moves away from it (24:13), to the second charge to which there were witnesses—his discussion of the resurrection as the hope of Israel (24:21, 23). Even though Paul is before Felix, he appeals to the Jews (24:14-15, 21).

When Paul is before Festus and Agrippa in Acts 25:1—26:32, there is hardly a defense speech in the unit. Paul only denies the charges (25:8) and appeals to Rome (25:11-12). Paul is not seeking release, but is fulfilling the divine purpose (23:11, *dei*) of being a witness of Jesus before Rome even if it will cost him his life before the capricious Caesar (25:11). Instead of defending himself, Paul turns the trial into a testimony making the resurrection, as the Jewish hope, the main issue. Paul is doing all he can to keep the mission to the Jews alive amidst enormous struggle.

Therefore, the three defense speeches are primarily an emphasis of the message to Israel in light of their rejection. Just as the Gentile temple riot led to an encouragement of the Gentile churches, the Jewish temple riot led to a prolonged encouragement to the Jews that the risen Jesus is the hope of Israel. This is Luke's way of emphasizing that the message is still for the Jews.

Finally, in Acts 21:1—28:31, Paul goes as God's vindicated messenger to Rome among receptive Gentiles, then he presents his message in Rome to Jews who reject it. In the long sea journey to the center of the Gentile world, God is sovereignly bringing Paul to Rome. Paul is vindicated, after his speeches, by the Lord in that (a) God speaks to Paul (27:23-24), (b) all that Paul says comes to pass (27:9-10, 21-26, 30-35), (c) Gentiles are physically saved as they listen to his words (27:30-32, 42-44; 28:8-9), and (d) he is not killed by a viper which bites him (28:3-6).

However, even though the Gentiles are receptive to Paul's words in Acts 27, the Jews are not in Acts 28. Paul once again explains to local Jews that he is not anti-Jewish (28:17-19), but a prisoner because he proclaims the hope of Israel (28:20). When the Jews return, Paul again proclaims the hope of Israel (i.e., the kingdom and Jesus from the Law and the Prophets (28:23; cf. 26:6-7, 22-23). Over a divided house (cf. Acts 2:12-13), Paul proclaimed from Isaiah 6:9-10 that they were falling into the national pattern of unbelief and thus becoming hard hearted (cf. Blind Elymas in 13:11) (28:14-27). Acts ends where Luke began—with a prophetic utterance that proves to be true. Paul proclaims that in light of Israel's hard heartedness, the message is going to the Gentiles because they will listen (as was proven in Acts 27).

Conclusion: The Cyclical Story and the Ending of Acts

Narrative "omissions" are also known as "gapping," or "narrative reticence."[38] These omissions may be due to the selectivity of the author,[39] and function as a literary technique to arouse interest and involvement in the narrative. The reader becomes curious, has a sense of suspense, or is surprised.[40] On the macro level the largest examples of gapping in Luke-Acts are in (1) the ending of the Gospel of Luke and the beginning of Acts, and (2) the ending of Acts.[41]

The ending of Acts certainly provides gaps for the reader. First, Paul was still speaking to the Jews after he turned from them to the Gentiles in 13:46 and 18:6. While some would argue that this marks the end of Paul's appeal to the Jews, other elements of the narrative and the closing scene support a different conclusion.[42] Second, the Jews in Rome had a mixed response to Paul's teaching. This led Tannehill to see the end of Acts as a tragedy since the "purpose of God" in Luke-Acts was thwarted by Israel's rejection.[43] But this pattern of the cyclical story has shown itself again and again throughout Acts. Does

---

[38]Tremper Longman III, *Foundations of Contemporary Interpretation,* ed. Moisés Silva, vol 3, *Literary Approaches to Biblical Interpretation,* (Grand Rapids: Academie Books), 97. William S. J. Kurz, *Reading Luke-Acts: Dynamics of Biblical Narrative* (Louisville: Westminster/John Knox Press, 1993), 31-36.

[39] They may also be due to the employment of different sources but the source critical theory has been over emphasized; see William S Kurz, "Narrative Approaches to Luke-Acts," *Biblica* 68 (1987): 201-202.

[40] Kurz, "Narrative Approaches to Luke-Acts," 203; Longman, *Foundations of Contemporary Interpretation,* 97; Meir Sternberg, *The Poetics of Biblical Narrative* (Bloomington: Indiana University Press, 1985), 186.
Kurz seems to go too far in his emphasis on reader response when he says, "the reader creates the narrative in the process of reading it, quite apart from the author, who might be long dead." Later he emphasizes the influential role of the author in guiding the reader's minds. *Reading Luke-Acts,* 31-32. An example of the unnecessary conclusions from such a reader response approach is Tannehill's thoughts that "the narrator allows readers and hearers to complete Paul's personal story in their own imaginations." Tannehill, *The Narrative Unity of Luke-Acts,* II:355. Does the reader "complete Paul's personal story?" It would seem that the historical reader(s) would know the rest of Paul's story, and the "completion of Paul's story" would probably not be the emphasis of *Luke's* ending.
Seymour Chatman argues that the text leads the reader to fill in gaps with causation in an attempt to find coherence. *Story and Discourse: Narrative Structure in Fiction and Film* (Ithaca, NY: Cornell University Press, 1978), 45-46.

[41] Kurz, *Reading Luke-Acts,* 33-36.

[42]Note the different views in Tyson, Joseph B. ed., *Luke-Acts and the Jewish People: Eight Critical Perspectives.* (Minneapolis: Augsburg Publishing House, 1988).

[43]Tannehill, *The Narrative Unity of Luke-Acts,* II:248-49.

Luke's closure in Acts argue for finality or emphasize continuity?[44] Third, Paul remained for two full years in his lodgings welcoming all, preaching the kingdom of God and teaching about Christ. The fact that the narrator knew that Paul remained in his lodgings for two years[45] argues that Luke did not complete Acts during Paul's imprisonment.[46] While the original readers probably knew what became of Paul, the writer did not convey this information.[47]

The significance may be found in Torgovnick's observation that, "endings invite the *retrospective analysis of a text* and create the illusion of *life halted and poised for analysis.*"[48] The ending of Acts emphasizes Paul poised in the cyclical story after the point of rejection continually proclaiming the message of the book, namely, that the gospel message continues to be available for both Gentiles and Jews.[49] In the last verse of the book (Acts 28:30) Paul welcomed "all" who came to see him, not just the Gentiles. In addition, Paul proclaimed to them the Jewish topics of the "kingdom of God" (cf. Acts 28:23) and Jesus as messiah (Christ, Jews?). As the cyclical story was repeated again-and-again throughout the book, the author freezes Paul at the next step in the cyclical story where the message continues to go out to an even larger audience—including all the readers of Acts.

---

[44] Again, Seymour Chatman argues that there is no true "end" to a story. "It is strictly an artifact of composition, not a function of raw story-material...." *Story and Discourse*, 47.

[45]*Luke* uses the aorist tense for "remained", Ἐνέμεινεν, implying that a simple past act is completed. See Kurz, *Reading Luke-Acts*, 34.

[46]See Hans Conzelmann, *Acts of the Apostles*, trans. James Limburg, Thomas Kraabel, and Donald H. Juel, Hermeneia (Philadelphia: Fortress Press, 1987), 228.

[47]Tannehill disagrees arguing that the final fate of Paul has been foreshadowed through Paul's speeches and Paul's echoes with Jesus' way of the cross. *The Narrative Unity of Luke-Acts*, II:354-56. While these elements do exist in the Acts narrative, the timing of Paul's "violent death" is not required to be with this trial before Caesar. See also J. Lee Magness, *Sense and Absence: Structure and Suspension in the Ending of Mark's Gospel*, Semeia Studies (Atlanta: Scholars Press, 1986), 85.

[48]Marianna Torgovnick, *Closure in the Novel* (Princeton, NJ: Princeton University Press, 1981), 209, cf. also, 5, (emphasis added).

[49]Tannehill also notes this emphasis in the ending of Acts. *The Narrative Unity of Luke-Acts*, II:356. Particularly he affirms, "In the meantime, Acts can only suggest that the church welcome those Jews who are still willing to listen and continue its mission to the more responsive gentile world." (Ibid., 357).

www.ingramcontent.com/pod-product-compliance
Lightning Source LLC
Chambersburg PA
CBHW050826160426
43192CB00010B/1907